STEP UP 成长 with CHINESE

TEXTBOOK 2

主编： 崔希亮
Series Editor Xiliang Cui

北京语言大学 Beijing Language & Culture University:

编者： 陈丽霞　　张兰欣　　徐式婧　　李耘达
Writers Lixia Chen Lanxin Zhang Shijing Xu Yunda Li

美国教育专家 American Educators:

陈少元　　陶洁琳　　竹露茜　　李艳惠　　谭大立
Carol Chen-Lin Janice Dowd Lucy Chu Lee Yen-hui Audrey Li Dali Tan

CENGAGE
Learning®

Andover • Melbourne • Mexico City • Boston, MA • Toronto • Hong Kong • New Delhi • Seoul • Singapore • Tokyo

Step Up with Chinese Textbook 2

Publishing Director:
Roy Lee

Editorial Manager, CLT:
Zhao Lan

Associate Development Editor:
Titus Teo

Creative Manager:
Melvin Chong

Senior Product Manager (Asia):
Joyce Tan

Product Manager (Outside Asia):
Mei Yun Loh

Regional Manager, Production and Rights:
Pauline Lim

Senior Production Executive:
Cindy Chai

Regional Director, Mainland China / Taiwan:
Steve Lee

Senior Project Executive (China):
Mana Wu

Compositor:
Sok Ling Ong

Editorial Assistant:
Zhi Li Tan

For product information and technology assistance, contact us at
Cengage Learning Asia Customer Support, 65-6410-1200

For permission to use material from this text or product,
submit all requests online at **www.cengageasia.com/permissions**
Further permissions questions can be emailed to
asia.permissionrequest@cengage.com

ISBN-13: 978-981-4455-17-6
ISBN-10: 981-4455-17-2

Cengage Learning Asia Pte Ltd
151 Lorong Chuan
#02-08 New Tech Park
Singapore 556741

Cengage Learning is a leading provider of customized learning solutions with office locations around the globe, including Andover, Melbourne, Mexico City, Boston (MA), Toronto, Hong Kong, New Delhi, Seoul, Singapore and Tokyo. Locate your local office at **www.cengage.com/global**

Cengage Learning products are represented in Canada by Nelson Education, Ltd.

For product information, visit **www.cengageasia.com**

Printed in Singapore
2 3 4 5 17 16 15

Welcome to Step Up with Chinese!

Step Up with Chinese is an innovative, standards-based Chinese textbook series for high school students with little or no Chinese background. Highly learner-friendly and task-centered, *Step Up* develops all four language skills while incorporating the principles of ACTFL Five C's – Communication, Cultures, Connections, Comparisons, and Communities. Students will learn all the necessary material to engage others in meaningful communication and gain a better understanding of the Chinese culture.

"The instructional framework is EXCELLENT! It is nicely aligned with the National Standards." – *Jianhua Bai, Kenyon College*

This series consists of three volumes covering three years of instruction. Each volume includes a Textbook and a Workbook. Each textbook offers ten themed lessons that are structured around key communicative goals. The textbook features a clear, step-by-step approach to help students progress from small "steps" of language usage towards larger communicative goals. Instead of the traditional text-and-vocabulary grammar centered approach, each chapter is broken down into small chunks of patterns to learn and practice. Students will get plenty of practice on new vocabulary and grammar. The activities have been carefully designed so that students develop confidence with the new material before moving to the next step. Each step builds upon previously learned vocabulary and sentence patterns in a systematic way. The integration section at the end of each chapter gives students the opportunity to synthesize and apply what they have learned in more challenging, authentic tasks, further reinforcing their interpretive, interpersonal and presentational skills.

"I like the way this textbook organizes each chapter. The step-by-step approach makes each task very clear." – *Lihua Li, Berkeley Preparatory School*

Interweaved a variety of cultural content, Chinese culture vis-a-vis Western culture, throughout the program—in the visuals, practice activities, readings, writing activities, cultural snippets and *Fun Time* section of each chapter, to foster students' cultural awareness from a global point of view. The program also reinforces language learning by making connections to students' prior knowledge, their personal experiences and other content areas that are relevant to them.

Step Up with Chinese provides ample support for students to gain a positive learning experience and to become a lifelong learner of Chinese.

"This is a very up-to-date book that is very appropriate for high school students in the States. The students can really relate to a lot of scenes in the book and see their own lives in the book instead of just knowing someone else's life in China." – *Jie Lei, George C. Marshall High School*

Textbook

The Student Textbook contains information and activities that the student need for in-class use and self-study. Each textbook contains 10 chapters structured around key communicative goals, and covers topics of high interest and relevance to high school students.

Each chapter opens with a clear learning agenda, and a warm-up activity to introduce the subject matter. Each chapter has three to four main communicative goals which are broken down into smaller steps to learn and practice. Each step comprises a short vocabulary list, a grammar section with usage examples and explanation, related cultural snippets, and activities for grammar and language practice. Following the last step is a collection of sample dialogs and reading passages; an integration section offering more challenging, authentic activities that require students to synthesize and apply what they have learned; and a *Fun Time* section with theme-related, enjoyable material such as songs, poems and rhymes to extend learning. The chapter ends with a complete list of all vocabulary and sentence patterns, and a self-assessment checklist.

"The text provides a lot of different ways for students to practice their reading, with ample pictures to maintain interest and mitigate character-reading fatigue, always a challenge for younger learners of Chinese."
– Adam Ross, Lakeside Upper School

Workbook

The Workbook offers a wide variety of activities to give students plenty of practice of what has been learned in each lesson on all the skills of listening, speaking, reading and writing. Listening exercises develop students listening comprehension skills through short oral exchanges (rejoinders) and longer spoken selections (dialogs and narratives). Scenario-based speaking activities develop students' oral communication skills in the interpersonal and presentational mode. Reading exercises develop their interpretative communication skills through a variety of reading texts (dialogs, short passages, notices, signs, emails, etc.). For writing, students learn to hand-write Chinese characters in the correct stroke order, and answer simple fill-in-the-blank questions to more challenging free-response questions. Also included in the Workbook are two review test sets—one mid-term review and one final-term review. The Workbook audio program may be accessed from the companion website.

"Excellent! The workbook is one of the first I have reviewed that appears not to waste students' time. Each activity was based on a scenario, encouraged development of a new skill, or give students specific practice for subsequent class interaction." *– Leslie Zimring, Summit School District*

Companion Website http://stepup.cengageasia.com

The companion website is open to all students and no registration is required. Students can access the *Pinyin* pronunciation guide, complete text and workbook audio program, chapter-by-chapter interactive vocabulary flashcards and extra online practice activities.

Instructors may register to download the complimentary instructors' resources including teaching suggestions, audio scripts and answer keys.

　　《成长》是一套具有开拓性的、专供初学者使用的中学中文教材。本教材的教学理念和目标是根据美国外语教学委员会(ACTFL)的国家语言教学标准(5C)制订的："沟通和交际能力(Communication)"、"文化理解和体验能力(Cultures)"、"与其他学科贯连的能力(Connections)"、"语言、文化比较能力(Comparisons)"和"在多元文化社区中学以致用的能力(Communities)"。

　　《成长》分三级。每级有十个单元,可以在一个学年内完成。教材所应用的教学方法是循序渐进的,能帮助学生从最基本、简单的表达,慢慢提升到更长、更复杂的表达。和传统教材以"生词 – 课文 – 语法"为中心的教学方法不同,《成长》每一个单元的内容根据交际目标分解成几个大步骤,每个大步骤下面又有几个小步骤,这样既能降低初学者的学习难度,又能让学生打好基础、不断巩固所学。每一单元都经过了精心设计,同时融合了人际交往的三种模式(语言沟通、理解诠释、表达演示)。

　　教材还在课文和活动中融入了许多中国传统与现代的文化内容,让学生可以更深入地了解中国、中国人、中国文化和中国习俗。课本里也安排了许多美国人熟悉的人物和场景,能够激发学生对用中文解释自己的本土文化产生兴趣。为了强化语言学习的效果,编者还在语言教学和其他学科之间设置了许多有意义的联系。

　　《成长》每一级教材都有课本和练习册。课本每单元开篇清楚列明学习目标,并通过热身活动导入正题。每个单元有三至四个主要教学步骤和交际目标。每个步骤都有一个生词表、语法解释、相关文化知识和练习。在主要步骤之后,设有阅读篇章、对话、综合练习、趣味活动,让学生能够延伸学习。单元末还列出该单元所介绍的所有生词和句型,以及一个自我评估表。课本附录则包括中英生词索引、主要句型表和中国地图。

　　练习册包括形式多样的练习题,有助于培养学生听、说、读、写等各方面的能力。听力练习通过录音片段训练学生的听力理解能力。情景活动培养学生在沟通交际和演示交际方面的口语表达能力。多样化的阅读篇章(对话、短文、书信、告示、电邮等)有助于培养学生的阅读理解能力。除此之外,在书写能力方面,学生会练习以正确的笔顺书写生字词,并用中文回答各种形式的问题,例如简单的填充题以及更具挑战性的自由题。

　　教材还配有专门的学习网站(http://stepup.cengageasia.com),提供汉语拼音总表、互动式词卡、课本和练习册录音(mp3)、额外的网上练习以及教师辅助资源(包括教师手册、课本和练习册录音稿和参考答案等等)。

　　《成长》可让学生积极、有效地学习中文,掌握应用中文的技能,并培养他们终身学习中文的兴趣。

STEP UP 成长 with CHINESE 2

CONTENTS

VII

STEP UP with CHINESE 2 成长

交际目标 Communicative Goals	主要步骤 Main Steps	核心词汇 Core Vocabulary	语言点 Language Focus

1 Starting a new school year 开学了!

交际目标 Communicative Goals	主要步骤 Main Steps	核心词汇 Core Vocabulary	语言点 Language Focus
◆ 在不同场合打招呼 Greeting people on different occasions ◆ 谈自己 Conversing about yourself ◆ 谈暑假活动 Learning about people's summer activities ◆ 时间的表达 Discussing when events occur ◆ 描述过去的事 Talking about the past ◆ 谈心情与感受 Expressing emotions and feelings	**Step 1** 打招呼 Meeting and Greeting People **Step 2** 询问活动发生的时间 Telling the Day and Time **Step 3** 描述暑假活动 Describing Your Summer Vacation	1. 打招呼 Greetings 2. 暑假活动 Summer activities 3. 心情 Emotions and feelings	1. 很高兴见到你! 2. 最近忙吗? 3. 中午我们吃饺子,好吗? 　好。 4. 今天礼拜几? 　今天礼拜三。 5. 学校什么时候开学? 　9月1号以后开学。 6. 从一月到六月是第二学期。 7. 暑假你参加夏令营了吗? 　没有,我去旅游了。 8. 你暑假过得怎么样? 　我暑假过得很开心。 9. 今天开学,我觉得很兴奋。

2 Moving to a new school 到新学校

交际目标 Communicative Goals	主要步骤 Main Steps	核心词汇 Core Vocabulary	语言点 Language Focus
◆ 谈交通工具 Telling modes of transportation ◆ 说明如何从某个地点到另一个地点 Stating how to get from one location to another ◆ 了解关于某人的文字介绍 Interpreting a written text about people ◆ 说明到某处的时间与地点 Talking about where and when people go to different places ◆ 比较事物特点 Using patterns that emphasize one key element over another ◆ 比较大小和形状 Comparing sizes, shapes, and colors	**Step 1** 谈交通 Going to Places **Step 2** 谈搬家和原因 Moving to a New Place **Step 3** 进行比较 Making Comparisons	1. 交通工具 Modes of transportation 2. 和交通工具有关的动词 Action verbs on taking transportation 3. 用于比较的形容词 Common adjectives for comparison	1. 我坐公交车去学校。 　我是走路回家的。 2. 我送你去学校。 3. 我从东边搬到西边。 4. 因为我家离学校很近,所以我走路去学校。 5. 我的学校跟你的学校一样。 6. 中文课比英语课有意思。 5. 他的学校比较大。 6. 我对中文感兴趣。

文化知识 Cultural Knowledge	贯连和比较 Connections and Comparisons	任务和实践 Tasks and Community Applications

1

1. 中国学校开学第一天 The beginning of school in China	座右铭 Mottos: • 美国和中国学校的校训 School mottos of American and Chinese schools	1. 情景演练：打招呼，问近况 (开学第一天)。 Role Work: Make a conversation with a partner on meeting on the first day of school.
2. 问私人问题 The cultural appropriateness of asking personal questions	比较 Comparison: • 美国、澳洲和中国的学年校历 School calendars in America, Australia, and China	2. 给中国网友发电邮，谈谈你的学校和暑假。 Write an email to a friend in China to share information about your school and your summer vacation.
3. 暑假 Summer vacations		3. 调查：同学如何过暑假，参加了什么暑假活动。 Survey: Find out how your classmates spent their vacation and the activities they did this past summer.

38

1. 中文名称在不同地方的使用习惯 Linguistic variation in Chinese	音乐 Music: • 跳皮筋歌谣 Chinese jump rope rhyme	1. 回应一则博文，描述你的学校和在校一天里的活动。 Respond to a blog entry by describing your school and your school day.
2. 生活在中国城市 Living in Chinese cities	数学 Mathematics: • 长度和大小 Length and size	2. 调查：同学们怎么来学校。 Survey: Find out how your classmates get to school.
3. 文理分科 Choosing liberal arts and science fields in Chinese high schools	比较 Comparison: • 各科目里克特量表科目难易度、喜好等的读数 Ratings (on difficulty level, interest, etc.) across all courses on a Likert scale	3. 两人一组：哪些科目相同，哪些不同。 Pair work: Talk about which courses you have in common and which ones you are taking that are different.

IX

交际目标 Communicative Goals	主要步骤 Main Steps	核心词汇 Core Vocabulary	语言点 Language Focus

3 ◆ Settling into a new home 搬进新家

◆ 说出房间的位置 Specifying the relative locations of rooms ◆ 表达动作的方向 Stating the direction of movement ◆ 描述家具和家中用品的位置 Describing where furniture and household items are ◆ 存在的表达 Expressing the existence of something ◆ 列举 Enumerating a list of items ◆ 形容形状和颜色 Describing shapes and colors	Step 1 描述房间 Describing the Rooms in a House Step 2 家具的摆放 Arranging Furniture Step 3 列举和形容物件 Listing and Describing Objects	1. 量词 (家中物品) Measure words for household items 2. 家中物品 Household items 3. 常用动词 Common action verbs 4. 颜色词 Colors 5. 形状 Shapes 6. 花草树木 Flowers and plants 7. 形容家具与住屋的形容词 Adjectives describing furniture and houses	1. 主卧室在哪儿? 主卧室在楼上。 2. 你们上来看我的书房。 3. 我的房间在左边。 4. 一台电冰箱、两盏台灯、三幅画、四张床、五块地毯、六面镜子 5. 花园里种着一些花。 6. 我把台灯放在书桌上。 7. 菜园里种着一些菜,像番茄、黄瓜、四季豆什么的。 8. 这张桌子是圆形的。 9. 我的房间是天蓝色的。

4 ◆ Adapting to the weather 适应气候

◆ 形容天气 Describing the weather ◆ 表达天气的异同 Expressing similarities and differences in the weather ◆ 描述服饰 Identifying clothing and accessories ◆ 谈论衣着的需要 Stating the need to wear something ◆ 形容人们的装束 Describing how people are dressed	Step 1 谈论天气 Talking about the Weather Step 2 按天气穿戴服饰 Dressing According to the Weather Step 3 形容人们的装束 Describing How People are Dressed	1. 天气 Weather 2. 形容天气的形容词 Adjectives describing the weather 3. 服饰 Clothing and accessories 4. 量词 (服饰) Measure words for clothing and accessories	1. 今天天气怎么样? 今天下雨,有点儿冷。 2. 今天气温多少度? 今天气温六十华氏度。 3. 今天没有昨天冷。 4. 一件毛衣、两条裙子、三双球鞋、四块手表、五顶帽子 5. 外面热极了,得戴太阳镜。 6. 夏天,人们穿着短裤、凉鞋。 7. 穿红裙子的女孩是我妹妹。

文化知识 Cultural Knowledge	贯连和比较 Connections and Comparisons	任务和实践 Tasks and Community Applications

文化知识 / Cultural Knowledge

1. 四合院
   Chinese courtyard houses

2. 风水
   Feng shui

3. 天圆地方
   The concept of "round sky and square earth" in Chinese architecture

4. 颜色的象征意义
   Color symbolism in Chinese culture

贯连和比较 / Connections and Comparisons

文字游戏 Word Game:

- 谜语
  Chinese riddles

比较 Comparison:

- 中式和美式房子
  Chinese and American houses

任务和实践 / Tasks and Community Applications

1. 根据客户要求，向他们推荐合适的房屋。
   Recommend apartments to clients according to their requirements.

2. 举出中国家庭生活和你的有什么不同。
   State the differences between your lifestyle and that of Chinese people.

3. 两人一组：根据对话内容，画出一个中国家庭住家的平面图，并以中文标示不同房间和部分。
   Pair work: Draw a floor plan of a Chinese host family's home according to a conversation, and label the rooms and areas in Chinese.

文化知识 / Cultural Knowledge

1. 中国最热和最冷的地方
   The hottest and coldest places in China

2. 中国服装
   Chinese clothing

3. 著名华人服装设计师
   Famous Chinese fashion designers

贯连和比较 / Connections and Comparisons

地理 Geography:

- 中国各地不同的天气情况
  Different climatic conditions in China

- 摄氏和华氏
  Celsius and Fahrenheit

文学 Literature:

- 中文诗歌和谚语中的春天主题
  Spring in Chinese poetry and proverbs

任务和实践 / Tasks and Community Applications

1. 两人一组：查一查某个著名城市的天气预报，然后向全班分享信息。
   Pair work: Find out the weather forecast for a well known city and present it to the class.

2. 阅读一段关于天气的对话，然后回答问题。
   Read a conversation on weather and answer the questions.

3. 形容同学的装束，并用图或表来呈现你所观察到的事物。
   Describe what your classmates are wearing and summarize your findings into a table or graph.

交际目标 Communicative Goals	主要步骤 Main Steps	核心词汇 Core Vocabulary	语言点 Language Focus

5 Discovering the community 熟悉新社区

交际目标	主要步骤	核心词汇	语言点
◆ 介绍社区场所 Describing the locations of community places	**Step 1** 介绍社区场所 Finding Places in the Community	1. 社区场所 Community places	1. 社区里不但有银行，而且还有邮局。
◆ 问路和指路 Asking for and giving directions	**Step 2** 在社区里活动 Getting around the Community	2. 复合方位词 Compound directional words	2. 电影院在社区的东北边。
◆ 表达具体距离 Expressing specific distances between two places	**Step 3** 在社区里生活 Living in the Community	3. 社区场所活动 Activities in the community	3. 请问，去邮局怎么走？ 往右拐，再往前走。
◆ 说明目的 Stating the purpose of an action		4. 量词(长度) Units of length	4. 请问，去便利店怎么走？ 前面往右拐就到了。
◆ 描述动作的顺序 Describing the sequence of actions			5. 这儿离地铁站有多远？ 这儿离地铁站有 3 英里。
			6. 我去商场购物。
			7. 先去药房，再去面包店。

6 Meeting new people 认识新朋友

交际目标	主要步骤	核心词汇	语言点
◆ 谈职业和工作场所 Talking about one's profession and workplace	**Step 1** 谈职业 Exploring Professions	1. 职业 Professions	1. 他是做什么的？ 他是工程师。
◆ 谈理想 Stating one's aspirations	**Step 2** 理想的工作 Finding One's Aspirations	2. 工作场所 Places of work	2. 他在学校里当教师。
◆ 描述一个假设的职业 Describing a possible profession	**Step 3** 旅游和名人 Discovering Famous People	3. 行业名称 Industries	3. 你以后打算在什么行业工作？ 我可能在金融业工作。
◆ 描述某人的特长 Describing one's strengths		4. 各行业的相关工作 Work related to each profession	4. 如果我是发型师，我就会设计新发型。
◆ 表达对某人的看法 Commenting on a person		5. 人物形容词 Adjectives describing people	5. 郎朗在音乐方面很有特长。
			6. 我觉得郑和不仅有学问，还非常能干。

文化知识 Cultural Knowledge	贯连和比较 Connections and Comparisons	任务和实践 Tasks and Community Applications

150

1. 指南针 The Chinese compass 2. 长度单位"里" Chinese measure of distance 3. 中国社区里的早晨活动 Morning activities in Chinese neighborhoods	地理 Geography: • 中国不同城市与景点之间的距离 Distance between Chinese cities and places of interest • 中国的小区 Residential areas in China	1. 看地图，形容不同社区场所的位置。 Read a map and describe the locations of community places. 2. 两人一组：用地图问路和指路。 Pair work: Ask for and give directions using a map. 3. 安排你周六的活动，列出需要做的事并按顺序排列。 Plan your schedule on Saturday by listing your tasks and activities in order.

182

1. 士农工商 The four main occupations in ancient China 2. 三百六十行，行行出状元 A Chinese saying on various professions 3. 不同行业里的杰出华人 Famous Chinese people in different professions	历史 History: • 中国古代名人 Famous historical Chinese figures 音乐 Music: • 中文歌曲欣赏 Chinese song appreciation	1. 两人一组：设计一段对话，谈谈你的理想，说明你想在哪个行业工作。 Pair work: Create a dialog on your aspirations, including details on which industry/field you would like to work in. 2. 搜集两位名人的资料以及他们所从事的工作，然后在三人小组里用中文互相提问。 Research information about two famous people and their professions. Sit in a group of three and ask each other questions in Chinese about the famous person. 3. 调查：向同学们查询他们家人从事什么行业，找出班里最普遍的行业是什么。 Survey: Find out the professions of your classmates' family members to see which professions are the most common.

SCOPE AND SEQUENCE

交际目标 Communicative Goals	主要步骤 Main Steps	核心词汇 Core Vocabulary	语言点 Language Focus

7 ◇ Maintaining a healthy lifestyle 保持健康的生活习惯

交际目标 Communicative Goals	主要步骤 Main Steps	核心词汇 Core Vocabulary	语言点 Language Focus
◆ 列出健康和不健康的食品 Identifying healthy and unhealthy foods ◆ 比较不同食品的益处 Comparing and contrasting the health benefits of foods ◆ 描述病情 Describing an illness ◆ 表达动作或者活动的次数或频率 Stating the frequency of an action ◆ 描述日常卫生习惯 Describing a daily hygiene routine	**Step 1** 吃得好 Eating Well **Step 2** 生病 Getting Sick **Step 3** 培养健康的生活习惯 Developing Healthy Habits	1. 食物 Foods 2. 疾病 Sickness 3. 健康习惯 Healthy habits	1. 我们去喝茶吧。 2. 豆类制品除了铁和钙以外，还有蛋白质。 3. 虽然可乐很好喝，但是糖份很高。 4. 你哪里不舒服？ 我肚子痛。 5. 感冒药一天吃三次。 6. 她用洗发液洗头发。 7. 吃饭以前应该先洗手。 8. 我每天运动半小时。 她每天刷两次牙。

8 ◇ Connecting with others 与人沟通

交际目标 Communicative Goals	主要步骤 Main Steps	核心词汇 Core Vocabulary	语言点 Language Focus
◆ 形容电脑和科技产品 Describing computers and gadgets ◆ 谈维修 Talking about maintenance and repair ◆ 和他人一起进行活动的表达 Describing activities done with others ◆ 说明新闻的来源 Stating the source of news	**Step 1** 在日常生活中使用科技 Using Technology in Daily Life **Step 2** 和他人沟通 Communicating with Others **Step 3** 搜索信息 Gathering Information	1. 科技产品 IT products 2. 常见网上活动 Common online activities 3. 新闻来源 News sources	1. 这台电脑既轻巧又耐用。 2. 电脑坏了。电脑修好了。打印机坏了，所以我买了一台新的。 3. 网断了，现在上不了网。 4. 我用网络视频电话跟朋友一起聊天。 5. 他不是玩网络游戏，就是在网上购物。 6. 我看了电视新闻才知道这个消息。 他一上网就看到了这条新闻。 7. 只要上网查一查，就可以找到资料。

1. 中华饮食里的主食 Chinese staple foods 2. 中国的清真食品 Halal food in China 3. 针灸 Acupuncture 4. 中医里的"冷""热"食物 "Hot" and "cold" foods in Chinese medicine 5. 推拿 Chinese therapeutic massage — *Tuina*	营养学 Food and Nutrition: • 食品标签上的营养标示 Nutrient information on a food label • 焦耳 The joule 比较 Comparison: • 中文和其他语言中关于健康生活的俗语与谚语 Proverbs and sayings on healthy living in Chinese and other cultures • 各国食品标签上所需列明的营养成分 Nutritional elements required on food labels in different countries	1. 两人一组：为谢师宴准备一份餐单，并确保食物不会超出预算。 Pair work: Come up with a list of foods for the teacher appreciation banquet and make sure it is within a given budget. 2. 情景演练：看医生，形容病症；医生开药，并提供健康贴士。 Role play: See a doctor and describe your symptoms. The doctor will prescribe medicine and recommend a health regimen. 3. 制订一个为期六个月的计划，让自己变得更健康。 Write up a plan for the next six months that you will do to become healthier. 4. 两人一组：为一个明星制订一份饮食与运动计划，让他/她在六个星期里能够有强健的体格、敏捷的身手，以及焕发的肌肤，可以参与某片的拍摄工作。 Pair work: Devise a diet plan and exercise routine for a celebrity so that in six weeks he/she will be fit, agile, flexible, and have a glowing complexion for a role in a film.

1. 联想集团和中关村 Lenovo and China's Silicon Valley 2. 淘宝、阿里巴巴和腾讯QQ E-commerce and instant messaging in China 3. 微博和百度 News in China	短信用语 Texting Language: • 中文短信里的数字 Use of numbers in Chinese text messages 比较 Comparison: • 中国和美国学生如何使用互联网 How Chinese and American students use the Internet	1. 和一位同学谈谈他/她对互联网的看法。一起探讨互联网如何改变现代人的生活、创造热门的网上活动，以及使用互联网所带来的利与弊。 Talk to a classmate to find out his/her opinion on the use of the Internet. Discuss how the Internet has changed everyone's life, created popular online activities, and caused both productive and unproductive use of the Internet. 2. 写一篇题为"互联网和美国学生生活"的文章。 Write an article on the topic of "The Internet and the Lives of American Students." 3. 调查：同学们喜欢在网上做的两个活动。 Survey: Find out from your classmates two things they like to do on the Internet.

交际目标 Communicative Goals	主要步骤 Main Steps	核心词汇 Core Vocabulary	语言点 Language Focus

9 ◆ Getting along with others 与他人相处

◆ 谈家务 Identifying household chores	Step 1 在家帮忙 Helping at Home	1. 家务事 Household chores	1. 我帮妈妈洗碗。
◆ 描述如何帮助别人 Stating how to help another person	Step 2 做个好邻居 Being a Good Heighbor	2. 寻求帮助 Seeking help	2. 你要是出门的话，我可以帮你喂狗。
◆ 形容同时进行的活动 Describing simultaneous actions	Step 3 与他人合作 Working with Others	3. 提供帮助 Offering help	3. 你可以帮我割草吗? 当然可以。
◆ 表示同意或不同意 Expressing agreement and disagreement			4. 我帮邻居把车子洗干净了。
◆ 表达看法 Stating opinions			5. 我一边帮他温习功课，一边和他讨论作业。
			6. 你同意我的看法吗? 我同意。
			7. 你说的我不是不同意，只是我觉得有点难。

10 ◆ Being a global citizen 做一个好公民

◆ 谈贡献社会的人士 Talking about community workers	Step 1 社会的一份子 Being Part of a Community	1. 人物性格 Personality traits	1. 志愿者对我的影响很大。
◆ 形容某人的性格 Describing people and getting along with them	Step 2 帮助社会 Helping the Community	2. 社区工作 Volunteer work	2. 芳芳很有耐心，所以很容易跟她相处。
◆ 描述如何为社区做出贡献 Stating ways to contribute to the community	Step 3 创造更美好的生活 Creating a Better Life	3. 环境问题 Environmental issues	3. 张安请我跟他一起去捐血。
◆ 谈环境 Talking about the environment		4. 环保好习惯 Eco-friendly habits	4. 空气被污染了。
◆ 描述如何保护环境 Describing how to protect the community			5. 我们应该节约用水。
			6. 当你离开房间的时候，应该把灯关掉。

282

文化知识 Cultural Knowledge	贯连和比较 Connections and Comparisons	任务和实践 Tasks and Community Applications
1. 摆碗筷 Ways to set the table 2. 远亲不如近邻 The value of good neighbors in Chinese culture 3. "面子"的意思 The meaning of "face" in China	家政 Home Economics: • 家务事 Helping with household chores 社区服务 Community Service: • 帮助社区里的年长者 Helping seniors in the community	1. 访问：问同学在家是否有帮父母做家务，然后在班上总结汇报。 Interview: Ask your classmates to find out whether they have been helping their parents with chores at home. Report your findings to the class. 2. 情景扮演：和另一个同学设计一段对话，针对某个课题发表看法。 Role play: Work with a partner to create a dialog on a given topic, stating your opinions and expressing agreement/disagreement. 3. 制订为期一个月的工作表，列出至少二十个任务，让同学们可以帮助社区里的年长者。 Come up with a schedule for a month of at least 20 tasks that students will undertake to help the seniors in the community.

310

文化知识 Cultural Knowledge	贯连和比较 Connections and Comparisons	任务和实践 Tasks and Community Applications
1. 孟子的故事 The story of Meng Zi 2. 希望工程 Project Hope 3. 中国环保热线 The Environmental Hotline in China 4. 再生艺术 Recycled art	慈善 Philanthropy: • 名人与慈善组织 Famous people and charitable organizations 义务工作 Volunteer Work: • 在不同慈善组织里做义工 Volunteering at different organizations 地理 Geography: • 环境问题和环境保护 Environmental issues and protection	1. 写一则广告，呼吁学生报名参加社区工作，帮助一个受影响的灾区。 Write a press release/advertisement/poster for the school newspaper to request students to sign up for volunteer work in an area hit by a severe disaster. 2. 两人一组：列出十个有益于环境的活动，打造一个绿色学校。 Pair work: Devise a list of 10 activities to create a more eco-friendly environment in school. 3. 制作宣传册，里头列出至少五项建议，鼓励学生减少碳足迹。 Create a brochure to inform students of at least five things they can do to reduce their carbon footprint.

Starting a new school year

开学了！

COMMUNICATIVE GOALS

◆ Greeting people on different occasions
◆ Conversing about yourself
◆ Learning about people's summer activities
◆ Discussing when events occur
◆ Talking about the past
◆ Expressing emotions and feelings

Cultural Knowledge

◆ The beginning of school in China
◆ The cultural appropriateness of asking personal questions
◆ Summer vacations

Get ready...

Look at the following three school calendars and compare the dates for holidays and school days. What are the similarities and what are the differences? Why do you think differences occur?

An Australian school calendar

Term 1: Jan 23 to Mar 30 **Term 3**: Jul 9 to Sept 21
Term 2: Apr 16 to Jun 22 **Term 4**: Oct 8 to Dec 14

☐ School holidays
■ Public holidays

JANUARY
S	M	T	W	T	F	S
1	2	3	4	5	6	7
8	9	10	11	12	13	14
15	16	17	18	19	20	21
22	23	24	25	26	27	28
29	30	31				

FEBRUARY
S	M	T	W	T	F	S
			1	2	3	4
5	6	7	8	9	10	11
12	13	14	15	16	17	18
19	20	21	22	23	24	25
26	27	28	29			

MARCH
S	M	T	W	T	F	S
			1	2	3	
4	5	6	7	8	9	10
11	12	13	14	15	16	17
18	19	20	21	22	23	24
25	26	27	28	29	30	31

APRIL
S	M	T	W	T	F	S
1	2	3	4	5	6	7
8	9	10	11	12	13	14
15	16	17	18	19	20	21
22	23	24	25	26	27	28
29	30					

MAY
S	M	T	W	T	F	S
		1	2	3	4	5
6	7	8	9	10	11	12
13	14	15	16	17	18	19
20	21	22	23	24	25	26
27	28	29	30	31		

JUNE
S	M	T	W	T	F	S
					1	2
3	4	5	6	7	8	9
10	11	12	13	14	15	16
17	18	19	20	21	22	23
24	25	26	27	28	29	30

JULY
S	M	T	W	T	F	S
1	2	3	4	5	6	7
8	9	10	11	12	13	14
15	16	17	18	19	20	21
22	23	24	25	26	27	28
29	30	31				

AUGUST
S	M	T	W	T	F	S
			1	2	3	4
5	6	7	8	9	10	11
12	13	14	15	16	17	18
19	20	21	22	23	24	25
26	27	28	29	30	31	

SEPTEMBER
S	M	T	W	T	F	S
						1
2	3	4	5	6	7	8
9	10	11	12	13	14	15
16	17	18	19	20	21	22
23	24	25	26	27	28	29
30						

OCTOBER
S	M	T	W	T	F	S
	1	2	3	4	5	6
7	8	9	10	11	12	13
14	15	16	17	18	19	20
21	22	23	24	25	26	27
28	29	30	31			

NOVEMBER
S	M	T	W	T	F	S
				1	2	3
4	5	6	7	8	9	10
11	12	13	14	15	16	17
18	19	20	21	22	23	24
25	26	27	28	29	30	

DECEMBER
S	M	T	W	T	F	S
						1
2	3	4	5	6	7	8
9	10	11	12	13	14	15
16	17	18	19	20	21	22
23	24	25	26	27	28	29
30	31					

An American school calendar

Semester 1: Sept 4 to Jan 25   **Semester 2**: Jan 28 to Jun 19   **School closed**

September — 15 days
S	M	T	W	T	F	S
						1
2	3	4	5	6	7	8
9	10	11	12	13	14	15
16	17	18	19	20	21	22
23	24	25	26	27	28	29
30						

October — 23 days
S	M	T	W	T	F	S
	1	2	3	4	5	6
7	8	9	10	11	12	13
14	15	16	17	18	19	20
21	22	23	24	25	26	27
28	29	30	31			

November — 19 days
S	M	T	W	T	F	S
				1	2	3
4	5	6	7	8	9	10
11	12	13	14	15	16	17
18	19	20	21	22	23	24
25	26	27	28	29	30	

December — 15 days
S	M	T	W	T	F	S
						1
2	3	4	5	6	7	8
9	10	11	12	13	14	15
16	17	18	19	20	21	22
23	24	25	26	27	28	29
30	31					

January — 21 days
S	M	T	W	T	F	S
	1	2	3	4	5	
6	7	8	9	10	11	12
13	14	15	16	17	18	19
20	21	22	23	24	25	26
27	28	29	30	31		

February — 20 days
S	M	T	W	T	F	S
					1	2
3	4	5	6	7	8	9
10	11	12	13	14	15	16
17	18	19	20	21	22	23
24	25	26	27	28		

March — 16 days
S	M	T	W	T	F	S
					1	2
3	4	5	6	7	8	9
10	11	12	13	14	15	16
17	18	19	20	21	22	23
24	25	26	27	28	29	30
31						

April — 22 days
S	M	T	W	T	F	S
	1	2	3	4	5	6
7	8	9	10	11	12	13
14	15	16	17	18	19	20
21	22	23	24	25	26	27
28	29	30				

May — 22 days
S	M	T	W	T	F	S
			1	2	3	4
5	6	7	8	9	10	11
12	13	14	15	16	17	18
19	20	21	22	23	24	25
26	27	28	29	30	31	

June — 13 days
S	M	T	W	T	F	S
						1
2	3	4	5	6	7	8
9	10	11	12	13	14	15
16	17	18	19	20	21	22
23	24	25	26	27	28	29
30	31					

A Chinese school calendar
2012 – 2013

第一学期 （九月三日到一月二十五日）

周次 (Week)	日	一	二	三	四	五	六	备注 (bèizhù, remarks)
九月三日开学 (kāixué, school starts)								
一		3	4	5	6	7	8	
二	9	10	11	12	13	14	15	九月十日：教师节
三	16	17	18	19	20	21	22	
四	23	24	25	26	27	28	29	
五	30	1/10	2	3	4	5	6	九月三十日：中秋节
六	7	8	9	10	11	12	13	十月一日：国庆节
七	14	15	16	17	18	19	20	
八	21	22	23	24	25	26	27	
九	28	29	30	31	1/11	2	3	
十	4	5	6	7	8	9	10	期中考试(qīzhōng kǎoshì, midterm examinations)
十一	11	12	13	14	15	16	17	
十二	18	19	20	21	22	23	24	
十三	25	26	27	28	29	30	1/12	
十四	2	3	4	5	6	7	8	
十五	9	10	11	12	13	14	15	
十六	16	17	18	19	20	21	22	
十七	23	24	25	26	27	28	29	
十八	30	31	1/1	2	3	4	5	一月一日：元旦 (Yuándàn, New Year's Day)
十九	6	7	8	9	10	11	12	
二十	13	14	15	16	17	18	19	
二一	20	21	22	23	24	25		期末考试(qīmò kǎoshì, final examinatios)

第二学期 （二月二十五日到七月五日）

周次 (Week)	日	一	二	三	四	五	六	备注 (bèizhù, remarks)
二月二十五日开学								
一		25	26	27	28	1/3	2	
二	3	4	5	6	7	8	9	
三	10	11	12	13	14	15	16	
四	17	18	19	20	21	22	23	
五	24	25	26	27	28	29	30	
六	31	1/4	2	3	4	5	6	四月四日：清明节
七	7	8	9	10	11	12	13	
八	14	15	16	17	18	19	20	期中考试
九	21	22	23	24	25	26	27	
十	28	29	30	1/5	2	3	4	五月一日：劳动节
十一	5	6	7	8	9	10	11	
十二	12	13	14	15	16	17	18	
十三	19	20	21	22	23	24	25	六月一日：儿童节 (Értóng Jié, Children's Day)
十四	26	27	28	29	30	31	1/6	
十五	2	3	4	5	6	7	8	
十六	9	10	11	12	13	14	15	六月十二日：端午节
十七	16	17	18	19	20	21	22	
十八	23	24	25	26	27	28	29	期末考试
十九	30	1/7	2	3	4	5		

STEPS *at a glance!*

 STEP 1

MEETING AND GREETING PEOPLE

A. Greetings and leave taking
   很高兴见到你！

B. Initiating conversations
   最近忙吗？

C. Using tag questions in conversations
   中午我们吃饺子，好吗？好。

 STEP 2

TELLING THE DAY AND TIME

A. More ways to tell days of the week
   今天礼拜几？今天礼拜三。

B. Asking the time and date
   学校什么时候开学？
   九月一号以后开学。

C. Specifying a time period
   从一月到六月是第二学期。

 STEP 3

DESCRIBING YOUR SUMMER VACATION

A. Stating what people did during the summer
   暑假你参加夏令营了吗？
   没有，我去旅游了。

B. Expressing how you feel about your vacation
   你暑假过得怎么样？
   我暑假过得很开心。

C. Expressing other emotions and feelings
   今天开学，我觉得很兴奋。

MEETING AND GREETING PEOPLE

A Greetings and leave taking

1
hǎojiǔ
好久不见!
Long time no see!

2
gāoxìng   dào
很高兴见到你!
Very glad to see you!

3
zuìjìn
最近好吗?
How have you been recently?

生
词

WORDS AND PHRASES
Common expressions for greetings and leave taking

hǎojiǔ 好久不见!	Long time no see!	huānyíng huílai 欢迎你们回来!	Welcome back! *(from teacher...)*
zuìjìn 最近好吗?	How have you been recently?	rènshi 很高兴认识你!	Very glad to meet you!
最近怎么样?	How have things been recently?	yíhuìr 一会儿见!	See you later!
gāoxìng dào 很高兴见到你!	Very glad to see you!	明天见!	See you tomorrow!
shǔjià guò 暑假过得好吗?	How was your summer vacation?		

Phrases you have learned

您好!	nín hǎo	Hello! *(formal)*	晚上好!	wǎnshang hǎo	Good evening
早上好!	zǎoshang hǎo	Good morning!	再见!	zàijiàn	Good-bye
下午好!	xiàwǔ hǎo	Good afternoon!			

The question word 怎么样 is commonly used among friends and young people as a general expression of greeting. It is placed at the end of the question:

Examples:

Nǐ zěnmeyàng?
你怎么样?
How are you?

Zuìjìn zěnmeyàng?
最近怎么样?
How have things been recently?

When saying goodbye to others in Chinese, 见 (to see) is often used to form the expression. You can specify the time you will see someone again by putting a time expression before 见:

Examples:

Zàijiàn.
再见。

Wǎnshang jiàn.
晚上见。

Yíhuìr jiàn.
一会儿见。

Xià xīngqīyī jiàn.
下星期一见。
See you next Monday.

Míngtiān jiàn.
明天见。

In China, there are often one or two dates (返校日 fǎnxiàorì) during the summer for students to return to school in order to turn in completed summer homework assignments, pick up some textbooks, and/or receive updated information about the next school year. How does your school prepare you for the new school year?

 CULTURAL HIGHLIGHTS

Opening Ceremony

In schools in China, on the first day there is always an opening ceremony to welcome back all of the students and faculty. The ceremony is referred to as 开学典礼 (kāixué diǎnlǐ). It begins with a flag salute and the singing of the national anthem. The principal gives a speech that states the expectations and sets the tone for the school year. During the opening ceremony, the principal will make an opening speech, followed by teacher and student representatives.

Try This!

1. Read the description and decide which expression you would use to greet this person. Refer to the expressions listed on page 4.

   ❶ You are a teacher and you see your students coming into the classroom on the first day of school.

   ❷ You see your good friend in the school yard after the long summer vacation.

   ❸ You see your friend and wonder how she's been recently.

   ❹ Your friend introduces you to a new student and you reply politely.

   ❺ You arrive at school and greet the principal.

   ❻ You are the principal and you greet the students back to school.

   ❼ You see your friend again and ask her how things have been going.

   ❽ You see your friend and comment that it has been a long time since you have seen each other.

   ❾ You are the president of the Chinese Club in school and you hold your first meeting of the year.

   ❿ You are a new teacher and have just been introduced to your department head.

2. Look at the following pictures and decide how you would specify the time you will see the same person again.

   再见　　下星期见　　明天见　　星期五见　　晚上见

Dad is going to work.

The teacher announced the class is over.

You see the principal as you leave your class.

The school team trains weekly.

Today is Tuesday and your grandparents are leaving for a three-day vacation.

Class is over and your classmate is going home.

3. Read the conversation below and decide if the statements afterwards are true or false.

丁强：你好，张安！好久不见！

张安：很高兴见到你，最近怎么样？

丁强：我最近很好。你呢？

张安：我也很好。

丁强：这是我们的新同学，马克。
　　　xīn
　　　new
　　　马克，这是张安。他是我的中国朋友。
　　　　　　　　　　　　　　　　　péngyou
　　　　　　　　　　　　　　　　　friend

张安：马克，你好！

马克：你好，张安，很高兴认识你！

丁强：上课了，我们一会儿见！

张安：好，再见！

True or False (是非题)：

❶ 丁强是一个学生。　　　　❺ 丁强最近不太好。

❷ 张安不认识丁强。　　　　❻ 张安是新同学。

❸ 马克是丁强的好朋友。　　❼ 马克很高兴认识张安。

❹ 张安是中国人。　　　　　❽ 丁强没有课。

最近忙吗？ or

最近忙不忙？

Have you been busy lately?

今天是星期一吗？ or

今天是不是星期一？

Is today Monday?

你明天有中文课吗？ or

你明天有没有中文课？

Do you have Chinese class tomorrow?

You have already learned to form questions with wh-words such as 谁 (shéi, who), 谁的 (shéi de, whose), 什么 (shénme, what), 几点 (jǐdiǎn, what time), and 哪里 (nǎli, where).

In daily conversations, people also use yes-no questions. They can be formed by the two methods listed below. To answer these yes-no questions, simply use the verb or adjective stated in the question.

❶ Add 吗 at the end of a statement to create a question.

Questions	Answers
最近好吗? *(adjective)* How have you been lately?	很好。 I've been fine.
明天是九月一号吗? *(verb)* Is it September 1st tomorrow?	不是。 No, it isn't.

❷ Use the affirmative verb or adjective followed by the negative form.

a) adjective + 不 + adjective

Questions	Answers
最近好不好? How have you been lately?	很好。 I've been very well.
你累不累? Are you tired?	不累。 No, I'm not tired.

b) verb + 不 + verb

Questions	Answers
明天是不是九月一号? Is it September 1st tomorrow?	不是。 No, it isn't.
你要不要吃饺子? Do you want to have some dumplings?	要。 Yes, I do (want).

c) verb + 没 + verb

Questions	Answers
他今天有没有英语课? Does he have English class today?	没有。 No, he doesn't (have).
你有没有弟弟? Do you have younger brothers?	有。 Yes, I do (have).

Try This!

1. Change the following statements into yes-no questions. Use the two methods as shown in the examples. Pay attention to the verb or adjective in the sentence.

❶ 他家有一只狗。 ＿＿ 他家有狗吗？ or 他家有没有狗？ ＿＿

❷ 明天是你的生日。 ＿＿＿＿＿＿＿＿＿＿＿＿＿＿

❸ 今天是星期三。 ＿＿＿＿＿＿＿＿＿＿＿＿＿＿

❹ 你的妈妈是医生。 ＿＿＿＿＿＿＿＿＿＿＿＿＿＿

❺ 这是你的书。 ＿＿＿＿＿＿＿＿＿＿＿＿＿＿

❻ 他们喜欢猫。 ＿＿＿＿＿＿＿＿＿＿＿＿＿＿

❼ 那是她们的狗。 ＿＿＿＿＿＿＿＿＿＿＿＿＿＿

❽ 安琪要吃牛肉。 ＿＿＿＿＿＿＿＿＿＿＿＿＿＿

❾ 现在是三点半。 ＿＿＿＿＿＿＿＿＿＿＿＿＿＿

❿ 我哥哥很高。 ＿＿＿＿＿＿＿＿＿＿＿＿＿＿

⓫ 他的西瓜很甜。 ＿＿＿＿＿＿＿＿＿＿＿＿＿＿

2. Use wh-words to create questions that elicit the answers circled. Use the question words provided to create the questions.

谁	谁的	什么	几点	哪里
who	whose	what	what time	where

❶ 我的好朋友姓王。

＿＿＿＿＿＿＿＿＿＿＿＿＿

❷ 我姐姐是大学生。

＿＿＿＿＿＿＿＿＿＿＿＿＿

❸ 他们喜欢吃热狗。

＿＿＿＿＿＿＿＿＿＿＿＿＿

❹ 我现在在学校上课。

＿＿＿＿＿＿＿＿＿＿＿＿＿

❺ 我们的学校有中文老师。

＿＿＿＿＿＿＿＿＿＿＿＿＿

❻ 那是我的书包。

＿＿＿＿＿＿＿＿＿＿＿＿＿

❼ 我下午两点半去游泳。

＿＿＿＿＿＿＿＿＿＿＿＿＿

❽ 他们在家看电视。

＿＿＿＿＿＿＿＿＿＿＿＿＿

❾ 我是北京人。

＿＿＿＿＿＿＿＿＿＿＿＿＿

❿ 你好，我姓张。

＿＿＿＿＿＿＿＿＿＿＿＿＿

3. **Role-play** Work with a partner to make a conversation on meeting on the first day of school. Come up with at least five yes-no questions. Role-play the conversation with your partner and then present it to the class.

我二十岁，你呢？
我十八岁。

你姓王，是吗？
是，我姓王。
Your surname is Wang, right? Yes, it is.

duì
你是美国人，对吗？
对，我是美国人。
You're American, right? Yes, I'm American.

中午我们吃饺子，好吗？
好。
Let's have Chinese dumplings for lunch, okay? Okay.

呢 is placed after a noun to ask a follow-up question on the preceding statement.

Examples: ❶ 我的暑假过得很好，你呢？
My summer vacation was good. How about yours?

❷ 我家有两只狗，你家呢？
I have two dogs. How about you?

是吗 and 对吗 are tag questions that seek confirmation to what is indicated in the preceding sentence. They can be used interchangeably.

Examples: ❶ 她有两个妹妹，是吗？
She has two sisters, right?

❷ 你学过中文，对吗？
You learned Chinese before, right?

The tag question 好吗 is used to seek agreement on a suggestion indicated in the preceding sentence.

Examples: ❶ 下午我们打篮球，好吗？
Let's play basketball this afternoon, okay?

❷ 晚上我们看电影，好吗？
Let's watch a movie tonight, okay?

1. Read the statements and add an appropriate tag question after them. There can be more than one type of tag question for each statement. Then work with a partner to ask and answer these questions.

Example: 他是美国人，对吗？ /是吗？

❶ 他姓李。

_____

❷ 你是中国人。

_____

❸ 她家在北京。

_____

❹ 我们今天在家吃饭。

_____

❺ 他喜欢狗和猫。

_____

❻ 星期三有中文课。

_____

❼ 咖啡很苦。

_____

❽ 他天天打乒乓球。

_____

❾ 你十六岁了。

_____

❿ 他昨天晚上上网了。

_____

2. Complete the dialog by filling in the correct tag questions. Some tag question(s) might be used more than once.

你呢　是吗　对吗　好吗

丁强：马克，你好！

马克：丁强，你好！好久不见，你暑假过得怎么样？

丁强：过得很好。_____？

马克：我过得也不错。

丁强：今天是星期二，_____？

马克：对。你今天有中文课，_____？

丁强：不是，我今天有英语课。

马克：我今天下午三点放学，_____？

丁强：我也是。

马克：放学后我们去踢足球，_____？
　　　　　　qù
　　　　　　go

丁强：好！

CULTURAL HIGHLIGHTS

Asking Personal Questions

Chinese people sometimes ask questions that other cultures consider too personal to answer. For example, it is a common practice for elders and even peers to ask someone's age, salary, marital status, or how much something costs (like a car). These are often asked out of concern. Do not be surprised if someone asks you the price of an article of clothing that you are wearing.

However, with Western influence, the notion of privacy is changing. Some Chinese people have found personal questions sensitive and have refrained from asking people about them. In your culture, what are some of the questions that are considered appropriate and inappropriate to ask?

你多大了？
有男朋友吗？

JANUARY						
S	M	T	W	T	F	S
1	2	3	4	5	6	7
8	9	10	(11)	12	13	14
15	16	17	18	19	20	21
22	23	24	25	26	27	28
29	30	31				

lǐbài

今天礼拜几？

今天礼拜三。

What day is today? Today is Wednesday.

A More ways to tell days of the week

zhōumò

大后天是周末吗？

对，大后天是礼拜天。

Is three days from now the weekend? Yes, it's a Sunday.

生 词

NEW WORDS

礼拜 n.	禮拜	lǐbài	week
周末 n.	週末	zhōumò	weekend
大前天 n.		dàqiántiān	three days ago
大后天 n.	大後天	dàhòutiān	three days from now

Words you have learned

xīngqī 星期 n. week	zuótiān 昨天 n. yesterday
jīntiān 今天 n. today	qiántiān 前天 n. the day before yesterday
míngtiān 明天 n. tomorrow	hòutiān 后天 n. the day after tomorrow

LANGUAGE FOCUS

In Chinese, there are three ways to express a week:

❶ 星期   ❷ 周   ❸ 礼拜

You have already learned to use 星期 and 周. The pattern with 礼拜 is the same as the patterns with 星期 and 周, i.e., just add the number after the Chinese word for "week":

Examples:

星期一 / 周一 / 礼拜一   星期五 / 周五 / 礼拜五

However, 礼拜 is more conversational. When referring to Sundays, 星期天/日, 礼拜天/日 and 周日 are all acceptable.

1. Complete the following sentences by writing the correct character(s).

❶ 今天是星期一，昨天是＿＿＿＿＿＿，后天是＿＿＿＿＿＿。

❷ 明天是星期五，今天是＿＿＿＿＿，昨天是＿＿＿＿＿。

❸ 昨天是礼拜天，大前天是＿＿＿＿＿，大后天是＿＿＿＿＿。

❹ 周末是＿＿＿＿＿和＿＿＿＿＿。

❺ 今天是五月一日。明天是＿＿＿＿＿。昨天是＿＿＿＿＿。

❻ 明天是九月三十号。后天是＿＿＿＿＿。前天是＿＿＿＿＿。

2. Look at the following calendar and make a statement about one day and then ask your partner to complete your sentence. You must create at least three sentences for your partner to complete and then your partner will create three different sentences for you.

Example: 今天是二月十八号，星期三。昨天是＿＿＿＿。大后天是＿＿＿＿。

二月						
星期一	星期二	星期三	星期四	星期五	星期六	星期日
						1 十三
2 十四	3 十五	4 立春	5 十七	6 十八	7 十九	8 二十
9 廿一	10 廿二	11 廿三	12 廿四	13 廿五	14 廿六	15 廿七
16 廿八	17 廿九	18 三十	19 春节	20 初二	21 初三	22 初四
23 初五	24 初六	25 初七	26 初八	27 初九	28 初十	

3. Look at the calendars in the beginning of this lesson (the Get Ready section). State in Chinese the country and dates for a holiday or vacation that occur in different months. You may refer to the holiday in English if you don't know its Chinese name.

Example: 在澳大利亚，一月二十六日是国庆节，是礼拜天。

Guóqìng Jié
National Day

你几点上中文课？

我上午九点上中文课。九点以前我有数学课。

What time do you have Chinese class? I have Chinese class at 9 a.m. Before 9 I have math class.

学校什么时候开学？

九月一号以后开学。

When does school start? School starts on September 1st.

NEW WORDS

生
词

时候 n.	時候	shíhou	time
什么时候 q.w.	什麼時候	shénme shíhou	when; what time
时间 n.	時間	shíjiān	time, period
开学 v.	開學	kāixué	school opens
考试 n.	考試	kǎoshì	exam, test
期中考试 phr.	期中考試	qīzhōng kǎoshì	midterm examination
期末考试 phr.	期末考試	qīmò kǎoshì	final examination
放假 v.		fàngjià	have a day off (holiday)
春假 n.		chūnjià	spring break/vacation
寒假 n.		hánjià	winter break/vacation
返校日 n.		fǎnxiàorì	a day in the summer for students to report back to school
交作业 phr.	交作業	jiāo zuòyè	hand in assignments/homework

Words you have learned

yǐqián
以前 n. before

yǐhòu
以后 n. after

jǐdiǎn
几点 pron. what time

LANGUAGE FOCUS

You have already learned how to ask time by using 几点, which only refers to clock time. To reply, replace 几点 with the time (i.e., place the time expression before the verb).

Examples: ❶ 你几点吃早餐？我早上八点吃早餐。
What time do you have breakfast? I have breakfast at 8 in the morning.

❷ 他几点下课？他下午三点下课。
What time does he get out of class? He gets out at 3 in the afternoon.

To ask the general question of when something takes place, use the question word 什么时候. It is placed before the verb to form a "when" question.

Examples: ❶ 你们什么时候放暑假？ ❷ 她什么时候考试？
When is your summer vacation? When are her exams?

To state that an activity or event takes place before or after a certain time, use 以前 or 以后.

Example: 九月五号以前开学。八点以后上课。
School starts before September 5th. Classes start after 8 o'clock.

Try This!

1. Read the following activities and the times when they take place. Then state in a complete sentence that you do these activities at the specified times. Remember that in Chinese the time expression occurs before the verb.

   Next, state that you do the activities before or after the stated time.

   Example: 起床 6.30 AM ⟶ 我早上六点半起床。
   or
   ⟶ 我早上六点半以前起床。

   ❶ 吃早饭　　7:00 AM ⟶ _____

   ❷ 上学　　　8:05 AM ⟶ _____

   ❸ 上中文课　8:20 AM ⟶ _____

   ❹ 吃中饭　　12:45 PM ⟶ _____

   ❺ 放学　　　2:50 PM ⟶ _____

   ❻ 回家　　　3:15 AM ⟶ _____

   ❼ 看电视　　5:30 PM ⟶ _____

   ❽ 吃晚饭　　6:45 PM ⟶ _____

   ❾ 做功课　　7:25 PM ⟶ _____

   ❿ 睡觉　　　11:15 PM ⟶ _____

2. Work with a partner to practice asking and answering questions on when the following activities take place. Use 什么时候 to make the questions. For the answers, you may give a specified date or a general time period using 以前 or 以后.

   Example: 学校什么时候开学？ ⟶ 学校九月三号开学。
   or
   ⟶ 学校九月二号以后开学。

   ❶ 交暑假作业　　　　❹ 放暑假

   ❷ 期中考试　　　　　❺ 放寒假

   ❸ 期末考试　　　　　❻ 放春假
   　　　　　　　　　　　spring break

3. Read the following text from a phone conversation and decide if the statements afterwards are true or false.

安琪：喂，是芳芳吗？
   wèi
   hello

芳芳：是，我是芳芳。

安琪：芳芳，我是安琪。

芳芳：啊，安琪，最近好吗？
   à
   express surprise

安琪：我很好。你怎么样？

芳芳：我也很好。

安琪：你知道学校什么时候开学吗？
   zhīdào
   know

芳芳：九月一号是返校日，去学校交作业。九月三号
       开学上课。

安琪：好，谢谢你！今天八月三十号，我们后天学校见！

芳芳：好，后天见！

True or False (是非题)：

❶ 芳芳很高兴认识安琪。

❷ 安琪说她最近很好。

❸ 芳芳不知道学校什么时候开学。

❹ 学校后天开学。

❺ 明天是八月三十一号。

❻ 今天安琪和芳芳去上学。

C Specifying a time period

你们从几月到几月放暑假？

When is your summer vacation?

我们从六月到八月放暑假。

Our summer vacation is from June to August.

second school term

JANUARY	FEBRUARY	MARCH
SUN MON TUE WED THU FRI SAT	SUN MON TUE WED THU FRI SAT	SUN MON TUE WED THU FRI SAT

xuéqī

从一月到六月是第二学期。

The second school term is from January to June.

NEW WORDS 生 词

第一学期 phr.	第一学期	dì-yī xuéqī	first school term (semester)
第二学期 phr.	第二学期	dì-èr xuéqī	second school term (semester)
春天(春季) n.		chūntiān (chūnjì)	spring
夏天(夏季) n.		xiàtiān (xiàjì)	summer
秋天(秋季) n.		qiūtiān (qiūjì)	fall
冬天(冬季) n.		dōngtiān (dōngjì)	winter

Words you have learned

cóng dào
从…到… n. from...to...

20

When you state that you do an activity from one time to another, use the expression 从⋯到⋯. For example, to say that you have spring break from one day to another, you would say, "从上个星期六到这个星期天我们放春假." Another example is the sentence, "从早上到下午我都没有时间." Can you guess what this sentence means?

从⋯到⋯ can also form 是–sentences to indicate the time period that a certain season or term spans.

Examples:

1 从六月到八月是夏季。
Summer is from June to August.

2 从九月到一月是第一学期。
The first semester is from September to January.

1. State from what time to what time you do or might do the following using a complete sentence.

Example: You go online on the computer: 从晚上七点到八点我上网。

1 You have Chinese class

2 You are in school

3 You sleep

4 You play a sport

5 You have vacation in the winter

6 You watch television

7 You have summer vacation

8 You do your homework

9 You eat lunch

10 You have a spring break

11 You start the first semester

12 You have midterm exams

2. State in a complete sentence in Chinese the duration of the following time periods using the 从⋯到⋯ construction:

Example: First semester: 从九月三日到一月二十五日是第一学期。

1 Spring *(March 21 – June 21)* _____

2 Summer *(June 21 – September 21)* _____

3 Fall *(September 21 – December 21)* _____

4 Winter *(December 21 – March 21)* _____

5 Final exams *(January 27 – January 30)* _____

6 Second semester *(February 1 – June 19)* _____

DESCRIBING YOUR SUMMER VACATION

cānjiā   xiàlìngyíng
你暑假参加夏令营了吗？
Did you attend summer camp during vacation?

qù   lǚyóu
没有，我去旅游了。你呢？
No, I went traveling. How about you?

A Stating what people did during the summer

shǔqī
我上暑期学校了。
I attended summer school.

cānjiā xiàlìngyíng
参加夏令营
參加夏令營
attend/go to summer camp

qù lǚyóu
去旅游
去旅遊
traveling

shàng shǔqī xuéxiào
上暑期学校
上暑期學校
attend summer school

shàng bǔxíbān
上补习班
上補習班
attend/go to a tutoring center

zuò shǔjià zuòyè
做暑假作业
做暑假作業
do summer assignments

zuò yìgōng
做义工
做義工
do volunteer work

dǎgōng
打工
work a temporary job

dāi zài jiā li
呆在家里
呆在家裏
stay at home

qù hǎibiān
去海边
去海邊
go to the beach

mǎi dōngxi
买东西
買東西
go shopping

guàng jiē
逛街
go to the mall, window shopping

Phrases you have learned

yóuyǒng 游泳 *v.* swimming	dǎ wǎngqiú 打网球 *phr.* play tennis	kàn diànyǐng 看电影 *phr.* watch a movie	dǎ diàndòng 打电动 *phr.* play console games
dǎ bàngqiú 打棒球 *phr.* play baseball	tī zúqiú 踢足球 *phr.* play soccer	wán diànnǎo yóuxì 玩电脑游戏 *phr.* play computer games	xiě bókè 写博客 *phr.* write a blog

In order to express that an activity happened in the past, we place 了 after the verb and its object. The use of 了 is to describe that an action has already been completed at one time.

Examples: ❶ 我暑假去旅游了。
I went traveling during the summer vacation.

❷ 我昨天晚上看电影了。
I saw a movie last night.

To state various summer activities that you have done, use the "verb + object" pattern:

Examples:

❧ 上 + 补习班 ➡ 我暑假上补习班了。
I attended a tutoring center during summer vacation.

❧ 做 + 义工 ➡ 我上个月做义工了。
I did volunteer work last month.

❧ 去 + 海边 ➡ 上个星期我去海边了。
I went to the beach last week.

❧ 打 + 篮球 ➡ 我前天下午打篮球了。
I played basketball in the afternoon the day before.

Note that when the time expression functions as an adverbial, it can be placed before or after the subject.

 CULTURAL HIGHLIGHTS

What Chinese Students Do in the Summer

Students in China have a summer vacation which is shorter than in the US. Summer vacation typically begins in July, though some schools start their vacations in June. Summer vacation generally lasts for about two months. During that time students may be engaged in a number of activities. Many of them will take extra classes at their regular school or at another school that will help in their academic studies. To improve their children's prospects of entering a good school, many parents will send them to training classes in music, dance, drawing, mathematics, etc. There are some who will take their children traveling in or outside of China.

Most Chinese students do not go to summer camp, but it is becoming more and more popular for students to travel to the countryside and engage in volunteer activities. Some students will teach younger children in rural villages to help supplement the rural children's education.

Try This!

1. Look at the pictures below and say what the people were doing during the summer. Be sure to state that the activities took place in the past.

2. Change the following sentences into the past tense by adding one of the time words below:

昨天晚上　前天下午　大前天早上

上个礼拜天　上个月　去年

Example: 我昨天晚上看电视了。_____

❶ 姐姐买衣服。 _____

❷ 马克的妈妈喝中国茶。 _____

❸ 哥哥吃饺子。 _____

❹ 我参加夏令营。 _____

❺ 他爸爸去法国。 _____

❻ 你们去海边。 _____

❼ 弟弟做作业。 _____

❽ 王老师看书。 _____

3. Read the following dialog and answer the questions.

丁强：马克，你好！

马克：丁强，你好！好久不见，你暑假过得怎么样？

丁强：过得很好。你呢？

马克：我过得也不错。你暑假做什么了？

丁强：我去墨西哥了，还参加夏令营了。你呢？
Mòxīgē
Mexico

马克：我做义工了，上个星期还去中国了。

❶ The relationship between Mark and Ding Qiang is

    a. 老师和学生   b. 学生和学生   c. 美国和中国   (   )

❷ Which expression indicates that they know each other?

    a. 怎么样？   b. 好久不见。   c. 我很高兴认识你。 (   )

❸ Who went to Mexico?

    a. 丁强   b. 丁强和马克   c. 马克   (   )

❹ Where did Mark go last week?

    a. 夏令营   b. 墨西哥   c. 中国   (   )

❺ What time period was mentioned in the dialog?

    a. 夏季   b. 秋季   c. 冬季   (   )

你暑假过得怎么样？
How was your summer vacation?

(1) 我暑假过得很开心。你呢？
kāixīn
I had a good time. What about you?

(2) 我过得很有意思。
yìsi
I had a good time.

(3) 我过得无聊极了。
wúliáo *jíle*
Mine was extremely boring.

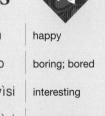

NEW WORDS 生词

开心 adj.	開心	kāixīn	happy
无聊 adj.	無聊	wúliáo	boring; bored
有意思 phr.		yǒu yìsi	interesting
没意思 phr.	沒意思	méi yìsi	not interesting
极了 adv.	極了	jíle	extremely

LANGUAGE FOCUS

As you have learned, 很 is used before an adjective but it does not intensify the degree of the adjective. To intensify an adjective to a high degree, we can place 极了 after the adjective.

Examples: ❶ 做暑假作业很无聊。   Doing summer assignments is boring.

❷ 做暑假作业无聊极了。   Doing summer assignments is extremely boring.

Or

❸ 参加夏令营很开心。   Going to summer camp makes me happy.

❹ 参加夏令营开心极了。   Going to summer camp makes me extremely happy.

The pattern 过得… is generally used to express how one spends his or her days/life. To express how you spend your vacation, you can also use this pattern. "很 + adjective" or "adjective + 极了" can be placed after 过得 to describe your vacation.

Examples: ❶ 你暑假过得怎么样？ 我暑假过得很无聊。
How was your summer vacation? It was boring.

❷ 你周末过得怎么样？ 我周末过得开心极了。
How was your weekend? It was extremely good.

1. Look at the following pictures of people and ask and answer questions on how their summer vacation is going. Use 很 or 极了 in your sentence.

    Example: 她暑假过得怎么样？她暑假过得……

2. Read the following dialog and decide if the statements afterwards are true or false.

芳芳：张安，好久不见！你好吗？

张安：嗨，芳芳！我很好。你暑假过得怎么样？

芳芳：我暑假天天呆在家里，过得无聊极了。你呢？

张安：我暑假去英国旅游了，还参加夏令营了，过得很有意思。

芳芳：你做暑假作业了吗？

张安：还没有！我今晚要在家里做。

芳芳：哈哈，现在快回家吧！
　　　　　　 kuài huí　 ba
　　　　　　 快回家吧！
　　　　 quickly return　making a mild
　　　　　　　　　 imperative sentence

张安：明天见！

True or False (是非题):

❶ 芳芳暑假天天逛街、买东西。　　　❹ 张安没有做暑假作业。

❷ 张安暑假过得很无聊。　　　　　　❺ 芳芳今晚要在家里做暑假作业。

❸ 芳芳暑假过得开心极了。

Expressing other emotions and feelings

juéde　　　xìngfèn
今天开学，我觉得很兴奋。
School starts today. I'm excited.

jǐnzhāng
我紧张极了！
I'm extremely nervous!

NEW WORDS

生词

觉得 v.	覺得	juéde	feel
感到 v.		gǎndào	feel
紧张 adj.	緊張	jǐnzhāng	nervous, intense
兴奋 adj.	興奮	xìngfèn	excited
难过 adj.	難過	nánguò	sad, aggrieved
伤心 adj.	傷心	shāngxīn	sad, heart-broken
生气 adj.	生氣	shēngqì	angry

LANGUAGE FOCUS

You can use 觉得 or 感到 to express how you feel. The adjectives describing your emotions and feelings will follow after these verbs.

Examples:　❶ 我觉得很难过。
　　　　　　　　I feel very sad.

　　　　　　❷ 我感到很生气。
　　　　　　　　I feel very angry.

Try This!

1. How do you feel about the following situations? Read the sentences and describe how you feel about the situations. Use the sentence pattern 我觉得/感到……．

> 开心　无聊　难过　有意思　生气
>
> 紧张　兴奋　伤心　没意思

For example:

明天是周末，大家觉得很开心。

 我的好朋友要打电话给我，

_____

 后天是我的生日，

_____

今天晚上看电影了，

_____

 这本书我看过了，

_____

 我没有做功课，老师

_____

 明天考试，

_____

 明天要去英国，

_____

 爸爸买新车了，

_____

 我考试考得不好，

_____

 我的小狗不见了，

_____

Reading *in Context*

STEP 1 MEETING AND GREETING PEOPLE

The teacher and students greeting each other on the first day of school

老师：同学们好！

同学：老师好！

老师：欢迎大家回来！很高兴
　　　见到你们！

同学：谢谢老师！

老师：你们暑假过得怎么样？

同学：很开心！老师呢？

老师：我过得也很好。

dàjiā

everyone

STEP 3 DESCRIBING YOUR SUMMER VACATION

Two students talking about how they spent their summer vacation

马克：丁强，你好啊！

丁强：马克，你好！好久不见，你
　　　暑假过得怎么样？

马克：过得很开心。你呢？

丁强：我过得也不错。你暑假做什
　　　么了？

马克：我去墨西哥旅行了。你呢？

丁强：我参加夏令营了。从夏令营
　　　回来以后我去上暑期学校。

马克：今天开学，我觉得很兴奋。

丁强：我紧张极了，因为我没
　　　做暑期作业！

马克：哈哈。上课了，我们
　　　一会儿见！

丁强：再见！

yīnwèi

because

STEP 2 TELLING THE DAY AND TIME

Two friends talking about what they want to do over the weekend

安琪：芳芳，学校什么时候
　　　开学？

芳芳：学校下个礼拜一开学。

安琪：明天是礼拜六，你这个
　　　周末做什么？

芳芳：我明天想去跑步，礼拜
　　　天想去看电影。你呢？

安琪：我明天下午从四点到
　　　六点打网球，礼拜天
　　　也想去看电影。你礼拜
　　　天几点去？

安琪：下午两点，你有时间吗？

芳芳：礼拜天下午两点到四点
　　　我要做功课，四点以后
　　　才有时间。

cái

only

安琪：那我们下个星期再看，
　　　好吗？

芳芳：好。

31

Step Up!

1. Below is a letter from your e-pal in China. Read the letter, complete the information and answer the questions about 陈红.

亲爱的美国笔友，
　　　　　bǐyǒu
　　　　　e-pal

　　我的名字叫陈红，今年十五岁。我是明德中学高一甲班的学
　　　　　　　　　　　　　　　　　　　dé　　　　jiǎ bān
　　　　　　　　　　　　　　　　　　　　　　　Class 1

生，很高兴做你的笔友。

　　新学期刚开始，我觉得很兴奋。这是我的新学校，我感到
　　　　　gāng kāishǐ
　　　　　just start

有点紧张。今天我想告诉你我暑假做了什么。
yǒudiǎn　　　　gàosu
slightly　　　　tell

　　刚放暑假的时候，我早上去上英语补习班，下午呆在家里做

暑假作业，觉得有点无聊。七月中我跟爸爸妈妈去上海看爷爷
　　　　　　　　　　　　　gēn
　　　　　　　　　　　　　with

奶奶以后，就去参加在北京的夏令营。在那儿我认识了很多新朋
　　　jiù
　　　right away

友，我们每天一起去逛街，有时候也去看电影。三个星期的夏令
　　　　　yìqǐ
　　　　　together

营，我们过得开心极了。

　　你的暑假过得怎么样？我想知道美国学生怎么过暑假，喜欢参

加什么活动。请你写电邮告诉我，好吗？
　　　qǐng
　　　please

你的中国笔友，
陈红

Identify the following information from the e-letter and write the answers in Chinese:

1 Name: _____

2 Age: _____

3 Name of school: _____

4 One person she traveled with: _____

5 Where her grandparents live: _____

6 The location of her summer camp: _____

7 One thing she did at summer camp: _____

Answer the following questions in Chinese:

1 Why is she writing the e-letter? **3** Why was she bored in the beginning?

2 Why does she feel nervous? **4** How does she feel about her camp experience?

2. After reading Chen Hong's letter, your assignment is to write her back and share information about your school and your summer vacation. Compose an e-letter that also describes you and your family. Your letter should be at least two paragraphs with each paragraph having a minimum of five sentences.

3. Do a survey of 10 students in your class to find out how they spent their vacation and at least two activities that they did this past summer. After you have surveyed 10 students, work with another student to complete a bar graph of the activities that all of the students you both interviewed did. Remember to ask each person his/her name, and what activity he/she did this past summer. (你叫什么名字？你暑假过的怎么样？你暑假做什么了？)

Use the chart below to get started:

	名字	暑假过得怎么样?	huódòng 活动 activity	活动
1				
2				
3				
4				
5				
6				
7				
8				
9				
10				

Fun Time!

When you walk into your school building or the main building, you often see a motto or slogan that encourages students to succeed in both their studies and in life. Here are two mottos from schools in China and two mottos from American schools. Read the Chinese mottos and try to determine their meanings. Then find out what the motto is for your school and compare it with one of the Chinese mottos. You may discover that the motto of your school is written in Latin so you may have to translate it into English first.

Chinese Mottos

Lai'an Zhongxin Primary School, *Jiangsu Province, China*

Renmin University of China, *Beijing*

English Mottos

Empowering All to Learn, Create, Contribute, and Grow

Livingston Public Schools, *U.S.*

I have learned...

Core Vocabulary

Verbs

到		dào	(used after verbs to indicate successful attainment of the action)	去		qù	go to (a place)
过	過	guò	spend	呆		dāi	stay (at a place)
欢迎	歡迎	huānyíng	welcome	买	買	mǎi	buy
回来	回來	huílai	come back	逛		guàng	stroll, roam
认识	認識	rènshi	know someone, be acquainted with	打工		dǎgōng	work a temporary job
开学	開學	kāixué	school opens	觉得	覺得	juéde	feel
放假		fàngjià	have a day off (holiday)	感到		gǎndào	feel
参加	參加	cānjiā	join, take part				

Nouns

最近		zuìjìn	recently	返校日		fǎnxiàorì	a day in the summer for students to report back to school
暑假		shǔjià	summer vacation	春天(春季)		chūntiān (chūnjì)	spring
一会儿	一會兒	yíhuìr	a little while	夏天(夏季)		xiàtiān (xiàjì)	summer
礼拜	禮拜	lǐbài	week	秋天(秋季)		qiūtiān (qiūjì)	fall
周末		zhōumò	weekend	冬天(冬季)		dōngtiān (dōngjì)	winter
大前天		dàqiántiān	three days ago	夏令营	夏令營	xiàlìngyíng	summer camp
大后天	大後天	dàhòutiān	three days from now	旅游	旅遊	lǚyóu	travel, tour
时候	時候	shíhou	time	补习班	補習班	bǔxíbān	tutoring center
时间	時間	shíjiān	time, period	义工	義工	yìgōng	volunteer work
考试	考試	kǎoshì	exam, test	海边	海邊	hǎibiān	beach
春假		chūnjià	spring break/vacation	东西	東西	dōngxi	things, items (in shopping)
寒假		hánjià	winter break/vacation				

Adjectives

高兴	高興	gāoxìng	glad, happy	兴奋	興奮	xìngfèn	excited
开心	開心	kāixīn	happy	难过	難過	nánguò	sad, aggrieved
无聊	無聊	wúliáo	boring; bored	伤心	傷心	shāngxīn	sad, heart-broken
紧张	緊張	jǐnzhāng	nervous, intense	生气	生氣	shēngqì	angry

I have learned...

Question word				Adverb			
什么时候	什麼時候	shénme shíhou	when; what time	极了	極了	jíle	extremely

Phrases

好久		hǎojiǔ	quite a while, a long time	暑期学校	暑期學校	shǔqī xuéxiào	summer school
期中考试	期中考試	qīzhōng kǎoshì	midterm examination	暑假作业	暑假作業	shǔjià zuòyè	summer assignments
期末考试	期末考試	qīmò kǎoshì	final examination	逛街		guàng jiē	go to the mall, window shopping
交作业	交作業	jiāo zuòyè	hand in assignments/homework	有意思		yǒu yìsi	interesting
第一学期	第一學期	dì-yī xuéqī	first school term (*semester*)	没意思	沒意思	méi yìsi	not interesting
第二学期	第二學期	dì-èr xuéqī	second school term (*semester*)				

Common expressions for greetings and leave taking

好久不见!	Hǎojiǔ bú jiàn!	Long time no see!
最近好吗?	Zuìjìn hǎo ma?	How have you been recently?
最近怎么样?	Zuìjìn zěnmeyàng?	How have things been recently?
很高兴见到你!	Hěn gāoxìng jiàndào nǐ!	Very glad to see you!
暑假过得好吗?	Shǔjià guò de hǎo ma?	How was your summer vacation?
欢迎你们回来!	Huānyíng nǐmen huílai!	Welcome back!
很高兴认识你!	Hěn gāoxìng rènshi nǐ!	Very glad to meet you!
一会儿见!	Yíhuìr jiàn!	See you later!
明天见!	Míngtiān jiàn!	See you tomorrow!

SENTENCE PATTERNS

很高兴见到你!

最近忙吗?

中午我们吃饺子，好吗? 好。

今天礼拜几? 今天礼拜三。

学校什么时候开学? 9月1号以后开学。

从一月到六月是第二学期。

暑假你参加夏令营了吗? 没有，我去旅游了。

你暑假过得怎么样? 我暑假过得很开心。

今天开学，我觉得很兴奋。

I can do!

Interpretive Communication

- ❏ I can understand when someone introduces himself/herself or introduces someone else to me.
- ❏ I can read and understand a short, simple dialog.
- ❏ I can understand when someone describes activities that he or she has done.
- ❏ I can understand when people talk about past activities.

Interpersonal Communication

- ❏ I can converse about people and their activities.
- ❏ I can talk to others about their likes, dislikes, and feelings.
- ❏ I can ask questions and get information about another student's summer activities.

Presentational Communication

- ❏ I can greet many different people.
- ❏ I can describe how I spent my vacation.
- ❏ I can tell about my leisure activities and preferences.
- ❏ I can write about what I did during summer vacation.

Cultural Knowledge

- ❏ I can talk about the first day of school in China.
- ❏ I can compare the appropriateness of questions in different cultural settings.
- ❏ I can compare Chinese and American students' vacations.

Moving to a new school

到新学校

COMMUNICATIVE GOALS

- Telling modes of transportation
- Stating how to get from one location to another
- Interpreting a written text about people
- Talking about where and when people go to different places
- Using patterns that emphasize one key element over another
- Comparing sizes, shapes, and colors

Cultural Knowledge

- Linguistic variation in Chinese
- Living in Chinese cities
- Choosing liberal arts and science fields in Chinese high schools

Get ready...

Imagine that you have just moved to a new city and will be attending a new school. Read the self-introductions (自我介绍 zìwǒ jièshào) of the students below and decide which of them you would like to have as a friend. Then write down in English at least two reasons why you would like to have one of them as a friend. Share your reasons with one other classmate and see if you agree with that classmate.

丁强

我叫丁强，上九年级 (niánjí, grade)。我十四岁，八月十五日是我的生日。我有两个哥哥和一个妹妹。我很喜欢吃巧克力 (qiǎokèlì, chocolate)。我家有一只小狗。我喜欢打棒球和篮球，也喜欢学中文。

林安琪

我是林安琪，上十二年级。三月二十九日是我的生日。我十七岁。我是美国人。我有一个姐姐，她在大学 (dàxué, university) 学中文。我们都喜欢说 (shuō, speak) 中文。我也喜欢画画，将来想一个画家。

张安

我是张安，上十年级。我十五岁。我属马，上个星期天是我的生日。我是中国人，我是去年来 (lái, come to) 美国的。我家有三口人，我没兄 (xiōng, older brother) 弟姐妹。我家有两只猫。我每天早上跑步，我很喜欢打电动。

马克

我叫马克，上十一年级。我的生日是七月三日。我有一个弟弟，他五岁。我的好朋友是张安。我不吃辣，我喜欢吃日本餐 (Rìběncān, Japanese food)。我很喜欢游泳和上中文课。李老师是我的中文老师。

刘芳芳

我是李芳芳，上海人，我九年级来美国，现在上高中 (gāozhōng, senior high) 十一年级。我属马，生日是十月三十一日。张安的爸爸是我的舅舅。我喜欢吃水果 (shuǐguǒ, fruits)，不喜欢喝牛奶。我喜欢的宠物是乌龟。我不喜欢数学课。我的爱好是弹钢琴。

zěnme qù
你怎么去学校？
How do you go to school?

zuò gōngjiāochē
我坐公交车去学校。
I go to school by bus.

dā dìtiě
我搭地铁去学校。
I go to school by subway.

A Talking about modes of transportation

NEW WORDS

怎么 q.w.	怎麼	zěnme	how	走 v.		zǒu	walk
来 v.	來	lái	come	回 v.		huí	return
去 v.		qù	go	开 v.	開	kāi	drive (a car)
坐 v.		zuò	go by, travel by	骑 v.	騎	qí	ride
搭 v.		dā	go by, travel by	上班 v.		shàngbān	go to work
打 v.		dǎ	ride, sit (a taxi/cab)				

Words you have learned

yǐqián
以前 n. before

xiànzài
现在 n. now

gōngjiāochē

坐公交车

坐公交車

public bus

xiàochē

坐校车

坐校車

school bus

dìtiě

坐地铁

坐地鐵

subway

huǒchē

坐火车

坐火車

train

fēijī

坐飞机

坐飛機

airplane

chuán

坐船

ship

zìxíngchē

骑自行车

騎自行車

bicycle

mótuōchē

骑摩托车

騎摩托車

motorcycle

chūzūchē

坐出租车

坐出租車

cab, taxi

dǎchē / dǎdī

打车/打的
打車/打的

take a cab/taxi

zǒulù

走路

walk

kāichē

开车
開車

drive

* 搭 (dā) has the same meaning as 坐 (zuò), but it is mainly used in spoken Chinese.

LANGUAGE FOCUS

To ask about how one gets to a certain place, put the question word 怎么 before the verb.

Examples: ❶ 你以前怎么去图书馆?
How did you go to the library in the past?

❷ 他现在怎么去上班?
How does he go to work now?

When telling how to get to a place, put the means of transportation before the verb.

Examples: ❶ 我以前 骑自行车   去图书馆。 In the past, I went to the library
(means of transportation)   *(destination)* by bicycle.

❷ 他现在 坐出租车(打的) 去上班。 He goes to work by taxi now.
(means of transportation)   *(destination)*

When time and means of transportation are in the same sentence, time goes before the means of transportation.

Examples: ❶ 我早上八点坐公交车去学校。
I go to school by bus at 8 a.m.

❷ 她下午三点开车回家。
She drives home at 3 p.m.

Linguistic Variation — Modes of Transportation

In various regions of the Chinese-speaking world, the terms for modes of transportation are different. Below is a comparison of these terms in several Chinese-speaking areas.

	Mainland China	Taiwan	Hong Kong	Singapore/ Malaysia
public bus	公共汽车/ *jiāo* 公交车	公车/ *kèyùn* 客运/ *bā* 巴士	巴士	巴士
cab/taxi	出租车	*jìchéng* 计程车	*dī* 的士	*dé* 德士
motorcycle	摩托车	机车	*diàndān* 电单车	摩托车
bicycle	自行车	*jiǎotà* 脚踏车	单车	脚车
subway	地铁/ *qīngguǐ* 轻轨 *(light rail, mostly not run underground)*	*jiéyùn* 捷运	地铁	地铁

1. Look at the following pictures and make a sentence stating the mode of transportation (first picture of each question) and where the person/people are going (second picture of each question). Next, make another sentence stating the time by referring to the clock display.

For example, for the first question, you can say:

❶ 他们坐校车去学校。

❷ 他们早上八点坐校车去学校。

❶

❷

❸

❹

❺

❻

❼

❽

❾

❿

2. Xiaoming just moved to a new school and must choose an alternate form of transportation. Look at the mode of transportation he first used and change the sentence to describe his new way of getting to school.

Example: 走路，地铁 ⟶ 小明以前走路去学校，现在他坐地铁去学校。

	yǐqián 以前		xiànzài 现在
❶	骑自行车		骑摩托车
❷	坐地铁		坐火车
❸	走路		坐校车
❹	打车		开车
❺	坐船		坐公交车

3. Do a survey of at least 10 members in your class and ask them how they get to school. Make a bar graph showing the different ways that the students in your class arrive at school. You can use the following table to help you get the information.

	名字	走路	开车	打车	坐公交车	坐校车	坐地铁/ 坐火车	骑自行车/ 骑摩托车
❶								
❷								
❸								
❹								
❺								
❻								
❼								
❽								
❾								
❿								

Means

lái
你是怎么来学校的？
How did you come to school?

我是走路来学校的。
I came to school on foot.

你是怎么回家的？
How did you go home?

我是坐地铁回家的。
I went home by subway.

Time

你是几点起床的？
What time did you get up?

我是早上七点起床的。
I got up at 7 a.m.

她是什么时候去北京的？
When did she go to Beijing?

她是昨天去北京的。
She went to Beijing yesterday.

你是在哪儿出生的？
Where were you born?

我是在美国出生的。
I was born in the U.S.

U.S.A.

你是在哪儿吃午餐的？
Where did you have lunch?

我是在餐厅吃午餐的。
I had lunch in the cafeteria.

LANGUAGE FOCUS

In Chinese, we use the expression 是…的 to show emphasis of when, where, or how an action took place.

For example: 他是开车来学校的。 He came to school <u>by car</u>.

Here the emphasis is on the fact that he arrived by car and not by any other means. As a result, to stress the mode of transportation, the transportation mode is placed immediately after 是 followed by the rest of the sentence and ended with 的. The words that are placed immediately after 是 represent the item being emphasized.

You can also place a time expression into the sentence to emphasize when an event occurred.

For example: 她是昨天去北京的。 It was <u>yesterday</u> that she went to Beijing.

In this sentence the emphasis is placed on yesterday which immediately follows 是.

This expression can also be used in a question.

For example: 你是怎么来的？ <u>How</u> did you get here?

The answer could be: 我是打车来的。 I came by <u>cab/taxi</u>.

1. Use the 是⋯的 construction to show that a person has arrived in (来) or gone to (去) a place using a specific mode of transportation. Be sure to emphasize the mode of transportation and use the proper verb 搭, 坐, 叫, 打 or 开.

    Example: 马丽⋯(火车)⋯北京 ⟶ 马丽是搭火车去北京的。

    ❶ 林老师⋯(飞机)⋯上海 ⟶ _____
    ❷ 马克的爸爸⋯(船)⋯英国 ⟶ _____
    ❸ 王阿姨⋯(公交车)⋯体育馆 ⟶ _____
    ❹ 我妹妹⋯(走路)⋯图书馆 ⟶ _____
    ❺ 你母亲⋯(地铁)⋯学校 ⟶ _____
    ❻ 大伟⋯(自行车)⋯餐厅 ⟶ _____
    ❼ 李芳芳⋯(火车)⋯西安 ⟶ _____
    ❽ 张医生⋯(出租车)⋯家 ⟶ _____
    ❾ 他的朋友⋯(开车)⋯我家 ⟶ _____
    ❿ 丁叔叔⋯(摩托车)⋯动物园 ⟶ _____

2. The following pictures give you a clue as to what needs to be emphasized in a sentence. Look at the pictures and create a sentence in which you describe the picture using the 是⋯的 pattern. Be sure to emphasize the item in the picture.

> 她是开车来学校的。

sòng

爸爸送弟弟去学校。

My dad takes my younger brother to school.

NEW WORDS

生词

| 送 v. | sòng | send someone, accompany someone |
| 接 v. | jiē | pick (someone) up |

jiē

爸爸来学校接妹妹。

My dad comes to school to pick up my younger sister.

爸爸开车送妹妹去学校。

My dad drives my younger sister to school.

妈妈开车来学校接我。

My mom drives to school to pick me up.

The verb 送 has the meaning of "to give" or "to send."

For example, you can say

我送你去图书馆。

I will take you to the library.

To distinguish how you will take someone to a place, you say 我开车送你去体育馆 which means "I will take you to the gymnasium by (driving a) car."

The verb 接 has the meaning of "receive/get." Thus, you can say "我来学校接你," which means "I will come to the school to get you." If you wish to expand the sentence by putting in a time expression and mode of transportation, you would say:

"我今天下午开车来学校接你."

This afternoon I will pick you up from school by car.

Try This!

1. Someone is taking you to various places. Use the words given and create sentences that reflect these events by adding a mode of transportation of your choice.

❶ 哥哥　电影院　哥哥开车送我去电影院。
diànyǐngyuàn
movie theater

❷ 姐姐　图书馆　_____

❸ 丁叔叔　动物园　_____

❹ 李芳芳　体育馆　_____

❺ 奶奶　学校　_____

❻ 张安　上海　_____

❼ 爸爸　教学楼　_____

❽ 哥哥　操场　_____

❾ 王老师　医务室　_____

❿ 张叔叔　北京　_____

⓫ 爷爷　餐厅　_____

2. Use the following words to create sentences about someone taking or picking up someone else to or from a place.

❶ 送　妈妈　妹妹　学校　去

_____

❷ 爸爸　来　开车　弟弟　图书馆　接

_____

❸ 图书馆　接　我　哥哥　来　坐地铁　今天下午

_____

❹ 姐姐　早上十点　我　送　骑自行车　去　体育馆

_____

❺ 老师　动物园　明天早上　送　坐校车　我们　去

_____

3. The people in the following exercise are picking you up. Create sentences using the words provided.

Example: 爸爸／开车／学校 ⟶ 爸爸开车来学校接我。

❶ 爷爷／开车／学校　　_____

❷ 奶奶／打车／体育馆　_____

❸ 姐姐／骑自行车／图书馆　_____

❹ 哥哥／骑摩托车／动物园　_____

❺ 张叔叔／搭飞机／上海　_____

❻ 李阿姨／搭地铁／我家　_____

❼ 妈妈／坐公交车／体育馆　_____

❽ 李芳芳／搭校车／我家　_____

❾ 马克／叫出租车／我家　_____

❿ 爸爸／走路／医务室　_____

xiāngcūn bān　　chéngshì
他从乡村搬到城市。
He moved from the countryside to the city.

NEW WORDS　生词

搬 v.		bān	move
城市 n.		chéngshì	city
乡村 n.	鄉村	xiāngcūn	countryside, rural area
地方 n.		dìfang	place

A Moving from one place to another

我从教学楼走到图书馆。
I walked from the school building to the library.

他从北京来到纽约。
He came to New York from Beijing.

The verb 到 can be placed after another verb of movement to indicate that the action has been completed and one has reached the destination.

Examples: ❶ 我搬到城东边。   I moved to the east side of the city.

❷ 他走到餐厅。   He walked to the cafeteria.

❸ 他们来到体育馆。   They came to the gymnasium.

To describe movement from one place to another, use the preposition 从 (from) to indicate the starting point in the pattern of " 从 + starting point." Place this 从-phrase before the verb.

Examples: ❶ 哥哥从家里走到学校。
My older brother walked to school from home.

❷ 他们从操场来到电脑室。
They came to the computer room from the sports field.

❸ 我们从这个地方搬到那个地方。
We moved from this place to that place.

To indicate the time, place the time expression before 从:

Examples: ❶ 哥哥今天早上从家里走到学校。
My older brother walked to school from home this morning.

❷ 他们下午两点从操场来到电脑室。
They came to the computer room from the sports field at 2 p.m.

❸ 我们去年三月从这个地方搬到那个地方。
We moved from this place to that place last March.

Try This!

1. Look at the pictures and use the names and times provided to state that these people move from one place to another place at different times.

Example: 王小伟2013年从上海搬到北京。

上海   北京

王小伟; 2013年

①

香港　　　　西安

阿姨；　2012 年

②

华盛顿　　　纽约

叔叔；　上个星期

③

墨西哥　　　美国

爷爷；　四月

④

中国　　　　法国

外婆；　六月二十号

⑤

城市　　　　乡村

王老师；　九月

⑥

伦敦　　　　悉尼

安琪；　2011 年

2. Below is Mark's schedule today, and it shows where he does various activities. Work with a partner to make at least five sentences describing how he moved from one place to another. Use 走 or 来 in your sentences.

Example:

马克早上九点从家里来到教学楼。

Time Schedule	
7:30	早餐 (家里)
9:00	中文 (教学楼)
10:00	数学 (教学楼)
11:00	电脑 (电脑室)
12:00	午饭 (餐厅)
1:00	—
2:00	历史 (教学楼)
3:00	体育 (体育馆)
4:00	做功课 (图书馆)

B Showing cause and effect

wèishénme

你为什么搬家？

Why did you move?

yīnwèi

因为我家离学校很远，

suǒyǐ

所以我从东边搬到西边。

Because my home was far from school, I moved from the east side to the west.

NEW WORDS

为什么 q.w.	爲什麼	wèishénme	why
搬家 v.		bānjiā	move (house)
交通 n.		jiāotōng	traffic
交通工具 phr.		jiāotōng gōngjù	mode of transportation
堵车 v.	堵車	dǔchē	traffic jam
郊区 n.	郊區	jiāoqū	suburbs
小区 n.	小區	xiǎoqū	residential area
方便 adj.		fāngbiàn	convenient
安静 adj.	安靜	ānjìng	quiet
吵 adj.		chǎo	noisy
因为…所以… conj.	因爲…所以…	yīnwèi…suǒyǐ…	because…therefore…

Words you have learned

离 prep.	lí	(in giving distances) from		当 v.	dāng	to be
远 adj.	yuǎn	far		想 v.	xiǎng	to think, wish
近 adj.	jìn	near		甜 v.	tián	sweet
将来 n.	jiānglái	in the future				

为什么 is used to ask "why" questions.

Examples: ❶ 你为什么搬家？　　Why are you moving?

❷ 你为什么住在郊区？　Why do you stay in the suburbs?

❸ 你为什么坐公交车去上学？　Why do you take the bus to school?

To answer "why" questions, use the paired conjunction 因为…所以…, which is used to show cause and effect.

Examples: ❶ 因为城西边很不方便，所以我搬到城东边。
Because it is inconvenient in the west area of the city, *(therefore)* I am moving to the east area.

❷ 因为城市里很吵，所以我住在郊区。
Because it is noisy in the city, *(therefore)* I am staying in the suburbs.

❸ 因为我家离学校很远，所以我坐公交车去上学。
Because my home is far away from school, *(therefore)* I take the bus to school.

1. Look at the pictures below and read the accompanying questions on why the person would like to be in the profession. Answer each of these questions by stating it is because he/she loves that field very much. Use 因为…所以… in your sentence.

Example:
你为什么想当歌手？
因为我很喜欢唱歌，
所以我将来想当歌

你为什么想当画家？

你为什么想当运动员？

你为什么想当钢琴家？

你为什么想当作家？

你为什么想当舞蹈家？

你为什么想当书法家？

2. Match the ideas found in column A with the ideas in column B, and make sentences by using 因为…所以… to indicate the reason that an event has occurred. The first sentence has been matched as an example.

Column A
因为

❶ 城市很吵
❷ 你家离火车站很近
❸ 我没吃中饭
❹ 他有九门课
❺ 爸爸现在很累
❻ 你喜欢吃鸡蛋
❼ 城市天天堵车
❽ 西瓜很甜

Column B
所以

a. 坐火车很方便
b. 天天都很忙
c. 他很想睡觉
d. 我们从城市搬到乡村
e. 想吃三明治
f. 我们点蛋花汤
g. 开车去上班很不方便
j. 很好吃

3. Read the text below and decide if the following statements are true or false based on the information found in the text.

我是陈红。我家住在郊区。前年我们住在上海。因为城市里很吵，每天堵车，所以去年我们从上海搬到郊区。我喜欢住在郊区的小区，因为很安静。我也喜欢我的新学校。星期一和星期五我妈妈开车送我上学，星期二、星期三和星期四我搭公交车去学校。你喜欢你的学校吗？你每天怎么去学校？

True or False
(是非题)

❶ 陈红不喜欢她的新学校。
❷ 城市每天堵车。
❸ 陈红是去年搬到郊区的。
❹ 星期四妈妈送陈红去学校。
❺ 郊区的小区很安静。
❻ 星期一陈红搭公交车上学。
❼ 陈红现在住在上海。

Living in Chinese Cities

In China, many people residing in the cities prefer to live near the center of the city for various reasons. First, since many offices and workplaces are located at the center of the city, living nearby reduces the daily commuting time. Second, the downtown area often has more amenities and offers more choices for food and entertainment, making it a convenient place to live. However, with rising property prices and cost of living, more and more people are unable to afford a place in the center of the city and are moving to the suburbs.

gēn　　　　yíyàng
我的学校跟你的学校一样。
My school is the same as yours.

fángzi
我家的房子跟你家的房子不一样。
My house is different from yours.

NEW WORDS 生 词

跟…(不)一样	跟…(不)一樣	gēn…(bù) yíyàng	(not) the same as…
形状 n.	形狀	xíngzhuàng	shape
颜色 n.	顏色	yánsè	color
大小 n.		dàxiǎo	size
房子 n.		fángzi	house
大 adj.		dà	big
小 adj.		xiǎo	small

LANGUAGE FOCUS

To state that some things are the same, use the construction 跟…一样 by placing 跟 between the two items for comparison and 一样 at the end of the sentence:

Examples: ❶ 我的教室跟你的教室一样。
My classroom is the same as yours.

❷ 他的书包跟我的书包一样。
His school bag is the same as mine.

To state that things are different, use the construction 跟…不一样:

Examples: ❶ 我以前的学校跟现在的学校不一样。
My previous school is not the same as my present school.

❷ 这个图书馆跟那个图书馆不一样。
This library is not the same as that library.

You may also use an adjective after 一样 to describe more specifically the condition or circumstance of the things that you are comparing.

Examples: ❶ 我的学校跟你的学校一样大。
My school is as big as yours.

❷ 教学楼跟图书馆楼不一样高。
The school building has a different height from the library building.

Try This!

1. Read the following sentences and see if you understand the meaning.

❶ 我的学校跟你的学校一样好。

❷ 我的家跟你的家一样大。

❸ 英文老师跟音乐老师一样高。

❹ 王叔叔跟李阿姨的年纪一样大。

❺ 这个星期跟下个星期一样忙。

❻ 西瓜跟苹果的颜色一样。

❼ 图书馆跟教学楼一样远。

❽ 星期三的课跟星期五的一样有意思。

❾ 餐厅跟体育馆的大小不一样。

❿ 上午跟下午的课不一样。

⓫ 住上海跟住北京一样方便。

⓬ 我们今天跟昨天一样累。

⓭ 这个男同学跟那个女同学一样好。

⓮ 网球跟棒球的形状一样。

2. Look at the pictures and tell the similarities or differences by using 跟…(不)一样 and the designated adjective following (不)一样.

Example:

交通 | 方便

这里的交通跟那里的交通一样方便。

老师 | 高

城市 | 吵

乡村 | 安静

房子 | 大

人 | 年纪

小区 | 安静

门 | 大

3. Compare the color (颜色), shape (形状), or size (大小) of the two objects in the pictures using 跟… (不) 一样.

Example:

草莓的颜色跟香蕉的颜色不一样。

❶

❷

❸

❹

❺

❻

❼

❽

❾

❿

bǐ

中文课比英语课有意思。
Chinese classes are more interesting than English classes.

róngyì   duō

历史课比数学课容易多了。
History class is much easier than math class.

A Comparing school subjects

NEW WORDS

多 adj.		duō	a lot, many	
少 adj.		shǎo	few, less	
长 adj.	長	cháng	long	
短 adj.		duǎn	short	

容易 adj.			róngyì	easy
难 adj.	難		nán	difficult
比 prep.			bǐ	compared to
一点 num.	一點		yìdiǎn	slightly, a little

School activities

早操 n.		zǎocāo	morning exercises
午休 n.		wǔxiū	noon break/lunch break
早自习 n.	早自習	zǎozìxí	morning study
晚自习 n.	晚自習	wǎnzìxí	night study
课间操 n.	課間操	kèjiāncāo	exercises between classes
课外活动 phr.	課外活動	kèwài huódòng	extra-curricular activities
时间表 n.	時間表	shíjiānbiǎo	time table/schedule
课程表 n.	課程表	kèchéngbiǎo	course schedule

Words you have learned

数学课 n.	shùxuékè	math class
化学课 n.	huàxuékè	chemistry class
物理课 n.	wùlǐkè	physics class
生物课 n.	shēngwùkè	biology class
历史课 n.	lìshǐkè	history class
美术课 n.	měishùkè	art class
体育课 n.	tǐyùkè	physical education
地理课 n.	dìlǐkè	geography
电脑课 n.	diànnǎokè	computer class

When comparing two items in Chinese, place 比 between the two items in the pattern of "A + 比 + B." An adjective is placed after B to describe the comparison.

Examples: ❶ 物理比化学难。
Physics is harder than chemistry.

❷ 早自习比午休短。
The morning study hall is shorter than the lunch break.

❸ 今天的功课比昨天的功课多。
Today's homework is more than yesterday's.

The degree of comparison can be made more specific by placing a degree complement after the adjective.

Examples: ❶ 物理课比化学课难一点。
Physics class is slightly harder than chemistry class.

❷ 早自习比午休短得多。
The morning study hall is much shorter than the lunch break.

❸ 今天的功课比昨天的功课多多了。
Today's homework is much more than yesterday's.

Try This!

1. Create sentences that contrast each pair of items in various degrees.

Example: 数学课	英文课	数学课比英文课难多了。
❶ 生物课	历史课	
❷ 化学课	物理课	
❸ 美术课	电脑课	
❹ 中文课	化学课	
❺ 体育课	地理课	
❻ 历史课	生物课	
❼ 英文课	美术课	
❽ 打棒球	跑步	
❾ 打乒乓球	登山	
❿ 滑雪	踢足球	

2. Complete the following Likert scale about the courses that you are taking this year or have taken. Mark an "X" on the scale which represents your rating for the course in terms of the adjectives. Compare your ratings across all courses and write at least 10 sentences that describe the differences in your ratings.

❶ 中文
1	2	3	4	5
难				容易

1	2	3	4	5
没有意思				有意思

1	2	3	4	5
不喜欢				喜欢

❷ 数学
1	2	3	4	5
难				容易

1	2	3	4	5
没有意思				有意思

1	2	3	4	5
不喜欢				喜欢

❸ 英语
1	2	3	4	5
难				容易

1	2	3	4	5
没有意思				有意思

1	2	3	4	5
不喜欢				喜欢

❹ 体育课
1	2	3	4	5
难				容易

1	2	3	4	5
没有意思				有意思

1	2	3	4	5
不喜欢				喜欢

3. Compare the two objects in the pictures by using the vocabulary from the word banks. It is not necessary to use all of the vocabulary.

Adjectives

难　容易　大　小　长　短　好吃
多　少　　快　慢　好　有意思

Degree complements

得多　一点　多了

①

Example:

乒乓球比足球小多了。

②

③

④

⑤

⑥

⑦

⑧

⑨

bǐjiào

他的学校比较大。

His school is relatively bigger.

$2.50

piányi

学校餐厅的三明治比较便宜。

The sandwiches in the school cafeteria are relatively cheaper.

NEW WORDS

生词

比较 adv.	比較	bǐjiào	relatively, rather, fairly, quite
贵 adj.	貴	guì	expensive
便宜 adj.		piányi	inexpensive
好看 adj.		hǎokàn	good looking
难看 adj.	難看	nánkàn	ugly, unpleasant to look at
可爱 adj.	可愛	kě'ài	cute
聪明 adj.	聰明	cōngmíng	smart
笨 adj.		bèn	stupid
有用 adj.		yǒuyòng	useful

66

The expression 比较 is used to make a comparison without stating specifically the item to which something is being compared. It is placed before the adjective. Using 比较 implies a comparison to another object. Thus, when comparing one school to another, we say, "我的新学校比较大." The statement means that "My new school is relatively bigger" and implies that it is being compared to another school. When we say "城市的房子比较贵," it is understood that the speakers were previously talking about other houses, for example, houses in the countryside.

Sometimes 比较 is used to make a comparison with what is considered the norm for that item. The sentence "这本书比较便宜" (This book is relatively inexpensive) states that the price for the book is inexpensive compared to what the normal price for it would be.

比较 can also be placed before a verb.

Examples: ❶ 他们比较喜欢吃中国菜。
They prefer to eat Chinese food.

❷ 我比较喜欢学中文。
I prefer to learn Chinese.

Try This!

1. Look at the following pictures and create a sentence that compares the two objects and uses the expression 比较.

$80 $60

Example:
物理课本比较贵。
or
英语课本比较便宜。

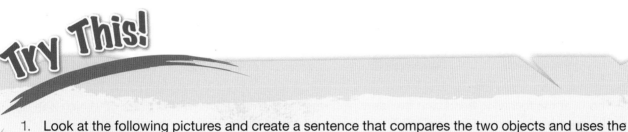

❶ 吵   安静

❷ 可爱

③ 好吃

⑥ 聪明

④ 容易　难

⑦ 有意思

⑤ 没意思　有意思

⑧ 大　小

2. Look at the following items and decide which one fits the adjective written under it. Which one is longer, shorter, bigger, or smaller? Then write a sentence that describes the picture.

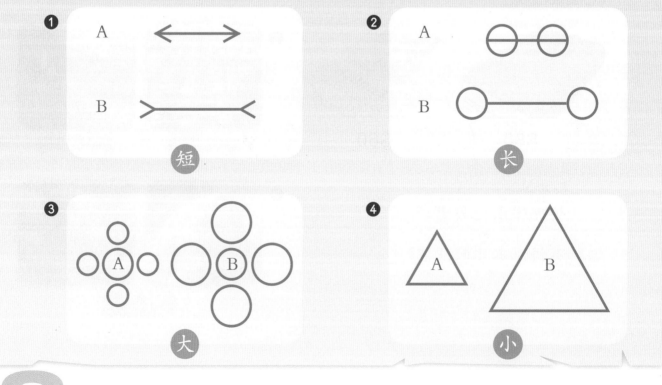

❶ A　B　短

❷ A　B　长

❸ A　B　大

❹ A　B　小

3. Read the statements from Column A and match them logically with statements from Column B.

A
❶ 因为乡村比较安静，
❷ 因为中文比较有用，
❸ 因为我比较喜欢吃水果，
❹ 因为我比较喜欢吃中国菜，
❺ 因为看电影比较有意思，
❻ 因为这个星期比较忙，
❼ 因为美术课比较容易，
❽ 因为坐火车比较方便，
❾ 因为教室比较吵，
❿ 因为妹妹比较小，

B
a. 所以他搬到乡村去住。
b. 所以我和哥哥今天去看电影。
c. 所以姐姐送她去学校。
d. 所以我们坐火车去纽约。
e. 所以他没有上网聊天。
f. 所以他去图书馆。
g. 所以我每天吃苹果。
h. 所以今天我去中国餐厅。
i. 所以很多人学中文。
j. 所以他喜欢美术课。

duì
你弟弟、妹妹对什么
xìngqù
科目感兴趣？
Which subjects are your younger brother and
yonger sister interested in?

弟弟对中文感兴趣。
My brother is interested in the Chinese language.

妹妹对数学感兴趣。
My sister is interested in math.

生 词

NEW WORDS

对 *prep.*	對	duì	to direct towards
科目 *n.*		kēmù	subject
兴趣 *n.*	興趣	xìngqù	interest

LANGUAGE FOCUS

When stating interest in something, use 对 followed by the field/object and then the expression
感兴趣 or 有兴趣.

Examples: ❶ 我对电脑感兴趣。 ❷ 她对美术有兴趣。
　　　　　　I'm interested in computers. 　She's interested in art.

To express that you are not interested in a field or object, place a negative adverb 不 before the
expression 感兴趣, or 没 before 有兴趣.

Examples: ❶ 我对物理不感兴趣。 ❷ 他对历史没有兴趣。
　　　　　　I'm not interested in physics. 　He's not interested in history.

1. Create a sentence describing the pictures by using the expression "对 + object + 感兴趣" or the negative form "对 + object + 不感兴趣."

他对踢足球感兴趣。

2. Based on the picture, ask and answer a question about the person and whether or not he/she is interested in that field.

Student A: Michael Phelps 对什么有兴趣?
Student B: 他对游泳有兴趣。

CULTURAL HIGHLIGHTS

Course Selections in Chinese High Schools

In China, when students enter the second year in high school they are asked to choose either the field of liberal arts (文科, wénkē) or science (理科, lǐkē) as a major focus of their studies. Thereafter, students of the liberal arts will take a subject that integrates history, geography, and political education; those in the sciences will take a subject that integrates physics, chemistry, and biology. Students in both liberal arts and science fields will study three core subjects: Chinese, mathematics, and a foreign language (usually English).

Students and parents often have a hard time deciding which field to choose. Factors influencing their decision include the student's strengths, future career options, personal interests, and future ambitions.

Reading *in Context*

STEP 1 GOING TO PLACES

A new student saying hello to two classmates in school

张安：你们好！

大卫、安琪：你好！你是新来的
同学，对吗？

张安：对，今天是我在学校的第
一天，我兴奋极了！

大卫：你喜欢这里吗？

张安：很喜欢！这里的教室都很新、
很大，餐厅里的东西也很
好吃。

安琪：你住哪儿？你今天怎么来
学校？

张安：我住西边，离学校不远。
今天我爸爸开车送我来
学校。明天开始，我想
自己坐公交车来。你们
是怎么来学校的？

kāishǐ
start
zìjǐ
oneself

大卫：我是开车来的，安琪是走
路来的，她家离学校很近。

安琪：有时候，我也骑自行车
来学校，骑自行车比走
路快。

kuài
fast

STEP 2 MOVING TO A NEW PLACE

Xiaowei just moved and is talking about it

小伟：我上周末搬家了，从南边搬到
北边。现在很累。

小明：哦，你为什么搬家？

小伟：因为南边很吵，离学校也很
远，所以我们搬到北边。这里
比较安静，离学校也比较近。

小明：我以前也跟你一样，从南边搬
到北边。北边确实比较方
便。那你喜欢你的新家吗？

quèshí
indeed

小伟：很喜欢，现在的家比以前
的大多了。

小明：什么时候请我去你新家玩？

qǐng
invite

小伟：下周六，怎么样？我们
一起打电动。

小明：好啊！下周六见！

STEP 3 MAKING COMPARISONS

Two students talking about the courses they are interested in

马克：你今天上了什么课？

丁强：历史课、数学课、英语课、
体育课、电脑课、美术课，
还有中文课。

马克：你最喜欢哪门课？

丁强：电脑课！我对电脑很感兴趣。
你呢？

马克：我喜欢数学课，美术课比较
无聊。

丁强：我跟你不一样。我觉得美术课
比数学课有意思多了。

马克：因为你对数学不感兴趣，所以
你觉得数学课无聊。

丁强：对，我对体育最感兴趣！

Step Up!

1. Read the following passage from 丁强's blog from the first day in a new school. Then complete the activities below.

2013 年 9 月 2 日

今天我非常开心，因为今天是我到新学校的第一天！

fēicháng
extremely

我的新学校比以前的学校大多了，我感到兴奋极了。

今天早上七点半，我从我家走到学校。因为我今天有七节课，所以我今天很忙。早上第一节课是早自习，这节课很安静，因为大家都在做功课。九点的时候，我上数学课，数学课比较难，我的同学都很聪明，他们都对数学课很感兴趣。从十点到十一点，我上历史课，历史课比数学课容易多了。十一点以后，我们上课间操。

下午，我上体育课、地理课和电脑课。体育课很有意思，我和我的同学一起打篮球！我不喜欢地理课和电脑课，我觉得地理课和电脑课很没意思。放学以后，我也是走路回家的。今天是一个非常有意思的一天！我喜欢我的新学校！

A. Number the following daily happenings in the chronological order in which they occur in 丁强's school day.

(   ) I go to physical education class.

(   ) I walk home.

(   ) I have history class.

(   ) I have my computer class.

(   ) I have my mathematics class.

(   ) I walk to school.

(   ) I have my geography class.

B. Answer the following questions based on 丁强's blog:

❶ How do the two schools compare?

❷ What is an easy class for 丁强?

❸ What class/classes doesn't he like and why?

2. Using 丁强's blog, respond to him by telling him about your school and your school day. Write an entry that is at least 10 sentences long. Compare the information that he gives with your day in your school.

3. Sit with a partner and talk about which courses you have in common and which ones you are taking that are different. Find out two courses that you have in common and two courses that are different. Then find out which teachers you have for each course and list those that are the same and those that are different. Write a summary of your findings in either graph form or in a narrative.

4. Talk with a different partner and find out at least two activities that you have in common (you both like to do or watch) and two activities that you don't have in common. Summarize your findings by writing a short biography/picture book of your friend's interests and dislikes but leave out his/her name. Share your summary with other members of the class and ask them to guess who that person is.

Fun Time!

Chinese jump rope (跳皮筋 tiào píjīn) is an interesting twist on American jump rope. In order to jump rope Chinese style, two children attach long elastic ropes or bands (橡皮筋 xiàngpíjīn) to their ankles so that the rope or band is held taut. Then other children jump in, jump out, and jump around the ropes in a manner that resembles Double Dutch jump rope in the US. Jumping rope leads to good eye and foot coordination, and it allows you to have fun with your friends!

Here is an authentic Chinese jump rope rhyme. Read the rhyme and circle the words that you know. Then try to read it out loud. Listen to your teacher read the rhyme and repeat the words. For fun, you can bring in some jump rope and go to the gymnasium to practice jumping rope while saying this rhyme.

Xiǎopíqiú,	yòng jiǎo tī,	mǎlán kāihuā èrshíyī,
小皮球，	用脚踢，	马兰开花二十一，

èr wǔ liù,	èr wǔ qī,	èr bā èr jiǔ sānshíyī,
二五六，	二五七，	二八二九三十一，

sān wǔ liù,	sān wǔ qī,	sān bā sān jiǔ sìshíyī,
三五六，	三五七，	三八三九四十一，

sì wǔ liù,	sì wǔ qī,	sì bā sì jiǔ wǔshíyī,
四五六，	四五七，	四八四九五十一，

wǔ wǔ liù,	wǔ wǔ qī,	wǔ bā wǔ jiǔ liùshíyī,
五五六，	五五七，	五八五九六十一，

liù wǔ liù,	liù wǔ qī,	liù bā liù jiǔ qīshíyī,
六五六，	六五七，	六八六九七十一，

qī wǔ liù,	qī wǔ qī,	qī bā qī jiǔ bāshíyī,
七五六，	七五七，	七八七九八十一，

bā wǔ liù,	bā wǔ qī,	bā bā bā jiǔ jiǔshíyī,
八五六，	八五七，	八八八九九十一，

jiǔ wǔ liù,	jiǔ wǔ qī,	jiǔ bā jiǔ jiǔ yìbǎiyī!
九五六，	九五七，	九八九九一百一！

Go online and watch some of the YouTube videos that demonstrate patterns for jumping rope.

I have learned...

Core Vocabulary

Verbs

去		qù	go	上班		shàngbān	go to work
来	來	lái	come	打车/打的	打車/打的	dǎchē/dǎdī	take a cab/taxi
坐		zuò	go by, travel by	走路		zǒulù	walk
搭		dā	go by, travel by	开车	開車	kāichē	drive
骑	騎	qí	ride	送		sòng	send someone, accompany someone
打		dǎ	ride, sit (a taxi/cab)	接		jiē	pick (someone) up
开	開	kāi	drive (a car)	搬		bān	move
走		zǒu	walk	搬家		bānjiā	move (house)
回		huí	return	堵车	堵車	dǔchē	traffic jam

Nouns

城市		chéngshì	city	早自习	早自習	zǎozìxí	morning study
乡村	鄉村	xiāngcūn	countryside, rural area	晚自习	晚自習	wǎnzìxí	night study
地方		dìfang	place	早操		zǎocāo	morning exercises
交通		jiāotōng	traffic	课间操	課間操	kèjiāncāo	exercises between classes
郊区	郊區	jiāoqū	suburbs	午休		wǔxiū	noon break/lunch break
小区	小區	xiǎoqū	residential area	时间表	時間表	shíjiānbiǎo	time table/schedule
形状	形狀	xíngzhuàng	shape	课程表	課間表	kèchéngbiǎo	course schedule
颜色	顏色	yánsè	color	兴趣	興趣	xìngqù	interest
大小		dàxiǎo	size	科目		kēmù	subject
房子		fángzi	house				

Adjectives

方便		fāngbiàn	convenient	短		duǎn	short
安静	安靜	ānjìng	quiet	容易		róngyì	easy
吵		chǎo	noisy	难	難	nán	difficult
大		dà	big	贵	貴	guì	expensive
小		xiǎo	small	便宜		piányi	inexpensive
多		duō	a lot, many	好看		hǎokàn	good looking
少		shǎo	few, less	难看	難看	nánkàn	ugly, unpleasant to look at
长	長	cháng	long	可爱	可愛	kě'ài	cute

I have learned...

聪明	聰明	cōngmíng	smart	有用		yǒuyòng	useful
笨		bèn	stupid				

Adverb

Numeral

比较	比較	bǐjiào	relatively, rather, fairly, quite	一点	一點	yìdiǎn	slightly, a little

Prepositions

Question Word

比		bǐ	compared to	怎么	怎麼	zěnme	how
对	對	duì	to direct towards	为什么	爲什麼	wèishénme	why

Conjunctions

因为…所以…	因爲…所以…	yīnwèi…suǒyǐ…	because…therefore…

Phrases

交通工具		jiāotōng gōngjù	mode of transportation
坐公交车	坐公交車	zuò gōngjiāochē	take a public bus
坐校车	坐校車	zuò xiàochē	take a school bus
坐地铁	坐地鐵	zuò dìtiě	take the subway
坐火车	坐火車	zuò huǒchē	take a train
坐飞机	坐飛機	zuò fēijī	go by airplane
坐船		zuò chuán	go by ship
骑自行车	騎自行車	qí zìxíngchē	ride a bicycle
骑摩托车	騎摩托車	qí mótuōchē	ride a motorcycle
坐出租车	坐出租車	zuò chūzūchē	take a cab, taxi
课外活动	課外活動	kèwài huódòng	extra-curricular activities

Constructions

跟…(不)一样	跟…(不)一樣	gēn…(bù) yíyàng	*(not) the same as…*
是…的		shì…de	*(used to emphasize time, location, and means)*

◇ SENTENCE PATTERNS ◇

我坐公交车去学校。

我是走路回家的。

我送你去学校。

我从东边搬到西边。

因为我家离学校很近，所以我走路去学校。

我的学校跟你的学校一样。

中文课比英语课有意思。

他的学校比较大。

我对中文感兴趣。

I can do!

Interpretive **Communication**

❏ I can understand when someone tells me the time or when I read a timetable.

❏ I can understand when someone tells me about his school day.

❏ I can read about someone's school day and organize the information provided in chronological order.

❏ I can understand when someone gives me directions.

❏ I understand when things and items are being compared.

Interpersonal **Communication**

❏ I can exchange information about my school and my school day.

❏ I can compare and contrast people, places, and things.

❏ I can share information on interests and preferences.

❏ I can find out how to get from one place to another.

Presentational **Communication**

❏ I can present information about my school verbally or in writing.

❏ I can talk and write about different ways of getting from one place to another.

❏ I can compare my school with someone else's school.

❏ I can describe when activities take place and the best time to make an appointment to engage in these activities.

❏ I can write information about my school day.

Cultural Knowledge

❏ I can talk about modes of transportation commonly used in the Chinese speaking world.

❏ I can describe the lives of people living in the cities in China.

❏ I can briefly describe the liberal arts and science fields of study in Chinese high schools.

Settling into a new home

搬进新家

COMMUNICATIVE GOALS

- Specifying the relative locations of rooms
- Stating the direction of movement
- Describing where furniture and household items are
- Expressing the existence of something
- Enumerating a list of items
- Describing shapes and colors

Cultural Knowledge

- Chinese courtyard houses
- Feng shui
- The concept of "round sky and square earth" in Chinese architecture
- Color symbolism in Chinese culture

Get ready...

Look at the following two photos of houses in China and the U.S. and compare them. What are the similarities and what are the differences? Why do you think there are such differences?

A type of traditional house in China

A type of house in the U.S.

STEP 1

DESCRIBING THE ROOMS IN A HOUSE

A. Specifying relative locations of rooms
主卧室在哪儿？主卧室在楼上。

B. Expressing directions of movement
你们上来看我的书房。

C. Expressing possession and locations
我的房间在左边。

STEP 2

ARRANGING FURNITURE

A. Using measure words for household items
一台电冰箱、两盏台灯、
三幅画、四张床、五块地毯、
六面镜子。

B. Expressing existence
花园里种着一些花。

C. Expressing movement and action
我把台灯放在书桌上。

STEP 3

LISTING AND DESCRIBING OBJECTS

A. Enumerating items
菜园里种着一些菜，像番茄、
黄瓜、四季豆什么的。

B. Describing shapes and colors
这张桌子是圆形的。
我的房间是天蓝色的。

81

zhǔwòshì
主卧室在哪儿？
Where is the master bedroom?

lóushang
主卧室在楼上。
The master bedroom is upstairs.

A Specifying relative locations of rooms

wèishēngjiān
卫生间在哪儿？
Where is the bathroom?

lóuxia
卫生间在楼下。
The bathroom is downstairs.

yángtái cháo
阳台朝哪儿？
Which direction does the balcony face?

阳台朝南。
The balcony faces south.

NEW WORDS 生词

朝 v.		cháo	face, towards
楼 n.	樓	lóu	floor, story
楼上 n.	樓上	lóushang	upstairs
楼下 n.	樓下	lóuxia	downstairs
门厅 n.	門廳	méntīng	foyer
主卧室 n.		zhǔwòshì	master bedroom
厨房 n.	厨房	chúfáng	kitchen
阁楼 n.	閣樓	gélóu	attic
地下室 n.		dìxiàshì	basement
阳台 n.	陽臺	yángtái	balcony
卫生间 n.	衛生間	wèishēngjiān	bathroom
房间 n.	房間	fángjiān	room
走廊 n.		zǒuláng	corridor; aisle

Words you have learned

shàng
上 n. up, above

shūfáng
书房 n. study

xià
下 n. down, below

kètīng
客厅 n. living room

yùshì
浴室 n. bathroom

wòshì
卧室 n. bedroom

cāntīng
餐厅 n. dining room

dōng (dōngbian)
东(东边) n. east (side)

nán (nánbian)
南(南边) n. south (side)

xī (xībian)
西(西边) n. west (side)

běi (běibian)
北(北边) n. north (side)

LANGUAGE FOCUS

❶ 上 and 下 can be added to nouns to indicate location:

楼上 upstairs   楼下 downstairs   桌子上 on the table   桌子下 under the table

❷ To express that something is at a certain location, place 在 before the location word.

For example: 浴室在楼下，卧室在楼上。
The bathroom is downstairs; the bedroom is upstairs.

阳台在主卧室外面，卫生间在厨房右边。
The balcony is outside the master bedroom; the toilet is on the right of the kitchen.

妈妈在楼上，爸爸在书房里。
Mom is upstairs; dad is in the study.

❸ To state the direction a place is facing, place 朝 before the directional word.

For example: 阁楼朝东。   The attic faces east.

主卧室朝西。   The master bedroom faces west.

Chinese Courtyard House

Siheyuan (四合院), or courtyard house, is a historical type of residence commonly found in China, most often in Beijing. Such a house is usually a one-story, rectangular structure built around a main room whose front door opens to the south. The main room is where the head of the family resides and is structured in a way that allows for cool summers and warm winters. The rooms adjoining the main house and facing east and west are called side houses. They are mainly occupied by the children and grandchildren of the family.

The courtyard is usually landscaped with plants, flowers, and fish ponds. The uniquely enclosed architectural structure fosters togetherness and harmony in the family and engenders a sense of belonging and security.

Throughout Chinese history, the courtyard house was the basic pattern used for residences, palaces, temples, monasteries, family businesses, and government offices.

The courtyard house is a traditional type of housing in Beijing. The majority of Chinese people today live in apartment buildings.

1. Study the following house plans and answer the questions. You may use the location and direction words provided.

左边　右边　前边　东　南
后边　里边　外边　西　北

Apartment A

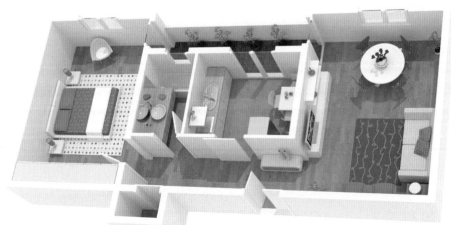

❶ 客厅在哪儿?

❷ 卫生间在哪儿?

❸ 主卧室朝哪儿?

Apartment B

④ 客厅在哪儿?

⑤ 厨房在哪儿?

⑥ 阳台朝哪儿?

Apartment C

⑦ 主卧室在哪儿?

⑧ 厨房在哪儿?

⑨ 客厅朝哪儿?

2. Imagine you are a real estate agent. You have three clients with different requirements for their apartments. Read their requirements listed below and recommend for each of your clients an appropriate apartment from those in Question 1.

 Client A

 Client B

 Client C

Client A

我家有三口人。我的孩子想要一个自己的房间。我喜欢做饭，也❶常常❷请❸朋友们来我家❹一起吃饭，所以我喜欢大的餐厅和客厅。我先生想要有个阳台，他喜欢在阳台上看书。

Your recommendation:

Apartment _____

Client B

我一个人住，想找一个不太大的房子。我自己做饭，所以要有厨房。❺有时候我的朋友们来我家吃饭聊天，所以我想要一个小客厅和小餐厅。

Your recommendation:

Apartment _____

Client C

我和太太两人住。我太太不喜欢朝东的卧室。我不喜欢朝西的客厅。我太太想要大一点的厨房。

Your recommendation:

Apartment _____

chángcháng	qǐng	péngyoumen	yìqǐ	yǒu shíhou
❶常常	❷请	❸朋友们	❹一起	❺有时候
often	invite	friends	together	sometimes

3. Imagine that you have just moved into your new house and your new friend at your new school is calling you on the phone to ask you about your new house. Work with a partner who will be your friend. Your friend is really curious about your new house and asks you a lot of questions. Your friend should have his/her book closed while asking questions. Answer his/her questions according to the house plan below.

For example:

Your friend:　你的卧室在哪儿？

You:　　　　我的卧室在楼上。

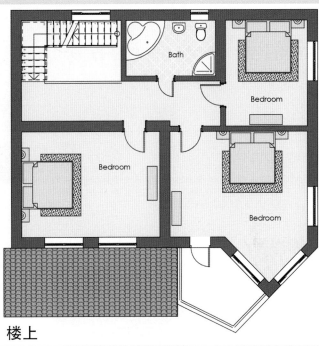

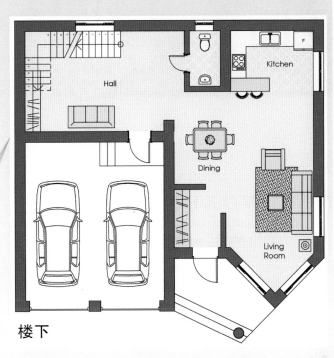

楼下

楼上

There are different Chinese terms for "restroom/toilet." 卫生间, 洗手间 (xǐshǒujiān) and 厕所 (cèsuǒ) are commonly used in China and Hong Kong. In Taiwan, 化妆室 (huàzhuāngshì) is also used.

你们上来看我的书房。
Come up to take a look at my study.

NEW WORDS 生词

上 v.		shàng	go or come up
下 v.		xià	go or come down
过 v.	過	guò	go or come over
进 v.	進	jìn	go or come in
出 v.		chū	go or come out
请 v.	請	qǐng	(used in polite requests) please

我们出去看阳台。
Let's go out to take a look at the balcony.

来 and 去 can be added to verbs to indicate the direction of movement. 来 indicates movement directed towards the speaker, while 去 indicates movement directed away from the speaker.

上来 come up	下来 come down	过来 come over	进来 come in	出来 come out
上去 go up	下去 go down	过去 go over	进去 go in	出去 go out

Here are some sentences that show the meaning using subjects. Can you guess what they mean?

❶ 你上来。   ❹ 你们进去。

❷ 我下去。   ❺ 他们出来。

❸ 他过来。

To express additional information, add a verb or verb phrase after 来/去.

❶ 你上来做功课。   ❸ 你们下来吃晚饭。

❷ 我下去看电视。   ❹ 我们出去踢足球。

Try This!

1. Imagine that you have invited your friends to visit your new house. Look at the following descriptions and give statements in Chinese according to the situations depicted.

To show politeness to your friends, add the word 请 before the verb.

❶ Your friends arrived in a car and you ask them to get out of the car.

❷ You and your friends are at your front door and you are gesturing for them to go in before you.

❸ Your parents are inside the house asking your friends to come in.

❹ Your younger brother is upstairs and asks your friends to come up.

❺ Your friends are upstairs. Your father is downstairs in the living room with tea and fruit and asks them to come down.

❻ After having tea and fruit in the living room, your older brother is in a nearby room playing a new videogame and asks your friends to come over to take a look.

❼ You suggest to your friends to go over to your brother's game station to take a look.

2. You have moved to a new house. Your friends are visiting you, and it is a beautiful day so you suggest that the group do the following activities. Note the current location for each question.

For example:

You are in the living room and your friends are in the adjacent dining room. You invite your friends to come and play console games.

请你们过来打电动。

❶ Your friends are watching TV in the living room. You take out a basketball and ask them to go out and play basketball.

❷ You and your friends just finished lunch in the dining room. You invite them to the living room next to the dining room to play console games.

❸ Your friends are chatting in the study room upstairs. There is a TV soccer match and you invite them to the living room downstairs to watch the game.

❹ You and your friends are watching the TV soccer match and feel like playing soccer. You ask them to go out to the backyard to play.

❺ Your friends are enjoying the sun on the balcony. You invite them to the study to play chess.

❻ After playing chess in the study, you feel like playing a game of table tennis outside.

我的房间在走廊左边。
My room is on the left.

右边的房间是我父母的。
The room on the right is my parents'.

生 词

NEW WORDS

壁橱 n.	壁櫥	bìchú	closet
衣柜 n.	衣櫃	yīguì	wardrobe
床 n.	床	chuáng	bed
床头柜 n.	床頭櫃	chuángtóuguì	bedside cabinet, night table
沙发 n.	沙發	shāfā	sofa
书桌 n.	書桌	shūzhuō	desk
书架 n.	書架	shūjià	bookshelf
台灯 n.	臺燈	táidēng	lamp
落地灯 n.	落地燈	luòdìdēng	standing lamp
电视柜 n.	電視櫃	diànshìguì	TV console
餐桌 n.		cānzhuō	dining room table

LANGUAGE FOCUS

You have already learned how 的 is used between two nouns to indicate possession or close association.

我的生日　红色的书包　他的爱好

1 When 的 is used after a location word and before a noun, it describes the location of the noun.

> 左边的房间
> the room on the left

> 右边的房间
> the room on the right

> 左边的房间是卧室。
> The room on the left is a bedroom.

> 右边的房间是书房。
> The room on the right is the study.

2 When 的 is used after a noun and before a location word, it describes a location relative to the noun.

> 房间的左边
> on the left of the room

> 房间的右边
> on the right of the room

> 房间的左边是桌子。
> There is a table on the left of the room.

> 房间的右边是窗户。
> There is a window on the right of the room.

3 的 may be added to a noun or pronoun to express that something belongs to somebody.

> 左边的房间是我的。
> The room on the left is mine.

> 右边的书架是我爸爸的。
> The bookshelf on the right is my dad's.

> 前边的衣柜是我姐姐的。
> The wardrobe in front is my sister's.

Try This!

1. Match following sentences with the correct pictures on the right.

❶ 右边的房间是卧室。

❷ 左边的书架是爸爸的。

❸ 左边的女孩是我姐姐。

❹ 右边的男孩是我哥哥。

❺ 前边的书桌是我的。

a.

b.

c.

d.

e.

2. Describe the pictures according to the hints provided.

Example:

窗户的右边是书架。

_____

(On the right of the window)

_____

_____

(On the right of the bed)

_____

_____

(On the left of the desk)

_____

_____

(Behind the sofa)

_____

_____

(On the right of the standing lamp)

_____

_____

(In front of the desk)

3. Look at the following pictures of household furniture and their owners and make a statement about their ownership.

前面的书桌是哥哥的。

哥哥

爸爸

妈妈

妹妹

爸爸

哥哥

ARRANGING FURNITURE

To describe things you find in a house, you need to know the measure words for common household items.

A Using measure words for household items

生 词
NEW WORDS

jiājū yòngpǐn
家居用品

Measure word

diànshìjī
电视机
電視機

diànbīngxiāng
电冰箱
電冰箱

tái
台
臺

(used for electrical appliances)

xǐwǎnjī
洗碗机
洗碗機

xǐyījī
洗衣机
洗衣機

hōnggānjī
烘干机
烘乾機

wēibōlú
微波炉
微波爐

táidēng
台灯
臺燈

zhǎn
盏
盞

(used for lamps)

huà

画
畫

chuānglián

窗帘
窗簾

fú

幅

(used for paintings, curtains, etc.)

chuáng

床

shāfā

沙发
沙發

zhāng

张

張

(used for beds, tables, sofas, etc.)

kāfēizhuō

咖啡桌

dìtǎn

地毯

kuài

块

塊

(used for things that are shaped like sheets)

jiājū yòngpǐn
家居用品

jìngzi
镜子
鏡 子

lúzi
炉子
爐 子
stove

huāpíng
花瓶

xǐshǒupén
洗手盆/
xǐliǎn chí
洗脸池
洗 臉 池

yùgāng
浴缸

mǎtǒng
马桶
馬 桶

Word you have learned

diànnǎo
电脑 *n.* computer

To state or count how many items there are, follow the pattern "number + measure word + item." Look at the examples below and see if you can determine the meanings.

number	+	measure word	+	item
一		台		电冰箱
两		盏		台灯
三		幅		画
四		张		床
五		块		地毯
六		面		镜子

Try This!

1. Wang An moved to a new house. Here are some pictures of the rooms in his house. State the various items and how many you find in each room using the correct measure words.

   For example:

   客厅里有一张咖啡桌。
   _____

zhòngzhe   yìxiē

花园里种着一些花。

There are some flowers (planted) in the garden.

yuànzi   liàng

院子里放着一辆自行车。

There is a bicycle (placed) in the yard.

NEW WORDS

花园 n.	花園	huāyuán	garden	花 n.		huā	flower
车库 n.	車庫	chēkù	garage	着 part.	著	zhe	(placed after verbs to indicate a continuing action or state)
院子 n.		yuànzi	yard	辆 m.w.	輛	liàng	(used for bicycles, cars, etc.)
菜园 n.	菜園	càiyuán	vegetable garden	棵 m.w.		kē	(used for trees)
果园 n.	果園	guǒyuán	fruit garden	朵 m.w.		duǒ	(used for flowers, clouds, etc.)
邻居 n.	鄰居	línjū	neighbor	一些 num.		yìxiē	some
树 n.	樹	shù	tree				

Verbs of placement

种	種	zhòng	to plant, grow	插		chā	to stick in, insert
放		fàng	to put down, place	摆	擺	bǎi	to put, place (more for display)
挂	掛	guà	to hang				

着 can be placed after verbs to indicate the existence of something or someone in a particular location. Here we focus on the use of 着 with verbs of placement, such as to plant (种), to put (放), and to hang (挂). When 着 follows a verb, it describes the state resulting from the action of that verb.

For example: ❶ 墙上挂着一幅画。
There is a painting (hung) on the wall. (a state resulting from the action of "hanging")

❷ 花瓶里插着两朵花。
There are two flowers (inserted) in the vase. (a state resulting from the action of "inserting")

❸ 客厅里摆着一个大花瓶。
There is a big vase (placed) in the living room. (a state resulting from the action of "placing")

When stating the location at the beginning of the sentence, a directional word (上, 下, 里, 外, 左边, 右边, etc.) needs to be added to the location noun to indicate the exact location.

◈ 墙上挂着一幅画。　　◈ 花瓶里插着两朵花。

Try This!

1. Look at the pictures below and use 着 to describe where the objects that you see are located.

咖啡桌上放着一个花瓶。

❶ (vase)

❷ (bicycles)

❸ (trees)

❹ (bowls)

❺ (paintings)

❻ (books)

❼ (cups)

❽ (milk)

2. Read the following passage and answer the questions.

邻居李阿姨的花园

我家的邻居李阿姨喜欢花，也喜欢种花。她家的院子里有一个小花园。花园中间种着一棵树。这棵树很高，也很大。树的两边种着一些花，很漂亮。看，
piàoliang
beautiful
我的桌子上放着一个花瓶。花瓶里插着三朵阿姨送给我的花，怎么样？很好看吧！

❶ 邻居李阿姨有什么爱好？

❷ 她的小花园在哪儿？

❸ 花园的中间有什么？

❹ 花园里的树长得怎么样？
zhǎng
grow

❺ 树的两边有什么？

❻ 我的桌子上有什么？

❼ 花瓶里有什么？

我把台灯放在书桌上。
I placed the lamp on the desk.

叔叔把画挂在墙上。
My uncle hung the painting on the wall.

NEW WORD

把 *prep.* | **bǎ** | *(used to move the object to the pre-verbal postion)*

LANGUAGE FOCUS

把 is often used to indicate that something is done to an item in a certain way. We can use 把 to describe someone moving an object to a location. 把 is generally placed after the subject. The basic structure is: subject + 把 + object + verb + 在 + location noun + directional word.

For example: ❶ 哥哥把书桌放在床旁边。
My brother moved the desk to the side of the bed.

❷ 妈妈把花插在花瓶里。
My mother put the flowers in the vase.

Feng Shui

Feng shui is a Chinese system of beliefs that uses the laws of Chinese astronomy and placement on Earth to help improve life by receiving positive *qi*, or energy. *Feng shui* involves many principles about the auspicious (or favorable) positioning of a house and the placement of items inside.

While many associate *feng shui* with superstitions, some of its principles seem to be based on science and logic. For example, one *feng shui* principle requires that houses face south. China is situated on the Northern Hemisphere with most of its land territory to the north of the Tropic of Cancer. Therefore, houses facing south are more accessible to sunshine. The principle of facing south also helps to avoid the cold north wind that usually occurs in winter in northern China. This principle is a reflection of people's understanding of natural phenomenon in ancient times.

Another *feng shui* principle is to avoid placing the bed opposite a door. The belief is that as air currents flow through the door, the opening and closing of the door will disrupt the air flow and harm one's health, similar to a sudden change of temperature. Moreover, wind can come into the room through openings like a door or window, so the belief is that one may catch a cold more easily if the bed is placed opposite a door.

Try This!

1. You and your parents have just moved into a new home and your Chinese friends are helping your family arrange the furniture. State where you want each of the items below to be placed. The desired location is given below each picture. Note that in Chinese you need to add a directional word after the location noun to express the location.

把沙发放在客厅里。

① (in the living room)

② (beside the sofa)

③ (on the left of the desk)

④ (beside the stove)

(in the vase)

(on the wall)

(beside the window)

(on the right of the bed)

(beside the dining table)

(in front of the door)

(beside the bed)

(in the kitchen)

2. Describe how you would arrange the list of items below in a study according to the picture provided. Use 把 in your sentences.

书桌　椅子　书柜　书　画　窗帘　沙发

Example: 我把书桌放在窗户前面。

菜 园 里 种 着 一 些 菜 ， 像 番 茄 、
黄 瓜 、 四 季 豆 什 么 的 。

There are some vegetables in the garden, such as tomatoes, cucumbers, string beans, etc.

A Enumerating items

餐 桌 上 放 着 一 些 水 果 ，

例 如 橙 子 、 苹 果 、 葡 萄 等 。

There are some fruits on the dining room table, such as oranges, apples, grapes, etc.

NEW WORDS 生 词

像…什么的	像…什麼的	xiàng…shěnme de	such as…etc.
例如…等		lìrú…děng	for example…etc.
菜 n.		cài	vegetable
食物 n.		shíwù	food
水果 n.		shuǐguǒ	fruit
家具 n.		jiājù	furniture
电器 n.	電器	diànqì	electrical appliance
东西 n.	東西	dōngxi	thing
文具 n.		wénjù	stationery

Words you have learned

báicài
白菜 n. Chinese cabbage

qíncài
芹菜 n. celery

104

Flowers and plants

玫瑰花		méiguīhuā	rose
茉莉花		mòlìhuā	jasmine
兰花	蘭花	lánhuā	orchid
菊花		júhuā	chrysanthemum

黄瓜	黃瓜	huángguā	cucumber
四季豆		sìjìdòu	string beans
灌木		guànmù	bushes
植物	植物	zhíwù	plants

LANGUAGE FOCUS

When listing things in Chinese, use the construction 像…什么的 to mean "such as." The list of items is placed between 像 and 什么的. This construction is normally used for non-exhaustive lists.

For example:

❶ 花园里种着一些花，像玫瑰花、兰花、菊花什么的。
There are some flowers in the garden, such as roses, orchids, chrysanthemums, etc.

❷ 餐桌上放着很多食物，像面包、火腿、香肠什么的。
There are many foods on the dining room table, such as bread, ham, sausage, etc.

The construction 例如…等 may also be used when referring to a list of items. Place the list of things between 例如 and 等.

For example:

❶ 果园里种着一些水果，例如西瓜、草莓、葡萄等。
There are some fruits in the orchard, such as watermelons, strawberries, grapes, etc.

❷ 厨房里里摆着一些电器，例如冰箱、炉子、微波炉等。
There are some electrical appliances in the kitchen, such as a refrigerator, stove, microwave oven, etc.

Try This!

1. Work with a partner to describe the following pictures using 像…什么的 or 如…等. Then compare your sentences with another student in the class to see which construction you used and how similar or different they are.

2. Read the following passage and answer the questions:

邻居王爷爷的菜园

王爷爷是我的邻居，他家后面有一个菜园，里面种着很多菜，像番茄、黄瓜、四季豆什么的。那个菜园很有意思。王爷爷今年七十岁，但是（dànshì but）他每天都在菜园里工作（gōngzuò work）。他菜园里的番茄很红，很甜。还有他花园里的芹菜很绿，很好吃。我最喜欢爷爷菜园里的生菜。上次他给了我很多，我高兴极了。他告诉（gàosu tell）我以后还要在菜园里种一些水果，例如苹果、草莓、葡萄等。真有意思！以后我也想要有一个菜园。

❶ 邻居王爷爷的菜园在哪儿？

❷ 菜园里有什么菜？

❸ 那个菜园怎么样？

❹ 邻居王爷爷多大年纪了？

❺ 他菜园里的番茄怎么样？

❻ 芹菜呢？

❼ 我最喜欢什么？

❽ 王爷爷以后还要种什么？

 生词 NEW WORDS

Shapes

zhèngfāngxíng

正方形

chángfāngxíng

长方形
長方形

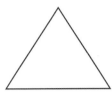

sānjiǎoxíng

三角形

wǔjiǎoxíng

五角形

yuánxíng

圆形
圓形

bànyuánxíng

半圆形
半圓形

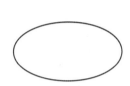

tuǒyuánxíng

椭圆形
橢圓形

língxíng

菱形

More colors

jīnhuángsè

金黄色
金黃色

gold

tiānlánsè

天蓝色
天藍色

sky blue

júhóngsè

桔红色
橘紅色

orange-red

yínhuīsè

银灰色
銀灰色

silver gray

yínbáisè

银白色
銀白色

silver white

zōngsè

棕色

brown

shēnsè 深色 dark color		qiǎnsè 浅色 淺色 light color	
shēnhóngsè 深红色 深紅色 dark red		qiǎnhóngsè 浅红色 淺紅色 light red	
shēnlánsè 深蓝色 深藍色 dark blue		qiǎnlánsè 浅蓝色 淺藍色 light blue	
shēnhuángsè 深黄色 深黃色 dark yellow		qiǎnhuángsè 浅黄色 淺黃色 light yellow	
shēnlǜsè 深绿色 深綠色 dark green		qiǎnlǜsè 浅绿色 淺綠色 light green	
shēnzǐsè 深紫色 dark purple		qiǎnzǐsè 浅紫色 淺紫色 light purple	
shēnfěnsè 深粉色 dark pink		qiǎnfěnsè 浅粉色 淺粉色 light pink	

To describe and identify the shape of something, use the 是⋯的 construction by placing the shape word in between.

For example: ❶ 这张桌子是圆形的。   This table is round.

❷ 那个书架是长方形的。   That bookshelf is rectangular.

To describe and identify the color of something, use the 是⋯的 construction by placing the color word in between.

For example: ❶ 这张沙发是棕色的。   The sofa is brown.

❷ 我的房间是天蓝色的。   My room is sky blue.

DO YOU KNOW ... 你知道吗?

Color Symbolism in Chinese Culture

As you may already know, the color red is a lucky and festive color in Chinese culture. White usually symbolizes bad luck, death, or something negative, such as lack of knowledge, intelligence, or experience. Traditionally, the color black indicates solemnity and uprightness. Yellow is the color of royalty and represents high status and power. The color blue represents calmness and tranquility, while the color green symbolizes peace and life.

 CULTURAL HIGHLIGHTS

Round Sky and Square Earth

The Temple of Heaven, Beijing

In ancient times, Chinese people viewed heaven as "rounded" and Earth as "square." This was known as "天圆地方" (tiān yuán dì fāng). Such perceptions of the world influenced various aspects of Chinese culture,

especially in Chinese architecture.

For example, the Temple of Heaven in Beijing occupies an area that is almost square, with the two southern corners being right-angled and those on the north corners rounded. This symbolizes the ancient Chinese belief that Heaven is round and the Earth is square.

The current Shanghai Museum building is designed in the shape of an ancient bronze cooking vessel called a  dǐng (鼎). The building has a round top and a square base, symbolizing the ancient Chinese perception of the world as "round sky, square earth."

Ding (鼎)

Try This!

1. Look at the pictures and check the correct shape and color for each item.

		正方形	长方形	三角形	圆形	深色	浅色
❶							
❷							
❸							
❹							
❺							
❻							
❼							

110

	正方形	长方形	三角形	圆形	深色	浅色
⑧						
⑨						
⑩						

2. Describe the color of each item below using the 是…的 construction. Use the following words to help you complete this exercise.

桔红色　銀灰色　深红色　　深蓝色
绿色　　棕色　　浅粉红色　血红色

STEP 1 DESCRIBING THE ROOMS IN A HOUSE

Anqi and Tony visit Mark's home for the first time. (I)

马克：嗨，安琪，东尼，你们好！欢迎你们来我家，请进，请进。

安琪：马克，你家的客厅真漂亮！

zhēn
very

piàoliang
beautiful

马克：谢谢。

东尼：你的房子真大。

马克：谢谢！这是厨房。我妈妈非常喜欢这个厨房。这是餐厅。那是甜甜和毛毛的房间。

fēicháng
extremely

Máomao

安琪：甜甜和毛毛是谁？

马克：是我们家的小狗。我们的卧室都在楼上，上去看看吧。

ba
(making suggestions)

（在二楼）

马克：二楼有卧室和书房。左边的房间是我父母的。右边的房间是我的。这是我的房间，你们进来吧。

东尼：你的房间真干净，东西真整齐！

gānjìng
clean

zhěngqí
neat

马克：谢谢！我妈妈天天都整理房间。

zhěnglǐ
tidy

安琪：前边是什么房间？

张安：前边的房间是书房。我每天都在书房里做作业。旁边是客房。那边还有一个大浴室和卫生间。

STEP 2 ARRANGING FURNITURE

Mother and daughter arranging items at home

小红：妈妈，我把花插在花瓶里，把花瓶摆在桌子上，行吗？

妈妈：不好，放在冰箱上面吧。你把那些水果和蔬菜放在冰箱里。

小红：好。

妈妈：我把厨具放在下面的柜子里。把碗和盘子、杯子、筷子什么的放在消毒柜里。

xiāodúguì
sterilizer

小红：把这些装饰品挂在墙上吧。

zhuàngshìpǐn
ornaments

妈妈：好。你挂吧。

小红：妈妈，你看，现在厨房很干净，也很整齐。

STEP 3 LISTING AND DESCRIBING OBJECTS

Anqi and Tony visit Mark's home for the first time. (II)

安琪：马克，你家的阳台真大啊！

马克：我爸爸喜欢在这里看书、喝茶。

安琪：你们看，外面还有一个花园呢。

ne
(to indicate emphasis)

马克：是啊。花园里种着很多花。

东尼：有玫瑰花、茉莉花、菊花什么的。玫瑰花是红色的，茉莉花是白色的，菊花是黄色的。红的、白的、黄的在一起真好看。

yìqǐ
together

马克：我和爸爸妈妈常常给花浇水、除草，还给花施肥。

chángcháng
often

jiāoshuǐ chúcǎo shīféi
water   weed   fertilize

安琪：那儿还种着一棵葡萄树呢。

shú
ripe

马克：秋天的时候，葡萄熟了，圆圆的葡萄甜极了。葡萄树旁边还有一个小菜园，里边种着一些菜，像番茄、胡萝卜、豆角什么的。这些菜都是我爱吃的。

húluóbo dòujiǎo
carrot   beans

Step Up!

1. Read the following passage and put the colors of the four seasons mentioned on a piece of paper. Then write a similar passage in Chinese about the colors of the four seasons in your eyes and share it with a partner.

一年四季的颜色

在我的眼里，春天是绿色的和粉红色的。夏天是绿色和红色的，

也是黄色和蓝色的，还是紫色和粉红色的。秋天是金黄色和红色

的。冬天是白色和蓝色的。朋友，请你告诉我，在你的眼里，一年

四季是什么颜色的呢？

<small>gàosu
tell</small>

2. 小伟 and 丽丽 are chatting online with 马丁, who is spending a school year overseas in Beijing. Read the conversation and complete the activities below.

 马丁
Martin online

 小伟
Xiaowei online

 丽丽
Lili online

小伟：　马丁，好久不见，北京怎么样？

丽丽：　马丁，好久不见，你在北京都好吗？

马丁：　你们好，看见你们真高兴！我在北京很好。
<small>zhēn / very</small>

丽丽：　我在你的脸书上看到一些照片，那是在你北京家里照的吗？
<small>liǎnshū / Facebook　　zhàopiàn / photos</small>

马丁：　是啊，我住在一个中国同学的家里，很有意思。

小伟：　住在中国人的家里？真好！

丽丽：　给我们说说吧。
<small>shuōshuo / tell</small>

马丁： 好啊，我的中国家庭有三口人，他们家有两个卧室，都朝

南。我和我的中国同学住在一个卧室里，主卧室是他父母

的。他们家的厨房不太大，旁边是餐厅，里面摆着一张大餐

桌，我们每天都一起在那儿吃早饭和晚饭。你们知道吗，

中国人的房子一般没有地下室和车库，也没有花园。

小伟： 我听说，中国人家里一般都没有烘干机。

马丁： 对，我的中国家里没有烘干机，只有一台洗衣机。洗了以

后，他们把衣服挂在阳台上。哦，他们家的阳台上种着很多

花，像月季、茉莉什么的。我的中国妈妈还在阳台上种了一

些辣椒和四季豆。

丽丽： 哈哈，我在照片上看见了，辣椒很多，也很红。

马丁： 是啊，她说，今天晚上我们吃宫保鸡丁，她要把她种的辣

椒放在里面。

小伟： 真好，我也想去中国学习，住在中国人家里，吃宫保鸡丁。

马丁： 哈哈，好啊，明年你们也一起来吧！

❶ Work with your partner and draw a map of the Chinese host family's home (马丁's host family) according to the conversation. Label in Chinese the rooms and the areas that you put on the map.

❷ After reading the conversation above, have you noticed any differences between the lifestyle of Chinese people and yours? List the differences in Chinese and compare your list with another classmate's. Then try to determine the reasons for the differences.

❸ Do you like 马丁's life in Beijing? Why? Tell his experiences in Chinese to others without referring to the conversation.

Fun Time!

Chinese riddles (谜语, míyǔ) are one of the most popular kinds of word games among Chinese people. Work with a partner to read the riddles below and try your best to solve them. See how quickly you can solve the riddle.

头上戴顶花花帽，坐在桌上微微笑，
dài dǐng mào (wear hat) zuò (sit) wēiwēixiào (smile)

每天晚上放光明，伴我读书到鸡叫。
guāngmíng (light) dú (read)

里边圆圆外边方，不是箱子不是缸，
xiāngzi (box)

喜欢清洁爱劳动，帮你洗衣工作忙。
qīngjié (cleanliness) láodòng (labor) gōngzuò (work)

小小白屋子，有门没窗子。
wū (house)

屋外很暖和，屋里冷冰冰。
nuǎnhuo (warm) lěngbīngbīng (cold)

小小一间房，只有一扇窗，
shàn

唱歌又演戏，天天翻花样。
yòu (also) yǎnxì (act) fān huāyàng (come up with new tricks)

I have learned...

Core Vocabulary

Verbs

朝		cháo	face, towards	请	請	qǐng	(used in polite requests) please
上		shàng	go or come up	种	種	zhòng	to plant, grow
下		xià	go or come down	放		fàng	to put down, place
过	過	guò	go or come over	挂	掛	guà	to hang
进	進	jìn	go or come in	插		chā	to stick in, insert
出		chū	go or come out	摆	擺	bǎi	to put, place (more for display)

Nouns

House interior

楼	樓	lóu	floor, story	阁楼	閣樓	gélóu	attic
楼上	樓上	lóushang	upstairs	地下室		dìxiàshì	basement
楼下	樓下	lóuxia	downstairs	阳台	陽臺	yángtái	balcony
门厅	門庭	méntīng	foyer	卫生间	衛生間	wèishēngjiān	bathroom
主卧室	主卧室	zhǔwòshì	master bedroom	房间	房間	fángjiān	room
厨房	廚房	chúfáng	kitchen	走廊		zǒuláng	corridor; aisle

Furniture & household appliances

壁橱	壁橱	bìchú	closet	电冰箱	電冰箱	diànbīngxiāng	refrigerator
衣柜	衣櫃	yīguì	wardrobe	洗碗机	洗碗機	xǐwǎnjī	dishwasher
床	床	chuáng	bed	洗衣机	洗衣機	xǐyījī	washing machine
床头柜	床頭櫃	chuángtóuguì	bedside cabinet, night table	烘干机	烘乾機	hōnggānjī	dryer
沙发	沙發	shāfā	sofa	微波炉	微波爐	wēibōlú	microwave oven
书桌	書桌	shūzhuō	desk	台灯	臺燈	táidēng	desk lamp
书架	書架	shūjià	bookshelf	画	畫	huà	painting
台灯	臺燈	táidēng	lamp	窗帘	窗簾	chuānglián	curtains
落地灯	落地燈	luòdìdēng	standing lamp	咖啡桌		kāfēizhuō	coffee table
电视柜	電視櫃	diànshìguì	TV console	地毯		dìtǎn	carpet
餐桌		cānzhuō	dining room table	镜子	鏡子	jìngzi	mirror
电视机	電視機	diànshìjī	television	炉子	爐子	lúzi	stove

洗手盆		xǐshǒupén	sink	花瓶		huāpíng	vase
洗脸池	洗臉池	xǐliǎnchí	sink	家具		jiājù	furniture
马桶	馬桶	mǎtǒng	toilet	电器	電器	diànqì	electrical appliance
浴缸		yùgāng	bathtub				

Flowers and plants

树	樹	shù	tree	黄瓜	黃瓜	huángguā	cucumber
花		huā	flower	四季豆		sìjìdòu	string beans
玫瑰花		méiguīhuā	rose	灌木		guànmù	bushes
茉莉花		mòlìhuā	jasmine	植物		zhíwù	plants
兰花	蘭花	lánhuā	orchid	菜		cài	vegetable
菊花		júhuā	chrysanthemum				

Shapes

正方形		zhèngfāngxíng	square	圆形	圓形	yuánxíng	circle
长方形	長方形	chángfāngxíng	rectangle	半圆形	半圓形	bànyuánxíng	semicircle
三角形		sānjiǎoxíng	triangle	椭圆形	橢圓形	tuǒyuánxíng	oval
五角形		wǔjiǎoxíng	pentagon	菱形		língxíng	diamond (shape)

Colors

金黄色	金黃色	jīnhuángsè	gold	深蓝色	深藍色	shēnlánsè	dark blue
天蓝色	天藍色	tiānlánsè	sky blue	浅蓝色	淺藍色	qiǎnlánsè	light blue
桔红色	橘紅色	júhóngsè	orange-red	深黄色	深黃色	shēnhuángsè	dark yellow
银灰色	銀灰色	yínhuīsè	silver gray	浅黄色	淺黃色	qiǎnhuángsè	light yellow
银白色	銀白色	yínbáisè	silver white	深绿色	深綠色	shēnlǜsè	dark green
棕色		zōngsè	brown	浅绿色	淺綠色	qiǎnlǜsè	light green
深色		shēnsè	dark color	深紫色		shēnzǐsè	dark purple
浅色	淺色	qiǎnsè	light color	浅紫色	淺紫色	qiǎnzǐsè	light purple
深红色	深紅色	shēnhóngsè	dark red	深粉色		shēnfěnsè	dark pink
浅红色	淺紅色	qiǎnhóngsè	light red	浅粉色	淺粉色	qiǎnfěnsè	light pink

I have learned...

Others

花园	花園	huāyuán	garden		邻居	鄰居	línjū	neighbor
车库	車庫	chēkù	garage		食物		shíwù	food
院子		yuànzi	yard		水果		shuǐguǒ	fruit
菜园	菜園	càiyuán	vegetable garden		东西	東西	dōngxi	thing
果园	果園	guǒyuán	fruit garden		文具		wénjù	stationery

Measure words

台	臺	tái	(used for electrical appliances)	面		miàn	(used for flat, smooth objects, such as mirrors, flags, etc.)
盏	盞	zhǎn	(used for lamps)	个		gè	(generic measure word)
幅		fú	(used for paintings, curtains, etc.)	辆	輛	liàng	(used for bicycles, cars, etc.)
张	張	zhāng	(used for beds, tables, sofas, etc.)	棵		kē	(used for trees)
块	塊	kuài	(used for things that are shaped like sheets)	朵		duǒ	(used for flowers, clouds, etc.)

Particle

着	著	zhe	(placed after verbs to indicate a continuing action or state)

Numeral

一些	yìxiē	some

Preposition

把	bǎ	(used to move the object to the pre-verbal position)

Constructions

像…什么的	像…什麼的	xiàng…shénme de	such as…etc.
例如…等		lìrú…děng	for example…etc.

◆ SENTENCE PATTERNS ◆

主卧室在哪儿？主卧室在楼上。	我把台灯放在书桌上。
你们上来看我的书房。	这张桌子是圆形的。
我的房间在左边。	我的房间是天蓝色的。
一台电冰箱、两盏台灯、三幅画、四张床、五块地毯、六面镜子	菜园里种着一些菜，像番茄、黄瓜、四季豆什么的。
花园里种着一些花。	

I can do!

Interpretive Communication

❑ I can understand when someone tells me the relative locations of rooms in a home.

❑ I can read information about the relative locations of rooms in a house and how furniture is placed in the house.

❑ I can understand when someone enumerates a list of items in a similar category.

❑ I understand when someone describes shapes and colors of some things.

❑ I can read and understand when someone talks about the existence of some things.

Interpersonal Communication

❑ I can exchange information about the relative locations of rooms and furniture.

❑ I can find out the relative location of rooms and furniture items.

❑ I can exchange information about the existence of something.

❑ I can share information on shapes and colors.

Presentational Communication

❑ I can talk about relative location of rooms, furniture, and other household items in a home.

❑ I can give directions orally or in writing stating where to put certain objects.

❑ I can list items.

❑ I can talk and write about colors and shapes.

Cultural Knowledge

❑ I can identify and recognize Chinese courtyard houses and know that they are called "四合院."

❑ I can identify and recognize houses with good *feng shui*.

❑ I can identify the concept of "round sky and square earth" in Chinese architecture.

❑ I can recognize and talk about the significance of certain colors in Chinese culture.

LESSON 4

Adapting to the weather

适应气候

Get ready...

Look at the following weather map of China and the table of weather symbols below. Describe the weather conditions of the cities on the map. Which city do you want to visit based on the weather condition at the moment?

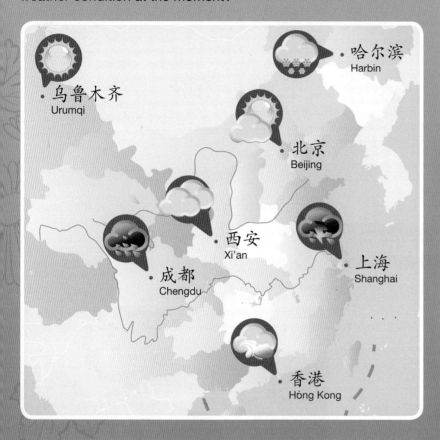

qíngtiān 晴天 sunny	yīntiān 阴天 overcast	duōyún 多云 cloudy	guāfēng 刮风 windy
yǔtiān 雨天 rainy	léizhènyǔ 雷阵雨 thunderstorm	xiàxuě 下雪 snow	

STEP 1

TALKING ABOUT THE WEATHER

A. Describing the weather
今天天气怎么样？
今天下雨，有点儿冷。

B. Telling specific temperatures
今天气温多少度？
今天气温六十华氏度。

C. Comparing the weather
今天没有昨天冷。

STEP 2

DRESSING ACCORDING TO THE WEATHER

A. Clothing and accessories
一件毛衣、两条裙子、三双球鞋、
四块手表、五顶帽子

B. Stating the need to wear certain clothing
外面热极了，得戴太阳镜。

STEP 3

DESCRIBING HOW PEOPLE ARE DRESSED

A. Stating what people wear
夏天，人们穿着短裤、凉鞋。

B. Identifying people by the way they dress
穿红裙子的女孩是我妹妹。

121

tiānqì
今天天气怎么样？
How's the weather today?

xiàyǔ　　　yǒudiǎnr　lěng
今天下雨，有点儿冷。
It's raining and a bit cold.

A Describing the weather

rè
现在外边热吗？
Is it hot outside now?

guā fēng
现在外边刮风，不热。
The wind is blowing now; it's not hot.

明天冷不冷？
Will tomorrow be cold?

qíngtiān　　　nuǎnhuo
明天是晴天，很暖和。
Tomorrow is a sunny day; it will be warm.

NEW WORDS

晴天 n.		qíngtiān	sunny day
阴天 n.	陰天	yīntiān	overcast
多云 adj.	多雲	duōyún	cloudy
刮风 phr.	刮風	guāfēng	wind blowing, windy
雨天 n.		yǔtiān	rainy day
下雨 phr.		xiàyǔ	raining
雷阵雨 n.	雷陣雨	léizhènyǔ	thunderstorm
下雪 phr.		xiàxuě	snowing
天气 n.	天氣	tiānqì	weather
冷 adj.		lěng	cold
热 adj.	熱	rè	hot
暖和 adj.		nuǎnhuo	warm
凉快 adj.	涼快	liángkuai	*(pleasantly)* cool
有点儿 adv.	有點兒	yǒudiǎnr	a little, a bit

LANGUAGE FOCUS

To ask about the weather, the following questions can be used:

❧ 明天天气怎么样？ ("how" question using 怎么样)
How's the weather tomorrow?

❧ 后天冷吗？ (yes-no question ending with 吗)
Will the day after tomorrow be cold?

❧ 大后天热不热？ (yes-no questions with an adjective followed by its negative)
Will the day after tomorrow be hot?

You have already learned how to express a higher degree by using 很 and 极了. When describing weather temperatures, the degree adverb 有点儿 can be used to express a slight degree. It is placed before the adjective.

For example: ❶ 明天有点儿热。 Tomorrow will be a bit hot.

❷ 后天有点儿冷。 The day after tomorrow will be a little cold.

❸ 大后天有点儿热。 Three days from now will be a bit hot.

Try This!

1. Study the weather forecast for the week and answer the following questions.

星期一	星期二	星期三	星期四	星期五	星期六	星期天
50–70°F	58–68°F	55–70°F	48–65°F	53–68°F	60–75°F	63–78°F
10 – 21.1°C	14.4 – 20°C	12.7 – 21.1°C	8.8 – 18.3°C	11.6 – 20°C	15.5 – 23.8°C	17.2 – 25.5°C

❶ 星期几是雨天？

❷ 星期几是晴天？

❸ 哪天最冷？

❹ 哪天最热？

❺ 你要去海边。哪天去最好？

2. Refer to the same weather forecast above. Work with a partner to practice asking and answering questions about the weather for the week.

Student A: 星期三天气怎么样？
Student B: 星期三是阴天，有点儿冷。

 CULTURAL HIGHLIGHTS

The hottest and coldest places in China

As the northernmost county in China, located in the Heilongjiang Province, Mohe County (漠河县 Mòhé Xiàn) is widely believed to be the coldest place in China. Temperatures there can fall as low as –52.3°C. A village, the northernmost settlement in China at the latitude of 53° 29' N, known as China's "Arctic Village," (北极村 Běijí Cūn) lies in this county on the Amur River, which forms the border with Russia. Here, the astronomical phenomenon of aurora borealis attracts local and foreign tourists to this village.

The hottest place in China is Turpan (吐鲁番 Tǔlǔfān), an oasis county-level city in Turpan Prefecture, in Xinjiang, China. On average, there are 152 summer days, and 28 really hot days with the temperature above 40°C (104°F). The Flaming Mountains (火焰山 Huǒyàn Shān), approximately 60 miles long and 3–6 miles wide, spans the Turpan Depression from east to west. The mountain climate is harsh, and the extremely high summer temperatures make this the hottest spot in China, frequently reaching 50°C (122°F) or higher.

qìwēn   duōshao   dù
今天气温多少度？
What's the temperature today?

huáshìdù
今天气温六十华氏度。
The temperature today is 60°F.

昨天气温七十五度，很暖和。
Yesterday's temperature was 75°F; it was warm.

生 词

NEW WORDS

气温 n.	氣温	qìwēn	temperature
多少 q.w.		duōshao	how many
度 n.		dù	degree
摄氏度 n.	攝氏度	shèshìdù	Celsius degree
华氏度 n.	華氏度	huáshìdù	Fahrenheit degree

LANGUAGE FOCUS

度 (degree) is the unit of measurement for temperatures. To ask about specific degrees, use the question word 多少.

For example: ❶ 明天气温多少度？
What will the temperature be tomorrow?

❷ 后天气温多少度？
What will the temperature be the day after tomorrow?

To specify the temperature scale (Celsius or Fahrenheit), use 摄氏度 or 华氏度 right after the numerals.

For example: ❶ 明天气温二十五摄氏度。
Tomorrow's temperature will be 25°C.

❷ 后天气温七十华氏度。
The temperature for the day after tomorrow will be 70°F.

It is fine to simply put 度 after the numerals when the temperature scale used is clear from the context.

For example: ❶ 明天气温二十五度。
Tomorrow's temperature will be 25 degrees.

❷ 后天气温七十度。
The temperature for the day after tomorrow will be 70 degrees.

1. Study the weather forecast for the week below. Work with a partner to ask and answer questions on the temperatures. Next, write a description of the weather in the spaces provided.

Adjectives:　　冷　　热　　凉快　　暖和

Degress adverbs:　很　　极了　　有点儿

Example: 星期一气温多少度？星期一气温五十八 (华氏) 度。

星期一	星期二	星期三	星期四	星期五	星期六	星期天
58°F	70°F	55°F	48°F	53°F	60°F	75°F
有点儿冷						

While the United States uses Fahrenheit to express temperatures, China and many other countries use Celsius.

Here is the conversion formula:

$$°C \times 9/5 + 32 = °F$$
$$(°F - 32) \times 5/9 = °C$$

C Comparing the weather

dī
今天气温比昨天低。
Today's temperature is lower than yesterday's.

这里跟那里一样冷。
This place is as cold as that place.

生 词

NEW WORDS

低 adj.		dī	low
和 prep.		hé	with
这么 adv.	這麼	zhème	so, like this
那么 adv.	那麼	nàme	so, like that

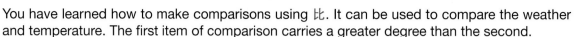

You have learned how to make comparisons using 比. It can be used to compare the weather and temperature. The first item of comparison carries a greater degree than the second.

For example:

❶ 今天比昨天冷。   Today is colder than yesterday.

❷ 今天比昨天冷一点。   Today is a little colder than yesterday.

❸ 今天比昨天冷多了。   Today is much colder than yesterday.

❹ 今天比昨天冷得多。   Today is much colder than yesterday.

比–sentences are negated by replacing 比 with 没有, in the pattern of "A + 没有 + B + (这么 / 那么) + adjective." Use 这么 when the speaker is near B, and 那么 when the speaker is far from B.

For example:

❶ 今天没有昨天(这么/那么)冷。   Today is not as cold as yesterday.
                                            (Both 这么 and 那么 are acceptable)

❷ 图书馆没有教室(这么)热。   The library is not as warm as the classroom.
                                            (The speaker is in the classroom.)

The construction 跟…一样 can be used to express similarities or differences in the weather and temperature. 和 can replace 跟 in this construction to express the same meaning.

For example:

❶ 今天跟昨天一样热。   Today is as hot as yesterday.

❷ 教室和图书馆一样冷。   The classroom is as cold as the library.

1. Combine each pair of sentences using 比. You may add an appropriate complement (一点，多了，得多) at the end.

Example: 今天24度。明天31度。

      ⟶ 今天比明天凉快得多。明天比今天热得多。

❶ 昨天10度。今天18度。

    ⟶ _____

❷ 前天35度。今天28度。

    ⟶ _____

❸ 明天20度。后天15度。

    ⟶ _____

❹ 我17岁。弟弟11岁。

    ⟶ _____

❺ 他的电脑1600美元。我的电脑700美元。

→ _____

❻ 北京现在的气温是21度。上海现在的气温是29度。

→ _____

❼ 我们学校寒假有三个星期。暑假有七个星期。

→ _____

❽ 我家有三只狗。他家有一只狗。

→ _____

2. Rewrite the following sentences using the construction 跟…(不)一样. You may add an appropriate adjective after 一样 to describe more specifically the similarity or difference.

> *Example:* 今天24度，明天31度。(temperature)
> → 今天的气温跟明天的气温不一样(高)。

❶ 昨天16度，今天16度。(temperature)

→ _____

❷ 明天36度，后天30度。(temperature)

→ _____

❸ 前天5度，昨天12度。(temperature)

→ _____

❹ 纽约0度，伦敦3度。(temperature)

→ _____

❺ 爷爷70岁，外公也是70岁。(age)

→ _____

❻ 我的书包是蓝色的，妹妹的书包是粉红色的。(color)

→ _____

❼ 我家有五个房间，他家有三个房间。(number of rooms)

→ _____

❽ 这张书桌是长方形的，那张餐桌是圆形的。(shapes)

→ _____

DRESSING ACCORDING TO THE WEATHER

In this section, you will learn some common vocabulary on clothing and accessories, and the verbs and measure words associated with them. Study the table below.

A Clothing and accessories 生词 NEW WORDS

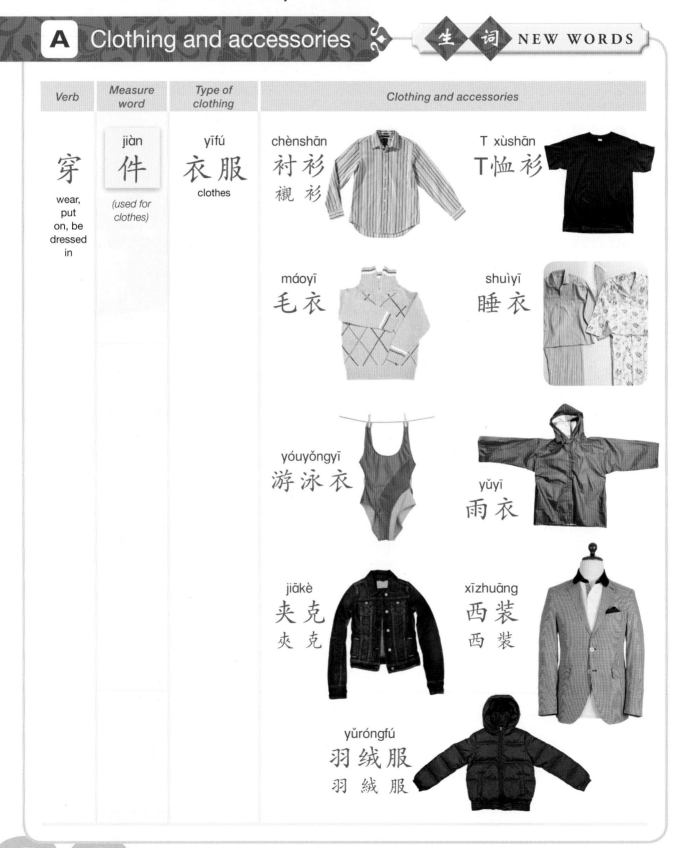

Verb	Measure word	Type of clothing	Clothing and accessories
穿 chuān wear, put on, be dressed in	jiàn 件 *(used for clothes)*	yīfú 衣服 clothes	chènshān 衬衫 襯衫 T xùshān T恤衫 máoyī 毛衣 shuìyī 睡衣 yóuyǒngyī 游泳衣 yǔyī 雨衣 jiākè 夹克 夾克 xīzhuāng 西装 西裝 yǔróngfú 羽绒服 羽絨服

Verb	Measure word	Types of clothing	Clothing and accessories
穿 wear, put on, be dressed in	条 條 (used for long, narrow things)	kùzi 裤子 褲子 trousers, pants	chángkù 长裤 長褲 niúzǎikù 牛仔裤 牛仔褲 duǎnkù 短裤 短褲
		qúnzi 裙子 skirt	chángqún 长裙 長裙 liányīqún 连衣裙 連衣裙 duǎnqún 短裙

Verb	Measure word	Type of clothing	Clothing and accessories
穿 wear, put on, be dressed in	shuāng 双 雙 *(used for things that come in twos)*	xiézi 鞋子 shoes	 qiúxié 球鞋 píxié 皮鞋  gāogēnxié 高跟鞋  liángxié　tuōxié 凉鞋 / 拖鞋　 涼鞋
		wàzi 袜子 襪子 socks	 zhōngtǒngwà 中筒袜 中筒襪  chángwà 长袜 長襪 duǎnwà 短袜 短襪

Verb	Measure word	Type of clothing	Clothing and accessories
dài 戴 (on the head, neck, wrist) put on, wear	dǐng 顶 頂 (used for hats, caps, or things with a top)		 màozi 帽子
	fù 副 (used for things that come in pairs or sets)		 tàiyángjìng 太阳镜 太 陽 鏡 shǒutào 手套
	条 條 (used for long, narrow things)		wéijīn 围 巾 圍 巾 lǐngdài 领 带 領 帶
	块 塊 (used for things that come in solid pieces)		shǒubiǎo 手 表 手 錶

* The measure words 个 and 支 can also be used for watches.

LANGUAGE FOCUS

In Chinese, there are two verbs for "to wear, to put on." 穿 is used for clothing items such as shirt, sweater, dress, shoes, socks, etc. 戴 is used for accessories such as hats, scarfs, watches, and jewels. Both are used in the "verb + object" pattern:

For example:
❶ 爸爸穿衬衫。
Dad is wearing a shirt.

❷ 妈妈穿连衣裙。
Mom is wearing a dress.

❸ 哥哥戴手表。
My older brother is wearing a watch.

❹ 姐姐戴围巾。
My older sister is wearing a scarf.

To state or count clothing items and accessories, just follow the pattern "numeral + measure word + item":

For example:
❶ 一件毛衣
a sweater

❷ 两条裙子
two skirts

❸ 三双球鞋
three pairs of sneakers

❹ 四块手表
four watches

❺ 五顶帽子
five hats

Try This!

1. State the quantity of the items in the pictures using the appropriate measure words.

❶

❷

❸

❹

❺

❻

❼

❽

❾

❿

2. Describe the following pictures using sentences containing 穿 or 戴.

妈妈戴手表。

妈妈　　姐姐　　叔叔　　妹妹　　弟弟

叔叔　　哥哥　　姐姐　　妈妈　　阿姨

3. You need to sort the laundry items below into the four laundry bags. Note that each bag is specifically for items that use a particular measure word. Sort the items by writing the words for each article of clothing in the spaces provided under each bag.

围巾　　外套　　凉鞋　　袜子　　毛衣　　短裤
衬衫　　领带　　T恤衫　　帽子　　长裤　　手套

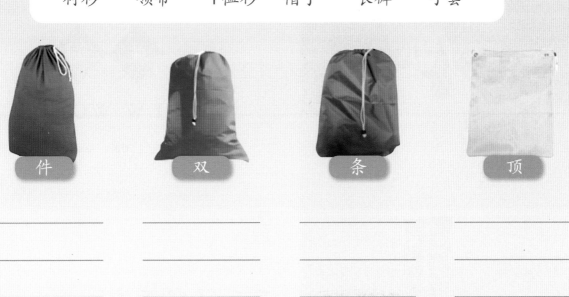

件　　　双　　　条　　　顶

_____　　_____　　_____　　_____

_____　　_____　　_____　　_____

_____　　_____　　_____　　_____

děi
外面热极了，得戴太阳镜。
It is extremely hot outside; there is a need to wear sunglasses.

冬天得穿羽绒服，戴手套。
There is a need to wear down jackets and gloves during winter.

生 词

NEW WORD

得 *aux. v.* | **děi** | need to, must

雨天得穿雨衣。
There is a need to wear a raincoat during rainy days.

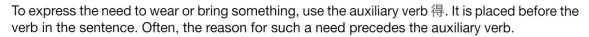
To express the need to wear or bring something, use the auxiliary verb 得. It is placed before the verb in the sentence. Often, the reason for such a need precedes the auxiliary verb.

Examples: ❶ 外面很冷，我得穿外套。
It is cold outside; I must wear a jacket.

❷ 现在是晴天，你得戴太阳镜。
It is sunny now; you need to wear sunglasses.

❸ 我下午要去打球，得穿球鞋。
I'm going to play a ball game in the afternoon; I need to wear sports shoes.

❹ 爸爸上班得戴领带。
Dad needs to wear a tie for work.

CULTURAL HIGHLIGHTS

Chinese Clothing

Chinese clothing comes in various forms. One of them is the *Zhongshan* suit (中山装 Zhōngshān zhuāng), a style of men's wear popularized by Sun Yat-sun (Zhongshan was one of Sun Yat-sen's given names in Chinese). It features a jacket and trousers instead of the robes worn previously. Adapted from Japanese student wear, this style of dress combined Western and Eastern fashions and was an attempt to cater to contemporary sensibilities without adopting Western styles.

A *Tangzhuang* (唐装 Tángzhuāng) is a Chinese jacket that originated at the end of the Qing Dynasty. The *Tangzhuang* evolved from the *Magua* (马褂 Mǎguà), a Manchurian piece of clothing, which was in turn adopted by the Han Chinese during the Qing Dynasty. *Tangzhuang* are made in different colors, most commonly red, navy, gold, black, and green. One common design is the usage of Chinese characters as a monogram such as 福 (fú, blessings) and 寿 (shòu, longevity) to spread good luck and wishes. At the Asia-Pacific Economic Cooperation summit in Shanghai in November 2001, the host presented silk-embroided *Tangzhuang* jackets as the Chinese traditional national costume.

The cheongsam or *qipao* (旗袍 qípáo) is a body-hugging one-piece Chinese dress for women. The original *qipao* was wide and loose. The stylish and often tight-fitting cheongsam that is most often seen today was created in the 1920s in Shanghai and was made fashionable by socialites and upper class women. In the Chinese movie *In the Mood for Love* (花样年华 Huāyàng Niánhuá), famous Chinese actress Maggie Cheung wore 23 different cheongsam dresses, perfectly portraying the beauty and charm of modern Chinese women.

1. Imagine you are at the following places at the specified time. What kind of clothing would you need to wear? First find out the weather in these places, and then fill in the blanks by describing the weather in Chinese and stating what you would need to wear.

Xiàwēiyí
❶ 夏威夷，七月　天气 _____
Hawaii
　　　　　　　　我得 _____

Bōshìdùn
❷ 波士顿，十一月　天气 _____
Boston
　　　　　　　　我得 _____

Yúnnán
❸ 云南，五月　天气 _____
Yunnan
　　　　　　　我得 _____

Sānfānshì
❹ 三藩市，四月　天气 _____
San Francisco
　　　　　　　我得 _____

2. Make sentences to express the need to wear certain clothing arising from the situations depicted in the pictures below.

去海边得穿凉鞋。

138

DESCRIBING HOW PEOPLE ARE DRESSED

夏天，人们穿着短裤、凉鞋。
During summer, people wear shorts and sandals.

A Stating what people wear

她戴着一条红色的围巾。
She is wearing a red scarf.

LANGUAGE FOCUS

Besides indicating the existence of something as introduced in Lesson 3, 着 is used after an action verb to show that the action is continuing at the point in time.

For example:
❶ 冬天，人们都穿着羽绒服，戴着手套。
During winter, people wear down jackets and gloves.

❷ 他戴着一顶蓝色的帽子。
He is wearing a blue hat.

Try This!

1. In the photos below, give each person a name and describe what he/she is wearning using 着.

奶奶穿着一件蓝色的衣服。

妈妈穿着一条黑色的长裤。

 CULTURAL HIGHLIGHTS

Famous Chinese Fashion Designers

Vera Wang (王薇薇 Wáng Wēiwēi) and Jason Wu (吴季刚 Wú Jìgāng) are famous Chinese fashion designers.

Vera Wang is an American fashion designer based in New York City. She is known for her wide range of haute couture bridesmaid gowns and wedding gown collections. By balancing modern designs with traditional elegance, Wang has acquired a large following, particularly in Hollywood. Her fashions are frequently worn to film premieres and award ceremonies by a number of high-profile actresses, including Halle Berry, Goldie Hawn, Charlize Theron, Anjelica Huston, and Meg Ryan.

Jason Wu is a Taiwanese-Canadian fashion designer based in New York City. From full-length gowns to more casual daywear, Wu's pieces have clean, classic lines and incorporate bright colors and prints without being flashy. The result is modern and wearable but consistently noteworthy. He is most famous for designing the dresses of Michelle Obama on several occasions, including during the first and second inaugurations of American President Barack Obama.

穿红裙子的女孩是我姐姐。

The girl who is wearing a red skirt is my sister.

LANGUAGE FOCUS

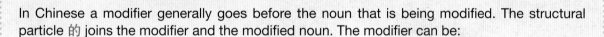

In Chinese a modifier generally goes before the noun that is being modified. The structural particle 的 joins the modifier and the modified noun. The modifier can be:

❶ a noun

For example: ▷ 哥哥的书桌 my older brother's desk

▷ 学校的操场 the school's sports field

❷ an adjective

For example: ▷ 开心的妹妹 my happy sister

▷ 生气的老师 an angry teacher

❸ a verb phrase (i.e., verb + object)

For example: ▷ 穿蓝球鞋的男孩 the boy who is wearing blue sneakers

▷ 戴紫围巾的女孩 the girl who is wearing a purple scarf

Look at number **❸**. The modifier and the modified noun can be the subject or object of a sentence, just like other noun phrases.

▷ 穿蓝球鞋的男孩是我哥哥。 The boy who is wearing blue sneakers is my older brother.

▷ 戴紫围巾的女孩是我姐姐。 The girl who is wearing a purple scarf is my older sister.

If the context is clear, the modified noun may be omitted.

▷ 穿红衣服的(女人)是我妈妈，穿蓝衣服的(男人)是我爸爸。
The lady who is wearing a red shirt is my mother, and the man who is wearing a blue shirt is my father.

1. Look at the following pictures and make sentences according to the way each person in the picture is dressed. The modified noun may be omitted.

穿红衣服的是王老师。

王老师

爸爸

妈妈

哥哥

姐姐

弟弟

妹妹

叔叔

阿姨

马克

2. Change the following sentences into 是–sentences.

❶ 姐姐戴着黄围巾。 ⟶ _____

❷ 哥哥穿着白T恤衫。 ⟶ _____

❸ 妹妹戴着紫帽子。 ⟶ _____

❹ 弟弟穿着绿球鞋。 ⟶ _____

❺ 爸爸戴着蓝领带。 ⟶ _____

❻ 妈妈穿着红裙子。 ⟶ _____

❼ 张老师戴黑手表。 ⟶ _____

❽ 叔叔穿着蓝衬衫。 ⟶ _____

Reading *in Context*

STEP 1 TALKING ABOUT THE WEATHER

Xiaohong asking her mom about the weather

小红：妈妈，今天天气好吗？

妈妈：不好。阴天。天气预报
说今天有雨。可是现
在还没有下。

小红：是吗？外面冷吗？

妈妈：今天比昨天冷。

小红：今天气温多少度？

妈妈：今天十九度，气温比昨天低。
有点儿冷。

小红：外面有没有风？

妈妈：有风。

小红：风大吗？

妈妈：没有昨天的风大。虽然风
不大，但是比昨天冷得多。
你要多穿一点儿衣服。

yùbào
forecast

shuō *kěshì*
say but

STEP 2 DRESSING ACCORDING TO THE WEATHER

Two brothers talking about what to wear tomorrow

哥哥：天气冷了，咱们
得注意身体。

弟弟：是啊。明天天气怎么样？
你知道吗？

哥哥：明天冷极了。只有8度。

弟弟：太冷了，明天得多穿
一点儿衣服。

哥哥：得穿羽绒服和靴子。

弟弟：明天你去哪儿？

哥哥：明天我去看足球
比赛，你呢？

弟弟：我和同学去爬山。

哥哥：你也要多穿点衣服，
得戴帽子和手套。

弟弟：好，谢谢！

zánmen *zhùyì*
we mind, watch

zhīdào
know

zhǐyǒu
only

tài
too

xuēzi
boots

bǐsài
match, competition

STEP 3 DESCRIBING HOW PEOPLE ARE DRESSED

Two students talking about their new teacher

安琪：马克，我们学校来了一位新老师。
你知道吗？

马克：我听说了。你知道她教什么课吗？

安琪：听说教我们中文。

马克：她是从中国来的吗？

安琪：是，从北京来的。我在路上见
过她。她戴着一副眼镜。你看，
说曹操曹操就到。

马克：什么意思？

安琪：新老师来了。

马克：在哪儿？

安琪：穿着红羽绒服和红靴子、戴着
眼镜的那位就是新老师。

马克：长得真漂亮啊！

wèi
(used for persons)

tīngshuō
heard of

Cáo Cāo *jiù*
说曹操曹操就到
Speak of the devil

zhǎng *zhēn* *piàoliang*
grow very beautiful

Step Up!

1. Divide into groups of two. Each group will be in charge of finding out the weather forecast for a well known city. The information they will need to know is:

   ❶ Name of city

   ❷ Dates of the forecast

   ❸ Number of clear and cloudy days in the week; number of days of rain and snow in the week

   ❹ The hottest and coldest days in the week, with their specific temperatures.

   Present your findings to the class in the form of presentation slides or a poster. The class will vote for the group that has the most creative presentation.

2. Read the following conversation and answer the questions.

小丁： 明天是雨天，天气会很冷，气温会在十度左右。
　　　　　　　　　　huì　　　　　　　　　　　　　　　　zuǒyòu
　　　　　　　　　　will　　　　　　　　　　　　　　　　approximately

李明： 是吗？我们开学两个星期，秋天就到了。我好想念夏天。
　　　　　　　　　　　　　　　　　　jiù　　　　　　　　　xiǎngniàn
　　　　　　　　　　　　　　　　as soon as　　　　　　　　miss

小丁： 我听说你暑假去云南做义工。云南夏天的天气怎么样？
　　　　tīngshuō
　　　　heard that

李明： 云南的夏天没有北京热，很舒服。白天穿T恤衫、短裤，
　　　　　　　　　　　　　　　　　　　　　　　daytime
　　　　晚上有时候比较凉快，有时候得穿毛衣。

小丁： 我有一个同学到美国去念书，他说美国天气也开始凉快了。
　　　　　　　　　　　　　　niànshū　　shuō　　　　　kāishǐ
　　　　　　　　　　　　　　study　　say　　　　　　start
　　　　早上和晚上要穿外套。冬天天气冷极了，常常下雪，得穿
　　　　　　　　　　　　　　　　　　　　chángcháng
　　　　羽绒服、戴围巾。　　　　　　　　often

李明： 我喜欢暖和的天气，我以后去美国念书，要到加州。冬天
　　　　　　　　　　　　　　　　　　　　　　　　　Jiāzhōu
　　　　tài　　　　　　　　　　　　　　　　　　　California
　　　　不太冷，夏天不太热。这样一年四季穿牛仔裤、衬衫，凉
　　　　too　　　　　　　　　in this way
　　　　　　　　　　　　　　xíng
　　　　快的时候多穿一件外套就行。
　　　　　　　　　　　　　then okay

小丁： 加州天气那么好，我一定常常去那里看你。
　　　　　　　　　　yídìng
　　　　so　　　　definitely

❶ Which time of the year does this conversation take place?

❷ How did Li Ming spend his summer vacation?

❸ Is summer in Beijing hotter than in Yunnan?

❹ What must one wear during winter in the U.S.?

❺ Where does Li Ming want to go for overseas studies? Why?

3. Sit with a partner and describe what your classmates are wearing. Write at least 10 sentences. Then summarize what you have observed into a table or graph showing what types of clothing and colors are the most popular.

姓名	衣服	颜色
安琪	围巾	红色

红色。

她的围巾是什么颜色?

Fun Time!

Spring is an important season to the Chinese people, and is a recurrent theme in Chinese poetry and proverbs. Here are some examples.

Spring in Chinese Poetry
Below is a famous Chinese poem of the Tang dynasty. First cover the English translation, then circle the Chinese characters that you know. Without referring to the translation, try to guess the meaning of the poem based on those characters. Then read the translation and see if your guess is correct.

xiǎo
春晓

mián   chù   wén   tí
春眠不觉晓，处处闻啼鸟。

yè   shēng   luò zhī
夜来风雨声，花落知多少。

Mèng Hàorán
孟浩然

In spring, I sleep, unaware that the morning is here,
From near then far, trilling songbirds I hear;
In the night's pitter-patter of winds and rains though mild,
How many petals had fallen? Know not, I fear!

Spring in Chinese Proverbs
Read the proverb below that is related to spring.

zhī jì yú   chén
一年之计在于春，一日之计在于晨
Plan your year in spring, your day at dawn.

Why is spring a good time for planning? Do you have any proverbs in your culture that are related to spring? Share them with your classmates.

I have learned...

Core Vocabulary

Verb

戴		dài	*(on the head, neck, wrist)* put on, wear

Nouns

Weather and temperature

晴天		qíngtiān	sunny day	气温	氣溫	qìwēn	temperature
阴天	陰天	yīntiān	overcast	度		dù	degree
雨天		yǔtiān	rainy day	摄氏度	攝氏度	shèshìdù	Celsius degree
雷阵雨	雷陣雨	léizhènyǔ	thunderstorm	华氏度	華氏度	huáshìdù	Fahrenheit degree
天气	天氣	tiānqì	weather				

Clothing and accessories

衬衫	襯衫	chènshān	shirt	连衣裙	連衣裙	liányīqún	dress
T恤衫		T xùshān	T-shirt	鞋子		xiézi	shoes
毛衣		máoyī	sweater	球鞋		qiúxié	sneakers
睡衣		shuìyī	pajamas	皮鞋		píxié	leather shoes
游泳衣		yóuyǒngyī	swimsuit	凉鞋/拖鞋	涼鞋	liángxié/tuōxié	sandals, slippers
雨衣		yǔyī	raincoat	高跟鞋		gāogēnxié	high-heel shoes
夹克	夾克	jiākè	jacket	袜子	襪子	wàzi	socks
西装	西裝	xīzhuāng	suit	短袜	短襪	duǎnwà	ankle socks
羽绒服	羽絨服	yǔróngfú	down jacket	中筒袜	中筒襪	zhōngtǒngwà	crew socks
裤子	褲子	kùzi	trousers, pants	长袜	長襪	chángwà	knee-high socks
长裤	長褲	chángkù	trousers, pants	帽子		màozi	hat, cap
短裤	短褲	duǎnkù	shorts, Bermuda shorts	太阳镜	太陽鏡	tàiyángjìng	sunglasses
牛仔裤	牛仔褲	niúzǎikù	jeans	手套		shǒutào	gloves
裙子		qúnzi	skirt	围巾	圍巾	wéijīn	scarf
长裙	長裙	chángqún	long skirt	领带	領帶	lǐngdài	tie
短裙		duǎnqún	short skirt	手表	手錶	shǒubiǎo	watch

I have learned...

Adjectives

多云	多雲	duōyún	cloudy		暖和		nuǎnhuo	warm
冷		lěng	cold		凉快	涼快	liángkuai	(pleasantly) cool
热	熱	rè	hot		低		dī	low

Question word

多少		duōshao	how many

Measure words

件		jiàn	(used for clothes)
双	雙	shuāng	(used for things that come in twos)
顶	頂	dǐng	(used for hats, caps, or things with a top)
副		fù	(used for things that come in pairs or sets)
块	塊	kuài	(used for things that come in solid pieces)

Adverb

有点儿	有點兒	yǒudiǎnr	a little, a bit
这么	這麼	zhème	so, like this
那么	那麼	nàme	so, like that

Auxiliary verb

得		děi	need to, must

Preposition

和		hé	with

Phrases

刮风	刮風	guāfēng	wind blowing, windy		下雪	xiàxuě	snowing
下雨		xiàyǔ	raining				

◆ SENTENCE PATTERNS ◆

今天天气怎么样？今天下雨，有点儿冷。

今天气温多少度？今天气温六十华氏度。

今天气温比昨天低。

一件毛衣、两条裙子、三双球鞋、四块手表、五顶帽子

外面热极了，得戴太阳镜。

夏天，人们穿着短裤、凉鞋。

穿红裙子的女孩是我妹妹。

I can do!

Interpretive Communication

❏ I can understand when someone tells me the temperature.

❏ I can understand when someone describes the weather in different seasons.

❏ I can read and understand weather forecasts; reports, and charts.

❏ I can understand when someone describes their clothing to me.

Interpersonal Communication

❏ I can exchange information about the weather.

❏ I can discuss the change of weather.

❏ I can compare and contrast different seasons.

❏ I can share information on clothing preferences.

Presentational Communication

❏ I can talk about the weather in China and other places.

❏ I can compare the weather of China and other parts of the world.

❏ I can state things that I need to do.

❏ I can discuss the weather and its impact on our activities.

Cultural Knowledge

❏ I can talk about the hottest place and the coldest place in China.

❏ I can describe different types of Chinese clothing.

❏ I can name some famous Chinese fashion designers.

LESSON 5

Discovering the community

熟悉新社区

COMMUNICATIVE GOALS
* Describing the locations of community places
* Asking for and giving directions
* Expressing specific distances between two places
* Stating the purpose of an action
* Describing the sequence of actions

Cultural Knowledge
* The Chinese compass
* Chinese measure of distance
* Morning activities in Chinese neighborhoods

Get ready...

1. There are many newly developed residential areas in the city of Beijing. These residential areas, known as 小区 (xiǎoqū), are quite self-sufficient like a small town with nurseries, schools, hospitals, police stations, groceries, shopping malls, and restaurants. Look at some of them below and compare them with the community you live in.

2. "望京" is one of the largest residential areas in the northeastern part of Beijing. Its name means "looking at the capital" and refers to its closeness to the Forbidden City, the political center in the Qing Dynasty. Now there are a lot of upscale apartments with a large Korean population, as can be seen by the surrounding Korean restaurants and groceries.

Use "望京" as a keyword to search online and find out three things about this community in Beijing.

望京

STEPS *at a glance!*

FINDING PLACES IN THE COMMUNITY

A. Introducing places in the community

社区里不但有银行，而且还有邮局。

B. Describing the locations of community places

电影院在社区的东北边。

GETTING AROUND THE COMMUNITY

A. Asking for and giving directions

请问，去邮局怎么走？

往右拐，再往前走。

B. Giving more specific directions

请问，去便利店怎么走？

前面往右拐就到了。

C. Expressing specific distances between two places

这儿离地铁站有多远？

这儿离地铁站有3英里。

LIVING IN THE COMMUNITY

A. Going to a place to do something

我去商场购物。

B. Describing the sequence of actions

先去药房，再去面包店。

151

A Introducing places in the community

shèqū　　búdàn　　yínháng　　érqiě　　yóujú
社区里不但有银行，而且还有邮局。
Not only does the community have a bank, it has a post office, too.

lǐfàdiàn　　　　　　　　　　　　zhěnsuǒ
社区里不但有理发店，而且还有诊所。
Not only does this place have a hairdresser's salon, it has a clinic, too.

NEW WORDS

不但…而且…conj.		búdàn…érqiè	not only...but also
社区 n.	社區	shèqū	community
邮局 n.	郵局	yóujú	post office
警察局 n.		jǐngchájú	police station
便利店 n.		biànlìdiàn	convenience store
面包店 n.	麵包店	miànbāodiàn	bakery
理发店 n.	理髮店	lǐfàdiàn	hairdresser's salon
洗衣店 n.		xǐyīdiàn	laundromat
花店 n.		huādiàn	florist
书店 n.	書店	shūdiàn	book store
超市 n.		chāoshì	supermarket
菜市场 n.	菜市場	càishìchǎng	(vegetable) market
商场 n.	商場	shāngchǎng	mall
停车场 n.	停車場	tíngchēchǎng	car park
篮球场 n.	籃球場	lánqiúchǎng	basketball court
足球场 n.	足球場	zúqiúchǎng	soccer field
网球场 n.	網球場	wǎngqiúchǎng	tennis court
餐馆 n.	餐館	cānguǎn	restaurant
银行 n.	銀行	yínháng	bank
电影院 n.	電影院	diànyǐngyuàn	movie theater
公园 n.	公園	gōngyuán	park
诊所 n.	診所	zhěnsuǒ	clinic
药房 n.	藥房	yàofáng	pharmacy
医院 n.	醫院	yīyuàn	hospital
加油站 n.		jiāyóuzhàn	gas station

生
词

The paired conjunctions 不但 (not only) and 而且 (moreover) are used to provide additional details on the same subject. 不但 is used in the first clause after the subject while 而且 leads the second clause to add more information.

For example: ❶ 社区里不但有便利店，而且还有超市。
Not only does the community have a convenience store, it has a supermarket, too.

❷ 我不但喜欢吃饺子，而且还喜欢吃面条。
Not only do I like dumplings, I like noodles, too.

❷ 弟弟不但聪明，而且很可爱。
My younger brother is not only smart, but also very adorable.

Many of the Chinese terms for community places have the same component expressing the nature or function of places or facilities. Some of the commonly used are 局, 店, 场 and 馆.

- 局 *(office):* This is usually used to refer to government buildings.
- 店 *(store):* This is usually used to refer to retail shops that sell goods or services.
- 场 *(site):* This is usually used to refer to large places where people gather or the grounds for ballgames.
- 馆 *(shop):* This is usually used to refer to restaurants or sports facilities.

Try This!

1. Use the words below to make sentences containing 不但…而且….

Example: 社区里　警察局　医院

　　　　　⟶ 社区里不但有警察局，而且还有医院。

❶ 社区里　电影院　商场

⟶ _____

❷ 哥哥　踢足球　打篮球

⟶ _____

❸ 电影院　美国电影　中国电影

　　→　_____

❹ 商场里　书店　理发店

　　→　_____

❺ 酸辣汤　酸　辣

　　→　_____

❻ 我　忙　累

　　→　_____

❼ 医院里　花店　书店

　　→　_____

❽ 去菜市场买东西　方便　便宜

　　→　_____

❾ 社区里的超市　大　热闹 rènao
　　　　　　　　　　　　 lively

　　→　_____

❿ 我暑假　补习班　打工

　　→　_____

2. Work with a partner to ask and answer at least five questions about places in your community. Use the question patterns "……有什么?" "有……吗?" or "有没有?"

　　　　　　　Examples: ❶ 你的社区里有什么?

　　　　　　　　　　　　　❷ 社区里有邮局吗?

　　　　　　　　　　　　　❸ 社区里有没有电影院?

3. Fill in the blanks with the appropriate words.

面包店　　邮局　　　书店　　　银行　　　篮球场
电影院　　诊所　　　理发店　　餐馆　　　警察局

❶ 我的头发长极了，得去＿＿＿＿＿＿＿＿。

chángcháng
often
❷ 他喜欢吃面包，常常去＿＿＿＿＿＿＿＿。

shēngbìng
sick
❸ 我生病了，得去＿＿＿＿＿＿＿＿。

jiǎndào　qiánbāo
found　wallet
❹ 他捡到一个钱包，得去＿＿＿＿＿＿＿＿。

❺ 我想看电影，我要去＿＿＿＿＿＿＿＿。

❻ 我想买本书，得去＿＿＿＿＿＿＿＿。

è
hungry
❼ 我饿了，想去＿＿＿＿＿＿＿＿。

cúnqián
make a deposit
❽ 妈妈要存钱，得去＿＿＿＿＿＿＿＿。

jì bāoguǒ
send a parcel
❾ 我要寄包裹，得去＿＿＿＿＿＿＿＿。

❿ 他们想打篮球，要去＿＿＿＿＿＿＿＿。

xībĕi

医院在社区的西北边。

The hospital is in the northwest side of the community.

dōngbèi

电影院在社区的东北边。

The movie theater is in the northeast side of the community.

北
西 东
南

xīnán

超市在社区的西南边。

The supermarket is in the southwest side of the community.

dōngnán

公园在社区的东南边。

The park is in the southeast side of the community.

NEW WORDS 生 词

东北 n.	東北	dōngbèi	northeast	西北 n.	西北	xībĕi	northwest
东南 n.	東南	dōngnán	southeast	西南 n.	西南	xīnán	southwest

When expressing compound directions in Chinese, "east" and "west" are used as the points of reference. The word order in Chinese compound directions is different from that of English. Compare the following:

- 东北 *(lit. eastnorth)* northeast
- 东南 *(lit. eastsouth)* southeast
- 西北 *(lit. westnorth)* northwest
- 西南 *(lit. westsouth)* southwest

Note: 边 is often used after the directional word.

 CULTURAL HIGHLIGHTS

The Chinese compass

The compass is one of the four great inventions of China. Before the invention of the compass, direction was determined mainly by landmarks and celestial bodies. The earliest compasses are believed to have been discovered by the Chinese as early as the 9th century B.C.E. This compass, however, was not used for navigational purposes, but rather for spiritual practices. The needles of these compasses were made out of lodestones, a mineral which consists of naturally magnetized iron ore; when suspended above a board the stone would turn to align with the north-south axis of the earth.

The discovery of the compass as a navigational tool is accredited to the Chinese who are believed to have begun use of this tool sometime between the 9th and 11th centuries. The traditional Chinese compass consisted of a magnetic needle floating in a bowl of water.

There are many references to the compass in Chinese literary texts. The first mention of the compass as a tool was in a book dating back to the Song Dynasty (960-1279); the compass was referred to as a "south-pointing fish." The first literary reference to the use of compasses for maritime navigation dates back to 1117 in the book *Pingzhou Table Talks* (萍洲可谈) by Zhu Yu (朱彧).

With the Chinese compass, the Chinese explorer and fleet admiral Zheng He (郑和) commanded voyages to Southeast Asia, South Asia, the Middle East, Somalia and the Swahili coast, collectively referred to as the "Voyages of Zheng He" from 1405 to 1433.

1. Study the map below and complete each sentence with the correct word.

① 花店在医院的 _____。

② 警察局在公园的 _____。

③ 公园在 _____ 的东北边。

④ 诊所在医院的 _____。

⑤ 电影院在 _____ 的西北边。

⑥ 商场在餐馆的 _____。

⑦ 医院在 _____ 的南边。

⑧ 花店在公园的 _____。

⑨ 电影院在 _____ 的西边。

⑩ 超市在警局的 _____。

2. Using the same map in Question 1, work with a partner to practice asking and answering questions on the relative location of the community places.

Example: 公园在哪儿？ _公园在餐馆的南边。_

qǐngwèn   zěnmè   zǒu
请问，去邮局怎么走？
Can you tell me how to get to the post office?

wǎng   guǎi   zài
往右拐，再往前走。
Turn right, then walk straight.

A   Asking for and giving directions

请问，去电影院怎么走？
Can you tell me how to get to the movie theater?

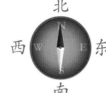

Go North

xiàng   ránhòu
向北走，然后向左拐。
Walk north, then turn left.

NEW WORDS

生词

请问 *v.*	請問	qǐngwèn	Please tell me
往 *prep.*		wǎng	toward, in the direction of
向 *prep.*		xiàng	toward, facing
拐 *v.*		guǎi	turn
再 *conj.*		zài	then, after
然后 *conj.*	然後	ránhòu	thereafter, afterward

LANGUAGE FOCUS

When we ask for directions to get to a place, we usually begin the question with a polite expression 请问. The destination is placed after the verb 去, followed by the question word 怎么走 (how to go).

Examples: ❶ 请问，去银行怎么走？
Can you tell me how to get to the bank?

❷ 请问，去医院怎么走？
Can you tell me how to get to the hospital?

In giving directions, we use a preposition 往 or 向, a directional word and a verb to form a prepositional phrase: 往/向 + directional all word + verb. This phrase indicates the direction of the verb.

✎ 往东走。 Walk east.

✎ 往左拐。 Turn left.

✎ 向南走。 Walk south.

✎ 向右拐。 Turn right.

When there is more than one direction to take, the conjunction 再 or 然后 can be used to link them up.

Examples: ❶ 往前走，再向左拐。
Walk straight, and then turn left.

❷ 往右拐，然后向前走。
Turn right, and then walk straight.

1. Study the community map below. Fill in the empty speech bubbles to explain how one can get to the movie theater and supermarket from the main road. Use the pattern "往/向 + direction word + verb."

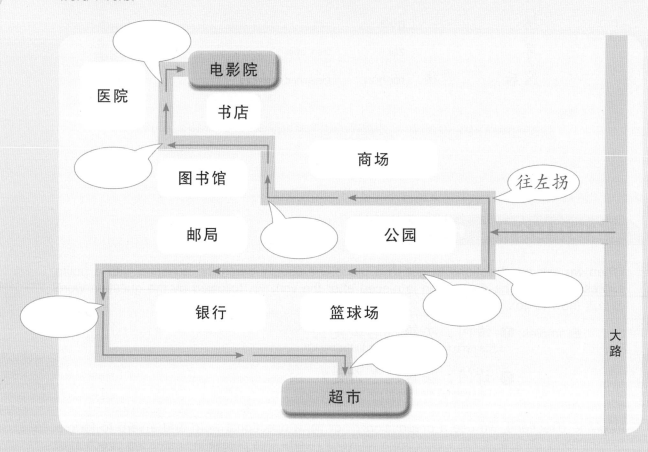

2. Draw a simple map of your community. Work with a partner to practice asking and answering questions on how to get to other community places indicated on the map.

Example: 请问，去公园怎么走？

往前走。

B Giving more specific directions

请问，去便利店怎么走？
Can you tell me how to get to the convenience store?

jiù
前面往右拐就到了。
Turn right in front and you will get there.

生 词

NEW WORDS

就 *adv.*		jiù	as soon as, right after
一直 *adv.*		yìzhí	straight, straight ahead
红绿灯 *n.*	紅綠燈	hónglùdēng	traffic lights

请问，去商场怎么走？
Can you tell me how to get to the mall?

yìzhí
从这里一直往南走是商场。
Keep walking south from here and you will reach the mall.

To give more specific directions, a location word or phrase can be placed before the prepositional phrase to indicate the starting point:

> 前面往左拐。
> Turn left in front.

> 这里向前走。
> Walk straight ahead from here.

> 邮局那里往右拐。
> Turn right at the post office.

The adverb 就 is used to link two actions with the second action taking place soon after the first action. In giving directions, it can be used to indicate that the person will reach the destination once the first action is completed. It is placed between the two verb phrases in the sentence.

> 前面往左拐就到了。
> Turn left in front and you will get there.

> 这里向前走就到了。
> Walk straight ahead from here and you will get there.

> 邮局那里往右拐就是银行。
> Turn right at the post office and you will see the bank.

To express a fixed direction of a motion, place the adverb 一直 before the verb.

> 一直走。
> Walk straight ahead.

> 前面往右拐，然后一直走就到了。
> Turn right in front, then go straight ahead and you will get there.

> 从银行这里一直走，到了红绿灯就是超市。
> Go straight ahead after the bank and you will reach the supermarket at the traffic light.

1. Use 一直 to complete the following sentences based on the map below.

① 从这儿一直往南走是_____。

② 从这儿一直往北走是_____。

③ 从这儿一直往西走是_____。

④ 从商场一直往西走是_____。

⑤ 从商场一直往_____走是电影院。

⑥ 从电影院一直往_____走是公园。

⑦ 从诊所一直往_____走是公园。

⑧ 从图书馆一直往_____走是便利店。

⑨ 从图书馆_____是药房。

⑩ 从药房_____是电影院。

2. Using the same map in Question 1, work with a partner to practice asking and answering questions on how to get to other community places indicated in the map. You can change the starting point. Use 就 in your answers.

 Example: 请问，从诊所去商场怎么走？ 往东走就到了。

图书馆　3 miles

地铁站

这儿离地铁站有多远？
How far is the subway station from here?

1 这儿离地铁站有3英里。
The subway station is three miles from here.

100 yards

你家离便利店有多远？
How far is the convenience store from your home?

2 我家离便利店有100码。
The convenience store is 100 yards away from my home.

NEW WORDS 生词

地铁站 n.	地鐵站	dìtiězhàn	subway station
英里 m.w.		yīnglǐ	mile
码 m.w.	碼	mǎ	yard
英尺 m.w.		yīngchǐ	foot
公里 m.w.		gōnglǐ	kilometer
米 m.w.		mǐ	meter

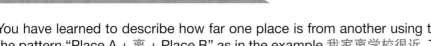
You have learned to describe how far one place is from another using the preposition 离. Use the pattern "Place A + 离 + Place B" as in the example 我家离学校很近. To ask questions about the actual distance between two places, place the verb 有 after this pattern, followed by the question word 多远 (how far):

Examples: ❶ 邮局离银行有多远？
How far is the bank from the post office?

❷ 书店离花店有多远？
How far is the florist from the book store?

To reply, simply replace the question word with the actual distance:

Examples: ❶ 邮局离银行有2英里。
The bank is two miles away from the post office.

❷ 书店离花店有200英尺。
The florist is 200 feet away from the book store.

里 is a traditional Chinese unit of distance. It has a standardized length of 500 meters or half a kilometer, and is about a third of a mile. 里 appears in many Chinese sayings, locations, and proverbs as an indicator of great distances. For example, the Great Wall of China is known as 万里长城 (Wànlǐ Chángchéng), which literally means "Ten-Thousand-Li Wall." It should be noted that the number "ten thousand" is used figuratively in Chinese to mean any "immeasurable" distance of great value.

1. Study the map below. Work with a partner to ask and answer questions about the distance between places in the community.

   Example: 加油站离商场有多远？ 加油站离商场有600英尺。

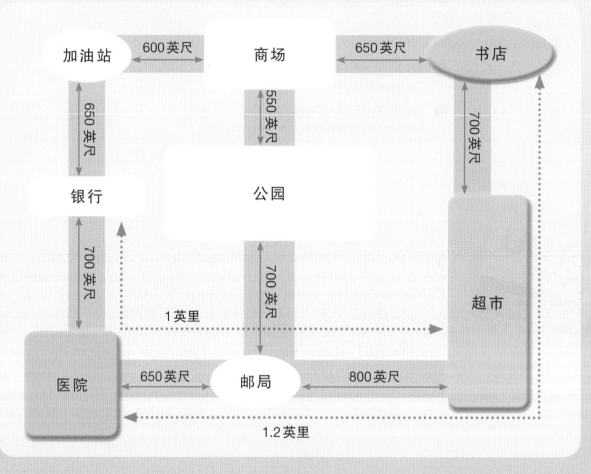

2. Do some research to answer the following questions. Then name the pair of cities that is furthest apart.

   ❶ 北京离上海有多远？

   ❷ 香港离西安有多远？

   ❸ 纽约离北京有多远？

   ❹ 华盛顿离伦敦有多远？

   ❺ 悉尼离巴黎有多远？

gòu wù
我们去商场购物。
We go to the mall to shop.

A Going to a place to do something

jì xìn
她去邮局寄信。
She goes to the post office to mail a letter.

生 词 WORDS AND PHRASES

gòu wù
购物 *phr.*
購物
shopping

jì xìn
寄信 *phr.*
mail a letter

mǎi yào
买药 *phr.*
買藥
buy medicine

kàn yīshēng

看医生 *phr.*

看醫生

see a doctor

jiāyóu

加油 *phr.*

buy fuel
(for car)

jiǎn tóufa

剪头发 *phr.*

剪頭髮

get a haircut

mǎi cài

买菜 *phr.*

買菜

buy groceries

sànbù

散步 *phr.*

take a stroll

xǐ yīfu

洗衣服 *phr.*

do laundry

kāi hù

开户 *phr.*

開戶

open a bank account

cúnkuǎn

存款 *phr.*

make a deposit
(at the bank)

qǔ qián

取钱 *phr.*

withdraw money
(from the bank)

LANGUAGE FOCUS

To say that you are going to a place to do something, put the phrase indicating the purpose after the place:

For example: **1** 妈妈去超市买菜。
Mom goes to the supermarket to buy groceries.

2 爸爸去银行开户。
Dad goes to the bank to open an account.

Try This!

1. Match the places on the left with the appropriate actions on the right. Then make a sentence for each match.

❶ 篮球场 •		• 买药	❶	他去篮球场打篮球。
❷ 加油站 •		• 剪头发	❷	_____
❸ 银行 •		• 买菜	❸	_____
❹ 邮局 •		• 散步	❹	_____
❺ 公园 •		• 看医生	❺	_____
❻ 菜市场 •		• 加油	❻	_____
❼ 药房 •		• 看电影	❼	_____
❽ 电影院 •		• 取钱	❽	_____
❾ 诊所 •		• 打篮球	❾	_____
❿ 理发店 •		• 寄信	❿	_____

2. Look at Mark's schedule for Saturday. Work with a partner to ask and answer question on his activities during different times of the day. Be sure to include where he goes and what you think he does at that time of day.

Example: 马克上午十点做什么？ 马克上午十点去篮球场打篮球。

十点	十二点	两点	四点	七点	九点
篮球场	餐馆	书店	商场	餐馆	电影院

xiān　　　　　zài
先去药房，再去面包店。
Go to the pharmacy first, then to the bakery.

我们先去书店买书，

再去餐馆吃饭，然后去电影院看电影。
Let's go to the book store to buy books first, then to the restaurant for dinner, followed by the movie theater for a movie.

172

NEW WORD

先⋯再⋯ *conj.* | xiān...zài... | first...then...

The paired conjunctions 先 (first) and 再 (then) are adverbs placed before verbs to indicate the sequence of actions. 然后 can replace 再 to indicate a second action, or can follow the 先⋯再⋯ construction to introduce a third action.

Examples: ❶ 我们先去邮局，再去银行。
Let's go to the post office first, then to the bank.

❷ 我们先去邮局，再去银行，然后回家。
Let's go to the post office first, followed by the bank, and then go home.

❸ 我们先去邮局寄信，再去银行取钱，然后回家洗衣服。
Let's go to the post office to mail letters first, followed by the bank to withdraw some money, and then go home to do laundry.

CULTURAL HIGHLIGHTS

Morning activities in Chinese neighborhoods

In residential districts in China, it is common to see people practicing *Taiji* in the morning. The parks are often filled with seniors who come early in the morning to practice *Taiji*. Besides exercising, this morning activity is also a good way to socialize and connect with each other.

In Guangzhou and Hong Kong, people often go to tea houses in the morning for *yum cha* (, yǐnchá), a Chinese style morning tea, which involves drinking Chinese tea and eating dim sum dishes. *Yum cha* in Cantonese literally means "drink tea." In traditional tea houses, freshly made dim sum dishes will be put

on a cart and pushed around the tables by a waiter or waitress. Any customer can just select a dish from the wide range of offerings on the cart.

Try This!

1. Based on the order of pictures, make sentences using 先⋯再⋯.

我先去邮局寄信，再去银行取钱。

2. Work with a partner to make sentences using 先⋯再⋯然后⋯. Use the following activities in your sentences.

Example:

我先看书，再做功课，
然后上网。

看书　做功课　洗澡　打球　买衣服
逛街　看电影　上网　发短信　打电动

174

Reading *in Context*

STEP 1 FINDING PLACES IN THE COMMUNITY

Describing a community

　　这是我住的社区。社区里不但有诊所，而且有医院，所以人们看病很方便。这个社区不大，购物和交通都很方便。这里不但有小超市，而且也有大商场和购物中心。社区里还有地铁和火车站。

　　我家附近有邮局、银行、电影院和篮球场。加油站在东边，离邮局不远。社区里还有一个健身房。我跟爸爸妈妈常常在那里锻炼身体。

kànbìng		fùjìn	jiànshēnfáng
看病	购物中心	附近	健身房
see the doctor	shopping mall	nearby	gym

chángcháng	duànliàn		
常常	锻炼		
often	train		

STEP 3 LIVING IN THE COMMUNITY

Moving to a new community

　　最近我搬家了。我很喜欢我的新社区。这里有商场、超市、医院、电影院，还有运动场、银行和邮局。生活很方便。

　　我家住的地方很安静，周围环境很好。附近有一大片绿地，还有很多树和花。

　　我家离商场和超市有5公里远。因为我家离超市比较远，所以我们常常开车去超市买东西。我家附近有个书店，每天放学后，我喜欢先去书店看书、买书，再回家做作业。

STEP 2 GETTING AROUND THE COMMUNITY

Asking for and giving directions

❶ A：劳驾，请问，去加油站怎么走？

　　B：一直往前走，到第二个路口往右拐，过了体育馆，马路对面就是加油站。

　　A：谢谢！

　　B：不谢。

❷ A：请问，去邮局怎么走？

　　B：一直往前走，到第三个路口往左拐，邮局在超市西边。

　　A：谢谢！

　　B：不客气。

❸ A：劳驾，请问，电影院在哪儿？

　　B：您一直往前走，过了第二个十字路口，电影院在马路左边。

　　A：谢谢！

　　B：不客气。

láojià			
劳驾	路口	马路	对面
excuse me	intersection	road	opposite

bú kèqi			
不客气	十字		
don't mention it	cross		

　　我家离网球场很近，我爸爸很喜欢去网球场打网球，他网球打得很好。现在我也很喜欢打网球。

shēnghuó	zhōuwéi	huánjìng	piàn
生活	周围	环境	片
life	surrounding	environment	piece

Step Up!

1. Read the passage and determine whether the following statements are true (T) or false (F).

我家在社区的中心。我家的周围(zhōuwéi)不但有超市和商场，而且还有体育馆和电影院。超市和商场在我家的西边，超市离我家有两百米，商场离我家有一千多米，买东西很方便。体育馆在我家的东边，离我家有两公里，周末我常(cháng)和爸爸妈妈一起去那儿锻炼(duànliàn)身体。电影院离我家比较远，有五公里。我们不常去看电影，我们常在家看影碟(yǐngdié)。我家离学校比较近，学校在马路对面，大概(dàgài)有一千米，我每天走路去学校。

我家离地铁站和公交车站都很近，离地铁站三百米，离公交车站二百米。

❶ 我家在社区的中心。 （　　）

❷ 超市和商场离我家不太(tài)远。 （　　）

❸ 体育馆在我家的东北边。 （　　）

❹ 我们常常去体育馆锻炼。 （　　）

❺ 电影院离我家很近。 （　　）

❻ 我们常常去电影院看电影。 （　　）

❼ 我家离学校比较远。 （　　）

❽ 我家在学校的对面。 （　　）

❾ 我家附近(fùjìn)的交通很方便。 （　　）

2. **Pair work** Practice asking for and giving directions with a classmate based on the map below. Each will take turns to play role A (asking for directions) and role B (giving directions). Take a die and toss it twice - the first time is to determine A's present location and the second time is to determine the destination.

Student A: 我在书店，请问去超市怎么走？
Student B: 向东走，到了路口往左拐，一直走就到了。

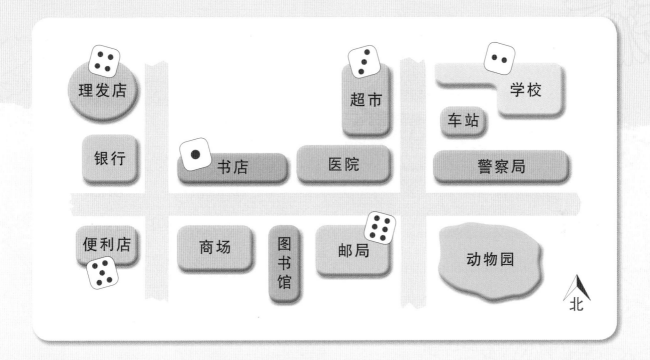

3. Imagine that your mom is sick and needs you to help with the tasks listed below on Saturday. Besides these tasks, you also have your own programs. Come up with at least three activities. Organize your day so that you can complete the tasks your mom asks you to do as well as those you have planned. Use 先…，再…，然后…. Share it with your classmates to see who has the most organized schedule on Saturday.

Task list from mom:
❶ Do laundry
❷ Buy groceries at the supermarket
❸ Buy medicine at the pharmacy

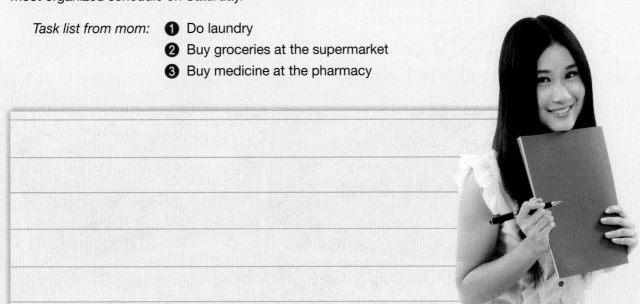

Fun Time!

China has a vast land area with many cities and places of interest that are miles apart. Research online and match each pair of cities or places of interest with the correct distance between them. Then, make sentences using 离 to describe the distance between each pair.

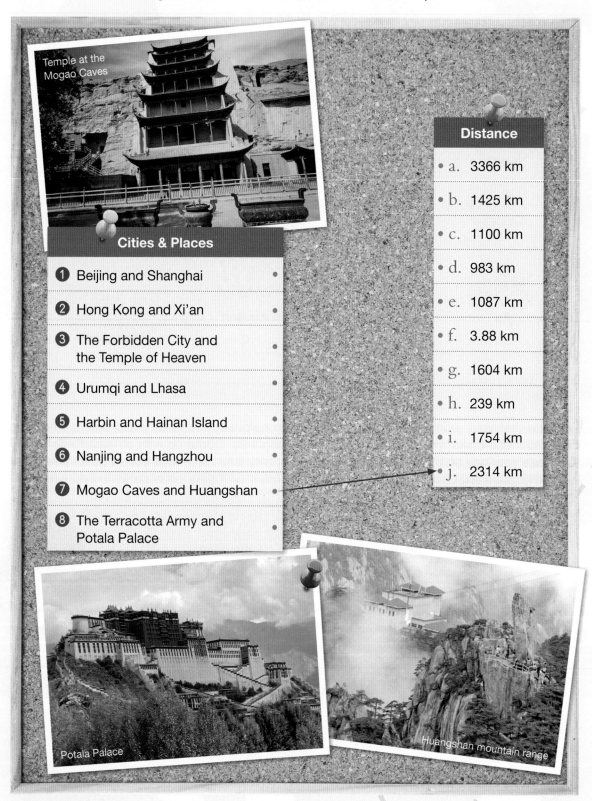

Temple at the Mogao Caves

Cities & Places

1. Beijing and Shanghai
2. Hong Kong and Xi'an
3. The Forbidden City and the Temple of Heaven
4. Urumqi and Lhasa
5. Harbin and Hainan Island
6. Nanjing and Hangzhou
7. Mogao Caves and Huangshan
8. The Terracotta Army and Potala Palace

Distance

- a. 3366 km
- b. 1425 km
- c. 1100 km
- d. 983 km
- e. 1087 km
- f. 3.88 km
- g. 1604 km
- h. 239 km
- i. 1754 km
- j. 2314 km

Potala Palace

Huangshan mountain range

I have learned...

Core Vocabulary

Verbs

请问	請問	qǐngwèn	Please tell me	拐		guǎi	turn

Nouns
Community places

社区	社區	shèqū	community	停车场	停車場	tíngchēchǎng	car park
邮局	郵局	yóujú	post office	篮球场	籃球場	lánqiúchǎng	basketball court
警察局		jǐngchájú	police station	足球场	足球場	zúqiúchǎng	soccer field
便利店		biànlìdiàn	convenience store	网球场	網球場	wǎngqiúchǎng	tennis court
面包店	麵包店	miànbāodiàn	bakery	餐馆	餐館	cānguǎn	restaurant
理发店	理發店	lǐfàdiàn	hairdresser's salon	银行	銀行	yínháng	bank
洗衣店		xǐyīdiàn	laundromat	电影院	電影院	diànyǐngyuàn	movie theater
花店		huādiàn	florist	公园	公園	gōngyuán	park
书店	書店	shūdiàn	book store	诊所	診所	zhěnsuǒ	clinic
超市		chāoshì	supermarket	药房	藥房	yàofáng	pharmacy
菜市场	菜市場	càishìchǎng	(vegetable) market	医院	醫院	yīyuàn	hospital
商场	商場	shāngchǎng	mall	加油站		jiāyóuzhàn	gas station

Compound directions

东北	東北	dōngběi	northeast	西北		xīběi	northwest
东南	東南	dōngnán	southeast	西南		xīnán	southwest

Others

红绿灯	紅綠燈	hónglǜdēng	traffic lights	地铁站	地鐵站	dìtiězhàn	subway station

Adverbs

就	jiù	as soon as, right after	一直		yìzhí	straight, straight ahead

Prepositions

往	wǎng	toward, in the direction of	向		xiàng	toward, facing

Conjunctions

不但…而且…	búdàn…érqiě	not only…but also	然后	然後	ránhòu	thereafter, afterward
再	zài	then, after	先…再…		xiān…zài…	first…then…

I have learned...

Measure words

英里		yīnglǐ	mile	公里		gōnglǐ	kilometer
码	碼	mǎ	yard	米		mǐ	meter
英尺		yīngchǐ	foot				

Phrases

购物	購物	gòu wù	shopping
寄信		jì xìn	mail a letter
买药	買藥	mǎi yào	buy medicine
看医生	看醫生	kàn yīshēng	see a doctor
加油		jiāyóu	buy fuel *(for car)*
剪头发	剪頭髮	jiǎn tóufa	get a haircut
买菜	買菜	mǎi cài	buy groceries
散步		sànbù	take a stroll
洗衣服		xǐ yīfu	do laundry
开户	開户	kāi hù	open a bank account
存款		cúnkuǎn	make a deposit *(at the bank)*
取钱		qǔ qián	withdraw money *(from the bank)*

❧ SENTENCE PATTERNS ☙

社区里<u>不但</u>有银行，<u>而且</u>还有邮局。

电影院在社区<u>的东北边</u>。

<u>请问</u>，去邮局<u>怎么走</u>？<u>往右拐</u>，<u>再往</u>前走。

<u>请问</u>，去便利店怎么走？前面往右拐<u>就</u>到了。

这儿<u>离</u>地铁站有多远？这儿<u>离</u>地铁站有3英里。

我去商场购<u>物</u>。

<u>先</u>去药房，<u>再</u>去面包店。

I can do!

Interpretive **Communication**

❑ I can understand when someone describes places in the community and their locations.

❑ I can understand when someone gives me directions on how to get to a place.

❑ I can read and understand descriptions of a community.

Interpersonal **Communication**

❑ I can talk about places in my community.

❑ I can ask and give directions.

❑ I can exchange information on daily activities.

Presentational **Communication**

❑ I can describe the community that I live in.

❑ I can state things that I do in a sequential order.

❑ I can write a list of tasks that I need to do.

❑ I can state the order in which I complete my tasks.

Cultural Knowledge

❑ I can describe the appearance of a traditional Chinese compass.

❑ I can tell the length of the traditional Chinese unit of distance 里.

❑ I can list some popular morning activities in Chinese neighborhoods.

LESSON 6

Meeting new people

认识新朋友

COMMUNICATIVE GOALS

- Talking about one's profession and workplace
- Stating one's aspirations
- Describing a possible profession
- Describing one's strengths
- Commenting on a person

Cultural Knowledge

- The four main occupations in ancient China
- A Chinese saying on various professions
- Famous Chinese people in different professions

Get ready...

In the past, many young boys dreamed of being fire fighters and many young girls dreamed of being elementary school teachers. Do you still remember your first ideal profession? Have your professional aspirations changed over time? What do you want to be when you grow up? Talk with a classmate and discuss how your aspirations have changed.

Below is an excerpt of a song lyric*. Some professions are mentioned in the song. Identify them and see if you can give the Chinese names for some of these professions. Compare with your classmates to see who has the most number of correct Chinese names for these professions.

Doctor, actor, lawyer or a singer
Why not president, be a dreamer
You can be just the one you want to be
Police man, fire fighter or a post man
Why not something like your old man
You can be just the one you want to be
Doctor, actor, lawyer or a singer
Why not president, be a dreamer
You can be just the one you want to be

I know that we all got one thing
That we all share together
We got that one nice dream
We live for
You never know what life could bring
Because nothing lasts for ever
Just hold on to the team you play for

I know you could reach the top
Make sure that you won't stop
Be the one that you want to be
Now sing this with me

* *The song title is "B What U Wanna Be" by Darin Zanyar.*
The excerpt above is slightly modified for learning purposes.
You may go online to read or listen to the full original song.

STEPS *at a glance!*

EXPLORING PROFESSIONS

A. Talking about one's profession
他是做什么的？他是工程师。

B. Describing one's workplace
他在学校里当教师。

FINDING ONE'S ASPIRATIONS

A. Stating one's aspirations
你以后打算在什么行业工作？
我可能在金融业工作。

B. Describing a possible profession
如果我是发型师，我就会设计新发型。

DISCOVERING FAMOUS PEOPLE

A. Talking about famous people
郎朗在音乐方面很有特长。

B. Expressing your views on a person
我觉得郑和不仅有学问，还非常能干。

183

gōngzuò
他是做什么工作的？
What is his job?

gōngchéngshī
他是工程师。
He's an engineer.

A Talking about one's profession

她是做什么的？
What is her job?

hùshi
她是护士。
She's a nurse.

NEW WORDS

工作 *n.* | gōngzuò | work

Common Professions

~师	工程师 *n.*	工程師	gōngchéngshī	engineer
	建筑师 *n.*	建築師	jiànzhùshī	architect
	会计师 *n.*	會計師	kuàijìshī	accountant
	发型师 *n.*	髮型師	fàxíngshī	hairdresser, hairstylist
	服装设计师 *n.*	服裝設計師	fúzhuāng shèjìshī	fashion designer

~员	公务员 n.	公務員	gōngwùyuán	civil servant
	售货员 n.	售貨員	shòuhuòyuán	salesperson
	服务员 n.	服務員	fúwùyuán	waiter, waitress
	收银员 n.	收銀員	shōuyínyuán	cashier
	消防员 n.	消防員	xiāofángyuán	firefighter
	邮递员 n.	郵遞員	yóudìyuán	mail carrier
	银行出纳员 n.	銀行出納員	yínháng chūnàyuán	bank teller

~家	企业家 n.	企業家	qǐyèjiā	entrepreneur
	银行家 n.	銀行家	yínhángjiā	banker
	音乐家 n.	音樂家	yīnyuèjiā	musician
	艺术家 n.	藝術家	yìshùjiā	artist

Others				
教授 n.		jiàoshòu	professor
护士 n.	護士	hùshi	nurse
导游 n.	導游	dǎoyóu	tour guide
军人 n.	軍人	jūnrén	businessman
商人 n.		shāngrén	artist
农民 n.	農民	nóngmín	farmer
工人 n.		gōngrén	worker

Words you have learned

jiàoshī	yùndòngyuán	wúdǎojiā
教师 n. teacher	运动员 n. athlete	舞蹈家 n. dancer
lùshī	huàjiā	kēxuéjiā
律师 n. lawyer	画家 n. artist	科学家 n. scientist
chúshī	zuòjiā	yáyī
厨师 n. chef	作家 n. writer	牙医 n. dentist
yǎnyuán	gāngqínjiā	jìzhě
演员 n. actor	钢琴家 n. pianist	记者 n. journalist

To ask about someone's profession, use the question "你是做什么工作的？" or "你是做什么的？" which means "What do you do [for a job]?" The subject can be replaced by any person whose profession you wish to find out. Look at the following sentences and see if you can figure out what they mean.

> 你是做什么工作的？

> 你爸爸是做什么工作的？

> 他妈妈是做什么的？

To answer the question, follow the pattern: person + 是 + profession.

> 我是服务员。

> 我爸爸是牙医。

> 他妈妈是会计师。

 CULTURAL HIGHLIGHTS

The Four Main Occupations in Ancient China

The four occupations 士农工商 (shì nóng gōng shāng) were formed according to a hierarchical social class structure in ancient China. In descending order, these were 士 (gentry scholars), 农 (peasant farmers), 工 (artisans and craftsmen), and 商 (merchants and traders).

Those who studied in order to occupy positions of rank were called 士 (shì). They were highly regarded because of their scholarship, abilities in administration, and sound ethics and morality. Many passed civil service examinations to hold high-ranking positions in the imperial court and assisted the emperor in governing the country. Those who cultivated the soil and grew grains were called 农 (nóng). Agriculture was an integral part of ancient China. The food that farmers produced sustained the whole of society, while the land tax exacted on farmers' lots and landholders' property produced much of the state revenue. Therefore, the farmer was a valuable member of society.

Those who manifested a skill and made utensils were called 工 (gōng). Like farmers, they produced essential goods needed by society. Although they could not provide the state with much of its revenues since they often had no land of their own to be taxed, artisans and craftsmen were still given a higher place than merchants. Those who transported valuable articles and sold commodities were called 商 (shāng). They were viewed by the scholarly elite as essential members of society, yet were placed on the lowest of the four grades in the official Chinese social hierarchy, due to the view that they did not produce anything, only profited from others' creations.

This social class structure is not applicable to modern China. However, the view that 士 is highly esteemed continues to remain rooted in the minds of parents and students today. A lot of time and resources are spent on education, which is widely believed to be the gateway to a good job and a better life in the future.

1. Work with a partner to practice asking and answering questions about the professions of the people in the pictures below.

芳芳的爸爸是做什么工作的？他是商人。

芳芳的爸爸

你的姐姐

马克的叔叔

张安的哥哥

丁强的姐姐

安琪的爸爸

李叔叔

安琪的姐姐

你的爸爸

马克的哥哥

2. Guess the profession of the following people according to the descriptions given.

❶ 芳芳的姐姐：我钢琴弹得很好。

❷ 张叔叔：我有很多学生。
student

❸ 安琪的妈妈：我喜欢跳舞。

❹ 马克的哥哥：我喜欢做菜。
cook

❺ 张安的哥哥：我喜欢剪头发。

❻ 李阿姨：我和医生一起工作
yìqǐ
with

❼ 丁强的爸爸：我天天送信。

❽ 芳芳的哥哥：我设计大楼。
design

❾ 王叔叔：我每天要见顾客。
gùkè
client

❿ 丁强的姐姐：我在商店工作。
shāngdiàn
retail shop

3. Conduct a survey to find out the professions of your classmates' family members. Limit it to one family member per classmate. Record your findings in a chart similar to the one below. Then plot a graph to see which professions are the most common among your classmates' families.

Student A: 你爸爸是做什么的？
Student B: 我爸爸是……。

Name	Profession
马克的爸爸	工程师

她在医院里工作。
She works in the hospital.

他在学校里当教师。
He works in school as a teacher.

生 词

NEW WORDS

工作 v. | gōngzuò | work

Common Workplaces

商店 n.		shāngdiàn	retail outlet, shop		工厂 n.	工廠	gōngchǎng	factory
餐馆 n.	餐館	cānguǎn	restaurant		农田 n.	農田	nóngtián	farmland
发廊 n.	髮廊	fàláng	hair salon		办公室 n.	辦公室	bàngōngshì	office
报社 n.	報社	bàoshè	news agency		化验室 n.	化驗室	huàyànshì	laboratory
军营 n.	軍營	jūnyíng	military camp		消防局 n.	消防局	xiāofángjú	fire station

Words you have learned

dāng	yínháng	yīyuàn
当 v. as	银行 n. bank	医院 n. hospital
xuéxiào	yóujú	zhěnsuǒ
学校 n. school	邮局 n. post office	诊所 n. clinic

LANGUAGE FOCUS

To describe where someone is working, use the pattern "在 + workplace + 里" and place it before the verb. Read the following sentences to determine their meaning.

For example ❶ 她在商店里工作。

❷ 他在餐馆里工作。

You can specify what the person is working as at the workplace using 当 after the pattern to introduce his or her profession. It can be translated as the word "as."

For example ❶ 哥哥在消防局里当消防员。
My older brother works at the fire station as a firefighter.

❷ 姐姐在诊所里当护士。
My older sister works at the clinic as a nurse.

Try This!

1. Look at each picture and make a sentence describing where the person is working.

马克的爸爸在银行里工作。/ 马克的爸爸在银行里当出纳员。

马克的爸爸

安琪的姐姐

张安的姐姐

丁强的哥哥

芳芳的爸爸

马克的哥哥

张叔叔

王阿姨

张阿姨

安琪的爸爸

2. Read the passage and determine whether the following statements are true (T) or false (F).

小明家有四口人，爸爸、妈妈、姐姐和他。他爸爸喜欢写作，在报社里当记者。他妈妈弹钢琴弹得很好，是个钢琴家。他姐姐对美术感兴趣，还喜欢剪头发，她在发廊里当发型师。小明天天打篮球，他将来想当篮球运动员。

❶ 小明没有哥哥。   （　　）

❷ 小明的爸爸是工程师。   （　　）

❸ 小明的爸爸在报社里工作。   （　　）

❹ 小明的妈妈是画家。   （　　）

❺ 小明的姐姐在发廊当发型师。 （　　）

❻ 小明是篮球运动员。   （　　）

A Stating one's aspirations

dǎsuàn hángyè
你将来打算在什么行业工作？
In which industry do you plan to work in the future?

jiànzhùyè
① 我打算在建筑业工作。
I plan to work in the building industry.

kěnéng shíshàngjiè
② 我可能在时尚界工作。
I may work in the fashion industry.

huì xīnwénjiè
③ 我可能会在新闻界工作。
I probably will be working in the news industry.

NEW WORDS

| 打算 v. | | dǎsuàn | plan to, intend to | 会 aux. v. | 會 | huì | will |
| 行业 n. | 行業 | hángyè | industry, trade, profession | 可能 aux. v. | | kěnéng | may, might, probably |

Common Industries and Fields of Work

~业	农业 n.	農業	nóngyè	agriculture industry
	建筑业 n.	建築業	jiànzhùyè	building industry
	医药业 n.	醫藥業	yīyàoyè	health industry
	金融业 n.	金融業	jīnróngyè	finance industry
	信息业 n.	信息業	xìnxīyè	IT industry
	服务业 n.	服務業	fúwùyè	service industry
	食品业 n.	食品業	shípǐnyè	food industry
	旅游业 n.	旅游業	lǚyóuyè	tourism industry

~界	法律界 n.		fǎlǜjiè	legal profession
	教育界 n.		jiàoyùjiè	education profession
	文学界 n.	文學界	wénxuéjiè	literary profession
	体育界 n.	體育界	tǐyùjiè	sports profession
	艺术界 n.	藝術界	yìshùjiè	arts profession
	音乐界 n.	音樂界	yīnyuèjiè	music profession
	娱乐界 n.	娛樂界	yúlèjiè	entertainment profession
	时尚界 n.	時尚界	shíshàngjiè	fashion industry
	新闻界 n.	新聞界	xīnwénjiè	news industry

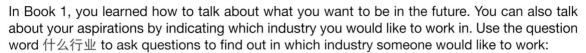
In Book 1, you learned how to talk about what you want to be in the future. You can also talk about your aspirations by indicating which industry you would like to work in. Use the question word 什么行业 to ask questions to find out in which industry someone would like to work:

> 你将来打算在**什么行业**工作?

In reply, keep the same word order but replace the question word with the industry term:

> 我打算在教育界工作。

> 我打算在食品业工作。

As you are talking about something that will take place in the future, the modal verbs 可能 and 会 could be used to indicate different degrees of certainty. They can be used separately, or together with 可能 before 会. Read the following sentences.

For example

❶ 我可能在娱乐界工作。
I might be working in the entertainment profession.

❷ 我会在金融业工作。
I will be working in the finance industry.

❸ 他可能会在信息业工作。
He probably will be working in the IT industry.

CULTURAL HIGHLIGHTS

A Chinese Saying on Various Professions

An old Chinese saying goes like this: 三百六十行，行行出状元 (sānbǎi liùshí háng, háng háng chū zhuàngyuán, There are masters in all 360 trades). It means that whatever trade you are engaged in, you could make great achievements if you put in effort. 行 here refers to "trade or business."

In ancient times, the number of trades was less than 360. In the Tang Dynasty, there were mainly 36 trades in social life. For example, selling meat was 肉肆行 (ròusì hǎng, the trade of meat), selling fish was 鲜鱼行 (xiānyú háng, the trade of fresh fish), making clothes was 成衣行 (chéngyī háng, the trade of ready-made garments), and playing acrobatics was 杂耍行 (záshuǎ háng, the trade of acrobatics). As society progressed, division of trades and occupations became more precise and specific and new trades emerged. As time went by, 36 trades could no longer include all the occupations at the time. In the Song Dynasty, 36 trades were replaced by 72 trades. In the Yuan Dynasty, the 72 trades could

not adequately describe all the trades in China, and the number increased to 120. In the Ming Dynasty, the number of trades rose up to 360.

Since then, the number of trades did not increase. In fact, no matter what the number is, no one really knows to which trades these numbers actually refer, and no one can tell how many trades actually exist today. Generally speaking, the number is just an approximation used to describe a fairly large quantity, and no one has ever clearly accounted for them one by one.

1. **Survey** Ask at least five of your classmates in which industry they intend to work in the future. Follow the speech pattern and record your findings. Next, share your findings with the class.

> Student A: 你将来打算在什么行业工作?
> Student B: 我打算/可能/可能会……。

姓名	在什么行业工作?

2. Read the dialog and answer the following questions in Chinese.

张安：丁强，你网球打得很好，将来想当网球运动员吗?

丁强：我可能会当网球运动员，但我也喜欢写作，可能会在新闻界工作。

张安：你是说，在报社里当记者吗?

丁强：是，我觉得当记者很有意思。你呢? 你将来打算在什么行业工作?

张安：我会在建筑业工作，我想当建筑师。

丁强：当建筑师要设计大楼，你一定很喜欢设计。

张安：是，我喜欢画画。

❶ 丁强将来想当什么?　　❸ 张安打算在什么行业工作?

❷ 丁强喜欢做什么?　　❹ 张安喜欢做什么?

B Describing a possible profession

rúguǒ

如果我是发型师，

　我就会设计新发型。

If I'm a hairstylist, I will design new hairstyles.

如果我是音乐家，

　我就会开很多音乐会。

If I'm a musician, I will hold a lot of musical concerts.

如果我是护士，

hǎohāo　zhàogù　bìngrén

我就会好好照顾病人。

If I'm a nurse, I will take care of my patients properly.

生　词

NEW WORDS

如果···就··· conj.	rúguǒ...jiù...	if...then...
努力 adv.	nǔlì	do one's best
好好 adv.	hǎohāo	properly, carefully

Profession-related words and phrases

做菜 _phr._		zuòcài	cook
设计大楼 _phr._	設計大樓	shèjì dàlóu	design buildings
设计新发型 _phr._	設計新髮型	shèjì xīn fàxíng	design new hairstyles
演戏 _phr._	演戲	yǎnxì	act
参加运动比赛 _phr._	參加運動比賽	cānjiā yùndòng bǐsài	take part in sports competitions
救火 _phr._		jiùhuǒ	put out a fire
开画展 _phr._	開書展	kāi huàzhǎn	hold an art exhibition
作曲 _phr._	作曲	zuò qǔ	compose music
开音乐会 _phr._	開音樂會	kāi yīnyuèhuì	hold musical concerts
表演 _phr._		biǎoyǎn	perform
医治病人 _phr._	醫治病人	yīzhì bìngrén	treat patients
照顾病人 _phr._	照顧病人	zhàogù bìngrén	take care of patients
报道新闻 _phr._	報道新聞	bàodào xīnwén	report news
保卫国家 _phr._	保衛國家	bǎowèi guójiā	defend the country

Extended

教导学生 _phr._	教導學生	jiàodǎo xuésheng	teach students
伸张正义 _phr._	伸張正義	shēnzhāng zhèngyì	uphold justice
维持治安 _phr._	維持治安	wéichí zhì'ān	maintain peace and order
管理财务 _phr._	管理財務	guǎnlǐ cáiwù	manage finances
做研究 _phr._		zuò yánjiū	do research

LANGUAGE FOCUS

The conjunction 如果 expresses supposition. It is placed before or after the subject in the first clause to introduce a situation or condition that might happen. The adverb 就 is used in the second clause to indicate the result produced from the situation or condition mentioned in the first clause. An adverb can be added before the verb to intensify the degree of the action.

Examples: ❶ 如果我是警察，我就会好好维持治安。
If I'm a policeman, I will do my best to maintain peace and order.

❷ 如果我是记者，我就会努力报道新闻。
If I'm a journalist, I will do my best to report news.

1. Imagine you are working in the professions depicted in the pictures. Use 如果…就… to make sentences describing what you would do if you were working in those professions.

2. Complete the following sentences.

❶ 如果我是音乐家，_____。

❷ 如果我是会计师，_____。

❸ 如果我是医生，_____。

❹ 如果明天下雨，_____。

❺ 如果你星期五没有课，_____。

❻ 如果外面很冷，_____。

❼ 如果我是演员，_____。

❽ 如果地铁站离这儿很近，_____。

A Talking about famous people

LángLǎng   fāngmiàn   tècháng

郎朗在音乐方面很有特长。

Lang Lang is skilled in music.

NEW WORDS

方面 n.		fāngmiàn	area, field
特长 n.	特長	tècháng	specialty, skill
成就 n.		chéngjiù	achievement

Guān Yǐngshān   chéngjiù

关颖珊在体育方面很有成就。

Michelle Kwan has made great achievements in sports.

LANGUAGE FOCUS

When talking about famous people, you can comment on their strengths or achievements in a particular area or field. The pattern "在 + name of area/field + 方面" is placed after the subject to identify the area or field, and is followed by an adjectival phrase to describe how well the subject performs in that area or field.

Examples: ❶ Stephen Hawking 在物理方面很有成就。
Stephen Hawking has accomplished a great deal in physics.

❷ Bill Gates 在电脑方面很有特长。
Bill Gates is very good at computers.

1. Research online to find out the professions of these famous Chinese people. Then, make sentences to describe how good they are in their respective fields.

Lǐ Liánjié
1 Jet Li (李连杰)

Wáng Wēiwēi
5 Vera Wang (王薇薇)

Chéng Lóng
9 Jackie Chan (成龙)

Bèi Yùmíng
2 I. M. Pei (贝聿铭)

Mò Yán
6 Mo Yan (莫言)

Yáo Míng
10 Yao Ming (姚明)

Lín Shūháo
3 Jeremy Lin (林书豪)

Zhōu Yǎngjié
7 Jimmy Choo (周仰杰)

Mǎ Yǒuyǒu
11 Yo-Yo Ma (马友友)

Wú Jìgāng
4 Jason Wu (吴季刚)

Zhào Xiǎolán
8 Elaine Chao (赵小兰)

Luò Jiāhuī
12 Gary Locke (骆家辉)

我觉得郑和不仅有学问，
还非常能干。

I feel that not only is Zheng He very knowledgeable,
he is very capable, too.

NEW WORDS

不仅…还… conj.	不僅…還…	bùjǐn…hái	not only…but also
非常 adv.		fēicháng	very, extremely

Positive Personality Traits

伟大 adj.	偉大	wěidà	great
正直 adj.		zhèngzhí	just, righteous
认真 adj.	認真	rènzhēn	serious
负责 adj.	負責	fùzé	responsible
勤劳 adj.	勤勞	qínláo	hardworking
风趣 adj.	風趣	fēngqù	humorous
友善 adj.		yǒushàn	friendly
能干 adj.	能幹	nénggàn	capable
勇敢 adj.		yǒnggǎn	brave, courageous
孝顺 adj.	孝順	xiàoshùn	filial
了不起 adj.		liǎobùqǐ	amazing
有创意 phr.	有創意	yǒu chuàngyì	creative
有才华 phr.	有才華	yǒu cáihuá	alented
有学问 phr.	有學問	yǒu xuéwèn	learned, scholarly, academic
有恒心 phr.	有恆心	yǒu héngxīn	persistent

Negative Personality Traits

自私 adj.		zìsī	selfish
小气 adj.	小氣	xiǎoqì	petty, stingy
懒惰 adj.	懶惰	lǎnduò	lazy
虚伪 adj.	虛僞	xūwěi	hypocritical
残暴 adj.	殘暴	cánbào	cruel
骄傲 adj.	驕傲	jiāo'ào	arrogant
冲动 adj.	衝動	chōngdòng	impulsive
粗俗 adj.		cūsú	vulgar

LANGUAGE FOCUS

In Lesson 5, you learned how to provide additional details on the same subject using the paired conjunctions 不但 (not only) and 而且 (moreover). Other paired conjunctions 不仅 and 还 work in a similar way and can be used to talk about additional traits or qualities that a person has. Note that the traits or qualities in such a construction must be positively correlated.

For example

❶ 我觉得安琪不仅认真，还非常负责。
I feel that not only is Anqi serious, she is very responsible, too.

❷ 我觉得他不仅自私，还非常小气。
I feel that not only is he selfish, he is also very petty.

1. Research online to find out more about these famous Chinese people, and give a statement expressing how you feel about each of them.

Example: 我觉得孔子不仅有学问，还非常正直。

Kǒng Zǐ ❶ Confucius (孔子)	*Cài Lún* ❺ Cai Lun (蔡伦)	*Lǐ Liánjié* ❾ Jet Li (李连杰)
Lǐ Bái ❷ Li Bai (李白)	*Zhāng Héng* ❻ Zhang Heng (张衡)	*Wú Jìgāng* ❿ Jason Wu (吴季刚)
Zhāng Dàqiān ❸ Zhang Daqian (张大千)	*Qín Shǐhuáng* ❼ Qin Shihuang (秦始皇)	*Zhōu Yǎngjié* ⓫ Jimmy Choo (周仰杰)
Zhèng Hé ❹ Zheng He (郑和)	*Huā Mùlán* ❽ Mulan (花木兰)	*Yáo Míng* ⓬ Yao Ming (姚明)

2. Read the dialog and decide if the following statements are true (T) or false (F).

张安：马克，你知道_{zhīdào}林书豪是谁吗？

马克：听过_{tīngguo}这个名字，但_{dàn}不知道他是谁。

张安：林书豪是篮球运动员，非常了不起。

马克：他今年多大？

张安：他的生日是1988年8月23日，今年25岁。

马克：你喜欢看他打球吗？

张安：很喜欢！他的球赛_{qiúsài}很精彩_{jīngcǎi}。我觉得他打球不仅非常认真，还很有恒心。

马克：听你这么说，我也开始_{kāishǐ}对他感兴趣了。

张安：他不仅球打得好，还非常聪明，以前是哈佛大学_{Hāfó Dàxué}的学生。

马克：太_{tài}了不起了！下次_{xiàcì}有他的球赛，记得_{jìde}叫我看。

张安：好！

❶ 张安不知道林书豪是谁。 （　　）

❷ 林书豪是网球运动员。 （　　）

❸ 张安觉得林书豪不仅能干，还很勇敢。 （　　）

❹ 张安觉得林书豪不仅球打得好，还很风趣。 （　　）

❺ 马克觉得林书豪很了不起。 （　　）

Reading *in Context*

STEP 1 EXPLORING PROFESSIONS

An introduction to Jack

　　他叫杰克，现在跟爸爸妈妈一起在中国生活。他爸爸在一家美国公司工作，是公司的经理。妈妈在一个大学里当教授，她教英语。杰克在北京的一个中学上学。他现在上四年级。

　　杰克的中文学得很好，他用中文跟同学们聊天，用中文跟餐馆的服务员说话，用中文买东西。他爸爸妈妈说，杰克是他们的中文翻译。

Jiékè	yìqǐ	gōngsī	jīnglǐ	
杰克	一起	公司	经理	大学
Jack	together	company	manager	university

	jí	yòng	fānyì	
中学	级	用	翻译	
high school	grade	use	translator	

STEP 3 DISCOVERING FAMOUS PEOPLE

Mark and Tony are talking about the Great Wall of China.

马克：东尼，你游览过北京的长城吗？　 yóulǎn Chángchéng — visit, Great Wall

东尼：没有。你游览过吗？

马克：我游览过两次。长城太伟大了！太了不起了！　 cì — time

东尼：我听说长城是文化古迹，是吗？　 wénhuà gǔjì — cultural and historical site

马克：对。长城是中国的奇迹。我游览长城以后，看了一本介绍长城的书。长城的历史挺长的，已经有两千年的历史了。中国古代有一个皇帝，叫秦始皇。是他统一中国，　 qíjì jièshào — wonder, introduce；yǐjīng gǔdài — already, ancient；huángdì tǒngyī — emperor, unify

STEP 2 FINDING ONE'S ASPIRATIONS

Mike and Tony are talking about what they aspire to be in the future.

迈克：东尼，你将来打算做什么工作？　 Màikè Dōngní — Mike, Tony

东尼：我想有自己的公司，自己当老板。你呢？　 lǎobǎn — boss

迈克：我想当航天员。　 hángtiānyuán — astronaunt

东尼：当航天员？

迈克：是啊！当航天员。你看，我的身体多棒啊！当航天员就得有个好身体。　 bàng — fantastic

东尼：当航天员不但要有好身体，而且还要有很多航天知识。　 zhīshi — knowledge

迈克：航天知识以后我可以学。

东尼：你的想法挺大胆的。　 xiǎngfǎ tǐng dàdǎn — idea, quite, bold

迈克：我非常羡慕航天员。他们坐着飞船在太空飞行，多有意思啊！　 xiànmù fēichuán tàikōng — envy, spacecraft, space

东尼：如果你以后当了航天员，你就可以去月球，在月球上生活，做宇宙人。以后你回来的时候，人们会说你是外星人。哈哈！　 yuèqiú — moon；shēnghuó yǔzhòu — live, universe；wàixīngrén — alien

是他把一段一段的长城连在了一起。你想想，那时候没有任何机械，修长城全都靠人力。你说容易吗？　 duàn lián — section, connect；jīxiè xiū — machinery, repair；quán kào rénlì — entire, depend, labor

东尼：是挺不容易的！

马克：所以我觉得秦始皇不仅是中国的第一个皇帝，而且是一个了不起的皇帝。

东尼：你借我看看这本书，行吗？

马克：行。

Step Up!

1. Read the dialog and answer the following questions in Chinese.

芳芳：张安，你 Facebook 上面的照片真多！

zhàopiàn / photos

张安：哈哈，是的，因为暑假的时候我们全家一起去海边

hāhā (sound of laughter) / quán all / yìqǐ together

玩，所以拍了很多照片。

pāile took

芳芳：那是你的父母吗？他们是做什么的？

张安：我父亲是个电脑工程师，母亲是牙医。

芳芳：这个漂亮的女孩是谁？是你的女朋友吗？

piàoliang beautiful

张安：哈哈，不是不是，那是我姐姐。她今年24岁。

芳芳：她看起来很年轻。她工作了吗？

niánqīng young

张安：她在商店里当售货员，不过，最近她想换工作。

búguò but / huàn change

芳芳：啊？为什么？

ā oh

张安：因为售货员的工作很累，所以她不太喜欢。

tài too

芳芳：她打算在什么行业工作？

张安：我姐姐很时髦，在设计方面很有特长。她可能会在

shímáo trendy

时尚界工作，当一个服装设计师。

芳芳：服装设计师？你姐姐真有才华。

zhēn really

张安：是啊，如果她是服装设计师，我们就有漂亮的衣服

穿了！

芳芳：那就太好了，希望她会成功！

xīwàng hope / chénggōng successful

Questions

❶ 张安的父母是做什么的？

❷ 张安的姐姐现在是做什么的？

❸ 张安的姐姐为什么不喜欢现在的工作？

❹ 张安的姐姐打算在什么行业工作？她想当什么？

❺ 张安觉得，如果他姐姐是服装设计师，就会怎么样？。

❻ 如果张安的姐姐不能当服装设计师，你觉得她还可以做什么工作？
bùnéng
cannot

2. Work with a classmate to create a dialog about your aspirations. Include details on which industry/field you and your partner would like to work in, and the possible work you would like to engage in if you were in that profession. Be sure that each of you gives information in at least 10 sentences and role play the dialog to the class.

> Student A: 你将来打算在什么行业工作？
>
> Student B: 我可能在……工作。你呢？
>
> Student A: 我可能会在……工作。
>
> Student B: ……

3. Research information about two famous people and their professions. Then, sit in a group of three students and ask each other questions in Chinese about the famous person. One student (Ⓐ) is the leader and answers the questions. Two students (Ⓑ and Ⓒ) ask questions until either Ⓑ or Ⓒ guesses who the person is. Start by asking "是男的还是女的？" and continue by asking about professions. The person who guesses the name of the famous person will then become the leader (student Ⓐ) and answer questions about his/her famous person. All students should have a chance to be the leader.

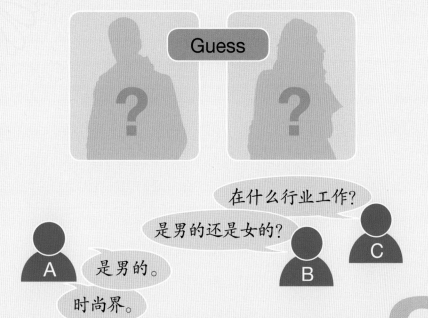

4. Research a famous person who is in the profession that you aspire to. Write a paragraph about him/her containing details about his/her profession, the area he/she is good in, and what you think about him/her. Introduce him/her to the class.

Fun Time!

Below are the lyrics of a Chinese song 相信自己. Listen to the song on YouTube and sing along.

Divide into groups of three or four. Each group is to work on a part of the lyrics to determine the meaning and explain it to the rest of the class. Check the dictionary for words that you do not know. Use pictures, actions, and/or animation clips to get the meaning across without using English.

Xiāngxìn Zìjǐ
相信自己

Língdiǎn Yuètuán
零点乐队

duōshao cì huī hàn rú yǔ
多 少 次 挥 汗 如 雨

shāngtòng céng tiánmǎn jìyì
伤 痛 曾 填 满 记 忆

zhǐ yīnwèi shǐzhōng xiāngxìn
只 因 为 始 终 相 信

qù pīnbó cái néng shènglì
去 拼 搏 才 能 胜 利

zǒngshì zài gǔlì zìjǐ
总 是 在 鼓 舞 自 己

yào chénggōng jiù děi nǔlì
要 成 功 就 得 努 力

rèxuè zài sàichǎng fèiténg
热 血 在 赛 场 沸 腾

jùrén zài dōngfāng shēngqǐ
巨 人 在 东 方 升 起

(X2)

xiāngxìn zìjǐ
相 信 自 己

nǐ jiāng yíngdé shènglì
你 将 赢 得 胜 利

chuàngzào qíjì
创 造 奇 迹

xiāngxìn zìjǐ
相 信 自 己

mèngxiǎng zài nǐ shǒu zhōng
梦 想 在 你 手 中

zhè shì nǐ de tiāndì
这 是 你 的 天 地

xiāngxìn zìjǐ
相 信 自 己

nǐ jiāng chāoyuè jíxiàn
你 将 超 越 极 限

chāoyuè zìjǐ
超 越 自 己

xiāngxìn zìjǐ
相 信 自 己

dāng zhè yíqiè guòqu
当 这 一 切 过 去

nímen jiāng shì dì yī
你 们 将 是 第 一

(X3)

I have learned...

Core Vocabulary				NEW WORDS			

Verbs

工作		gōngzuò	work	保卫	保衛	bǎowèi	defend, protect
打算		dǎsuàn	plan to, intend to	教导	教導	jiàodǎo	teach
设计	設計	shèjì	design	伸张	伸張	shēnzhāng	uphold
医治	醫治	yīzhì	cure, treat, heal	维持	維持	wéichí	maintain
照顾	照顧	zhàogù	take care of	管理		guǎnlǐ	manage
报道	報道	bàodào	report	开	開	kāi	hold (exhibitions, etc.)

Nouns

工作		gōngzuò	work	特长	特長	tècháng	specialty, skill
行业	行業	hángyè	industry, trade, profession	成就		chéngjiù	achievement
方面		fāngmiàn	area, field				

Common professions

工程师	工程師	gōngchéngshī	engineer	企业家	企業家	qǐyèjiā	entrepreneur
建筑师	建築師	jiànzhùshī	architect	银行家	銀行家	yínhángjiā	banker
会计师	會計師	kuàijìshī	accountant	音乐家	音樂家	yīnyuèjiā	musician
发型师	髮型師	fàxíngshī	hairdresser, hairstylist	艺术家	藝術家	yìshùjiā	artist
服装设计师	服裝設計師	fúzhuāng shèjìshī	fashion designer	教授		jiàoshòu	professor
公务员	公務員	gōngwùyuán	civil servant	护士	護士	hùshi	nurse
售货员	售貨員	shòuhuòyuán	salesperson	导游	導游	dǎoyóu	tour guide
服务员	服務員	fúwùyuán	waiter, waitress	军人	軍人	jūnrén	soldier
收银员	收銀員	shōuyínyuán	cashier	商人		shāngrén	businessman
消防员	消防員	xiāofángyuán	firefighter	农民	農民	nóngmín	farmer
银行出纳员	銀行出納員	yínháng chūnàyuán	bank teller	工人		gōngrén	worker
邮递员	郵遞員	yóudìyuán	mail carrier				

Common workplaces

商店		shāngdiàn	retail outlet, shop	工厂	工廠	gōngchǎng	factory
餐馆	餐館	cānguǎn	restaurant	农田	農田	nóngtián	farmland
发廊	髮廊	fàláng	hair salon	办公室	辦公室	bàngōngshì	office
报社	報社	bàoshè	news agency	化验室	化驗室	huàyànshì	laboratory
军营	軍營	jūnyíng	military camp	消防局	消防局	xiāofángjú	fire station

Common industries and fields of work

农业	農業	nóngyè	agriculture industry	教育界		jiàoyùjiè	education profession
建筑业	建築業	jiànzhùyè	building industry	文学界	文學界	wénxuéjiè	literary profession
医药业	醫藥業	yīyàoyè	health industry	体育界	體育界	tǐyùjiè	sports profession
金融业	金融業	jīnróngyè	finance industry	艺术界	藝術界	yìshùjiè	arts profession
信息业	信息業	xìnxīyè	IT industry	音乐界	音樂界	yīnyuèjiè	music profession
服务业	服務業	fúwùyè	service industry	娱乐界	娛樂界	yúlèjiè	entertainment profession
食品业	食品業	shípǐnyè	food industry	时尚界	時尚界	shíshàngjiè	fashion industry
旅游业	旅游業	lǚyóuyè	tourism industry	新闻界	新聞界	xīnwénjiè	news industry
法律界		fǎlùjiè	legal profession				

Others

病人	病人	bìngrén	patients	研究		yánjiū	research
新闻	新聞	xīnwén	news	比赛	比賽	bǐsài	competitions
国家	國家	guójiā	country, nation	运动	運動	yùndòng	sports
学生	學生	xuésheng	students	发型	髮型	fàxíng	hairstyle
正义	正義	zhèngyì	justice	画展	畫展	huàzhǎn	art exhibition
治安		zhì'ān	peace and order	音乐会	音樂會	yīnyuèhuì	musical concerts
财务	財務	cáiwù	finances				

Adjective
Positive personality traits

伟大	偉大	wěidà	great	友善		yǒushàn	friendly
正直		zhèngzhí	just, righteous	能干	能幹	nénggàn	capable
认真	認真	rènzhēn	serious	勇敢		yǒnggǎn	brave, courageous
负责	負責	fùzé	responsible	孝顺	孝順	xiàoshùn	filial
勤劳	勤勞	qínláo	hardworking	了不起		liǎobùqǐ	amazing
风趣	風趣	fēngqù	humorous				

Negative personality traits

自私		zìsī	selfish	残暴	殘暴	cánbào	cruel
小气	小氣	xiǎoqì	petty, stingy	骄傲	驕傲	jiāo'ào	arrogant
懒惰	懶惰	lǎnduò	lazy	冲动	衝動	chōngdòng	impulsive
虚伪	虛偽	xūwěi	hypocritical	粗俗		cūsú	vulgar

I have learned...

Negative personality traits

自私		zìsī	selfish	残暴	殘暴	cánbào	cruel
小气	小氣	xiǎoqì	petty, stingy	骄傲	驕傲	jiāo'ào	arrogant
懒惰	懶惰	lǎnduò	lazy	冲动	衝動	chōngdòng	impulsive
虚伪	虛偽	xūwěi	hypocritical	粗俗		cūsú	vulgar

Adverbs

努力	nǔlì	do one's best
好好	hǎohāo	properly, carefully
非常	fēicháng	very, extremely

Conjunctions

如果…就…	rúguǒ…jiù…	if...then...
不仅…还… 不僅…還…	bùjǐn…hái…	not only...but also

Auxiliary verbs

会	會	huì	will	可能		kěnéng	may, might, probably

Phrases
Positive personality traits

有创意	有創意	yǒu chuàngyì	creative	有学问	有學問	yǒu xuéwèn	learned, scholarly, academic
有才华	有才華	yǒu cáihuá	talented	有恒心	有恆心	yǒu héngxīn	talented

Profession-related words and phrases

做菜		zuòcài	cook	医治病人	醫治病人	yīzhì bìngrén	treat patients
设计大楼	設計大樓	shèjì dàlóu	design buildings	照顾病人	照顧病人	zhàogù bìngrén	take care of patients
设计新发型	設計新髮型	shèjì xīn fàxíng	design new hairstyles	报道新闻	報道新聞	bàodào xīnwén	report news
演戏	演戲	yǎnxì	act	保卫国家	保衛國家	bǎowèi guójiā	defend the country
参加运动比赛	參加運動比賽	cānjiā yùndòng bǐsài	take part in sports competitions	教导学生	教導學生	jiàodǎo xuésheng	teach students
救火		jiùhuǒ	put out a fire	伸张正义	伸張正義	shēnzhāng zhèngyì	uphold justice
开画展	開畫展	kāi huàzhǎn	hold an art exhibition	维持治安	偉持治安	wéichí zhì'ān	maintain peace and order
作曲	作曲	zuò qǔ	compose music	管理财务	管理財務	guǎnlǐ cáiwù	manage finances
开音乐会	開音樂會	kāi yīnyuèhuì	hold musical concerts	做研究		zuò yánjiū	do research
表演		biǎoyǎn	perform				

 SENTENCE PATTERNS

他是做什么的？他是工程师。	你将来打算在什么行业工作？	如果我是发型师，
他在学校里当教师。	我可能在时尚界工作。	我就会设计新发型。
我觉得郑和不仅有学问，还非常能干。	郎朗在音乐方面很有特长。	

I can do!

Interpretive Communication

❑ I can understand when someone talks about his/her profession and place of work.

❑ I can read and understand short, simple descriptions about one's profession and aspirations.

❑ I can understand when someone describes the area a person excels in.

❑ I can understand when someone comments on a person's personality.

Interpersonal Communication

❑ I can converse about people's professions and their personality traits.

❑ I can talk to others about my career aspirations.

❑ I can ask questions and get information about other people's professions and career aspirations.

Presentational Communication

❑ I can write about, introduce, and describe someone's profession.

❑ I can talk about my career aspirations.

❑ I can give a short presentation on a famous person.

Cultural Knowledge

❑ I can talk about the four main social classes in ancient China.

❑ I can explain the meaning of the Chinese saying 三百六十行，行行出状元.

❑ I can describe and comment on some famous Chinese people in ancient and modern times.

LESSON 7

Maintaining a healthy lifestyle

保持健康的生活习惯

COMMUNICATIVE GOALS

- Identifying healthy and unhealthy foods
- Comparing and contrasting the health benefits of foods
- Describing an illness
- Stating the frequency of an action
- Describing a daily hygiene routine

Cultural Knowledge

- Chinese staple foods
- Halal food in China
- Acupuncture
- "Hot" and "cold" foods in Chinese medicine
- Chinese therapeutic massage — Tuina

Get ready...

Look at the following bilingual label of milk tea and match the words from the following list.

每份	
热量	95大卡
蛋白质	1公克
脂肪	3公克
饱和脂肪	1公克
碳水化合物	15公克
糖	12公克
钠	53毫克

营养标示	
每一份量	20公克
本包装含	12份

NUTRITION INFORMATION

Servings per package: 12
Serving size: 20g (1 sachet made as directed)

	Quantity* per serving	Quantity* per 100m
Energy	397kj (95Cal)	1985kj (475Cal)
Protein	1g	5g
Fat (total)	3g	15g
– saturated	1g	5g
Carbohydrate	15g	75g
– sugars	12g	60g
Sodium	53mg	265mg

All quantities are average values. Contains 3g fat per serving.

Match the two columns.

English	Chinese
❶ Gram	a. 糖 (táng)
❷ Sodium	b. 碳水化合物 (tànshuǐhuàhéwù)
❸ Sugar	c. 公克 (gōngkè)
❹ Fat	d. 饱和脂肪 (bǎohé zhīfáng)
❺ Protein	e. 蛋白质 (dànbáizhì)
❻ Carbohydrate	f. 钠 (nà)
❼ Saturated fat	g. 脂肪 (zhīfáng)

Talk to a friend and discuss whether you think this tea is good for you or not. Examine the nutritional values and decide which parts are healthy and why.

STEPS at a glance!

STEP 1

EATING WELL

A. Making suggestions and classifying foods
我们去喝茶吧。

B. Reading the label
豆类制品除了铁和钙以外，还有蛋白质。

C. Eating healthy foods
虽然可乐很好喝，但是糖份很高。

STEP 2

GETTING SICK

A. Seeing the doctor
你哪里不舒服？我肚子痛。

B. Giving and following instructions
感冒药一天吃三次。

STEP 3

DEVELOPING HEALTHY HABITS

A. Maintaining daily hygiene
她用洗发液洗头发。

B. Keeping fit
吃饭以前应该先洗手。

C. Indicating duration and frequency of healthy habits
我每天运动半小时。
她每天刷两次牙。

我们吃水果沙拉吧。
Let's eat fruit salad.

A Making suggestions and classifying foods

我们喝茶吧。
Let's drink Chinese tea.

生 词

NEW WORDS

吧 *part.*		ba	(giving suggestions)
面食 *n.*	麵食	miànshí	flour products (pasta, pancakes, bread, dumplings, etc.)
主食 *n.*		zhǔshí	staple foods (rice, noodles, dumplings, etc.)
副食 *n.*		fùshí	non-staple foods (meat and vegetable dishes)
甜点 *n.*	甜點	tiándiǎn	dessert

饮料 *n.*	飲料	yǐnliào	beverages
零食 *n.*		língshí	snacks
食品 *n.*		shípǐn	food products (cooked or processed items)
种类 *n.*	種類	zhǒnglèi	category

214

Food categories

谷物类 phr.	穀物類	gǔwù lèi	grains
奶类 phr.	奶類	nǎi lèi	milk (category)
奶制品 phr.	奶製品	nǎizhìpǐn	dairy products
豆类 phr.	豆類	dòu lèi	beans (category)
豆制品 phr.	豆製品	dòuzhìpǐn	bean products
蔬菜类 phr.	蔬菜類	shūcài lèi	vegetables (category)
肉类 phr.	肉類	ròu lèi	meats (category)

海鲜类 phr.	海鮮類	hǎixiān lèi	seafood (category)
油脂类 phr.	油脂類	yóuzhī lèi	fats and oils (category)
水果类 phr.	水果類	shuǐguǒ lèi	fruits (category)
坚果类 phr.	堅果類	jiānguǒ lèi	nuts (category)

Word you have learned   shíwù
食物 n. food

LANGUAGE FOCUS

The word 吧 is very useful when speaking Chinese. It has many different meanings in different contexts. One of the meanings is to use it to suggest that someone do an activity. For example, if you want to suggest that someone do an activity, such as eating a certain food, use the expression, "吃水果吧！" This sentence is sometimes translated as "Let's eat fruit," but the implication is a suggestion, not a command.

Look at the following sentences and think of an English equivalent.

- 我们现在走吧！
- 你先吃吧！
- 我们搭地铁去吧！
- 你们少喝点可乐吧！
- 我们去看电影吧！
- 今天有点冷，穿一件毛衣吧！
- 你少吃点薯条吧！

CULTURAL HIGHLIGHTS

Staple Food

The word 主食 (zhǔshí) is used to refer to a "staple" food and literally means "a main food." In China, they usually refer to grains such as rice, wheat, millet, sorghum, maize (corn), oats, and barley.

Rice is a major staple food for people from the rice farming areas of southern China. Steamed white rice 米饭 (mǐfàn) is the most commonly eaten form in this region of China. It is found in many popular Chinese dishes such as rice porridge 粥 (zhōu), rice noodles 米粉 (mǐfěn), wide rice noodles

河粉 (héfěn), rice dumplings 粽子 (zòngzi), and sweet dumplings 汤圆/元宵 (tāngyuán/yuánxiāo). In the wheat farming areas of Northern China, people rely largely on flour-based foods 面食 (miànshí), such as dumplings 饺子 (jiǎozi), steamed buns 包子 (bāozi), and steamed bread 馒头 (mántou).

Chinese noodles 面 (miàn) can be made with rice or wheat flour. They can be fresh or dry and come in a variety of sizes, shapes, and textures. They are often served in soups or fried as toppings. They can be served hot or cold, with different sauces or toppings, in a broth 汤面 (tāngmiàn), or dry 炒米粉 (chǎomǐfěn).

1. In your health class, you are asked to tell your classmate the foods that you suggest he/she eat or drink or not. Be sure to end with 吧. Look at the list below and advise your friend which foods to eat and which ones not to eat.

Example:

píngguǒ
苹果： <u>你吃苹果吧！</u>

1
bōcài
菠菜

2
niúpái
牛排

3
dòujiāng
豆浆

4
jiǎozi
饺子

5
pútao
葡萄

6
nǎilào
奶酪

7
dàngāo
蛋糕

8
yú
鱼

9
pīsà
披萨

10
fānqié
番茄

11
hànbǎobāo
汉堡包

12
húntuntāng
馄饨汤

13
shālā
沙拉

14
kělè
可乐

15
bīngqílín
冰淇淋

2. Look at the foods and decide into which of the following categories each food belongs. Using the graphic organizer below, check the category into which each food falls. Some foods will only fit into one category and some foods will fit into more than one category. Then write a sentence stating the category into which it belongs.

Example: 红豆汤是豆类也是甜点。

食物	Shíwù zhǒnglèi 食物种类										Shípǐn zhǒnglèi 食品种类			
	谷物类	奶制品	肉类	蔬菜类	水果类	豆制品	奶类	豆类	油脂类	坚果类	主食	零食	饮料	甜品
hóngdòutāng 红豆汤 red bean soup								✗						✗
❶ xīlánhuā 西兰花 broccoli														
❷ xiāngjiāo 香蕉 banana														
❸ Běijīng kǎoyā 北京烤鸭 Peking duck														
❹ dòufu 豆腐 beancurd														
❺ xiánròu 咸肉 bacon														
❻ nǎilào 奶酪 cheese														
❼ bāozi 包子 meat bun														
❽ chǎofàn 炒饭 fried rice														
❾ xīguā 西瓜 watermelon														
❿ gōngbǎo jīdīng 宫保鸡丁 spicy chicken														
⓫ chéngzi 橙子 orange														
⓬ chǎomiàn 炒面 fried noodles														

食物	Shíwù zhǒnglèi 食物种类										Shípǐn zhǒnglèi 食品种类			
	谷物类	奶制品	肉类	蔬菜类	水果类	豆制品	奶类	豆类	油脂类	坚果类	主食	零食	饮料	甜品
⑬ huāshēng 花生 peanuts														
⑭ huángyóu 黄油 butter														
⑮ niúnǎi 牛奶 milk														
⑯ bīngqílín 冰淇淋 ice-cream														
⑰ báicài 白菜 Chinese cabbage														
⑱ zhōu 粥 porridge														
⑲ gǎnlǎnyóu 橄榄油 olive oil														
⑳ hétáo 核桃 walnut														

3. With a partner, make a list in English of all of the food that you both ate yesterday. Afterwards, write in Chinese the category into which the food falls. Create a similar graphic organizer like the one above and be sure to organize the foods into the three main meals and snacks: 早饭, 午饭, 晚饭, 零食.

Do YOU KNOW . . . 你知道吗?

One of the most popular meats in Chinese food is pork. On a Chinese menu, if the word 肉 (ròu, meat) is used alone, it always refers to a pork dish, such as 酸甜肉 (suāntiánròu, sweet and sour pork) or 回锅肉 (huíguōròu, double cooked pork). However, there are groups in China that do not eat pork. For example, Muslims, who constitute one of the largest of the 55 minorities, live in every region of China and have opened a number of restaurants to serve food that is appropriate to their religious beliefs. In their religion, they do not eat pork and will have a sign on their restaurants that says 清真 (qīngzhēn, "pure and true"), meaning "halal," to indicate that they are conforming to Islamic dietary laws. In those restaurants, you can eat some of the best "non-pork" meats in the country, such as lamb, mutton, and beef.

chúle   yǐwài
除了张安以外，他们都喜欢吃奶制品。
Except for Zhang An, all of them love dairy products.

tiě   gài
豆制品除了铁和钙以外，
dànbáizhì
还有蛋白质。
In addition to iron and calcium, bean products also contain protein.

fǎnshì   zhīfáng
有的零食有反式脂肪，
有的没有。
Some snacks contain trans fat while some don't.

NEW WORDS

除了……以外 conj.		chúle...yǐwài	except for; in addition to
有的 adj.		yǒude	some
食物标签 phr.	食物標簽	shíwù biāoqiān	food label
营养 n.	營養	yíngyǎng	nutrition
营养成分 phr.	營養成分	yíngyǎng chéngfèn	nutritional content
能量 n.		néngliàng	energy
卡路里 n.		kǎlùlǐ	calories
蛋白质 n.	蛋白質	dànbáizhì	protein
碳水化合物 n.		tànshuǐhuàhéwù	carbohydrate
脂肪 n.		zhīfáng	fat
饱和脂肪 phr.	飽和脂肪	bǎohé zhīfáng	saturated fat
反式脂肪 phr.		fǎnshì zhīfáng	trans fat
维生素 n.	維生素	wéishēngsù	vitamin
纤维 n.	纖維	xiānwéi	fiber
钠 n.	鈉	nà	sodium
钙 n.	鈣	gài	calcium
铁 n.	鐵	tiě	iron
糖份 n.		tángfèn	sugar content
胆固醇 n.	膽固醇	dǎngùchún	cholesterol

LANGUAGE FOCUS

The expression 除了……以外 is used to describe that the thing(s) or person(s) expressed between 除了 and 以外 are not included. If you want to say that everyone is here except one person, use the combination 除了……以外. The following sentences illustrate how to use this expression.

Examples: ❶ 除了马克以外，每个人都喜欢吃甜点。
Except for Mark, everyone likes dessert.

❷ 除了周末以外，他每天跑步。
Except for the weekends, he goes jogging every day.

The expression 除了……以外 has the meaning of "in addition to" when combined with either the word 还 or 也.

Examples: ❶ 除了米饭以外，有的时候她还吃面包。
In addition to rice, she sometimes also eats bread.

❷ 除了冰淇淋以外，我也喜欢吃蛋糕。
In addition to ice cream, I also like cake.

The expression 有的 is used before a noun to describe an unspecific quantity, like "some" in English.

For example: 有的人 some people

Can you guess the meaning of the following sentences?

▷ 有的人喜欢吃肉，有的人不喜欢吃肉。

▷ 有的食物好吃，有的食物不好吃。

▷ 有的食品的卡路里很高。

1. Most countries in the world require that food be labeled with nutrients. However, each country requires different nutritional elements to be included in a label. Look at the following table and answer the questions concerning the core nutrients that each country requires on its labels.

国家	Nutrients required on the food label
Àodàlìyà 澳大利亚	能量、蛋白质、脂肪、碳水化合物、糖、钠
Mǎláixīyà 马来西亚	能量、蛋白质、脂肪、碳水化合物
Xīnjiāpō 新加坡	能量、蛋白质、*总脂肪、饱和脂肪、反式脂肪、胆固醇、碳水化合物、*膳食纤维、钠
Rìběn 日本	能量、蛋白质、脂肪、碳水化合物、钠
Táiwān 台湾	能量、蛋白质、脂肪、碳水化合物、钠
Xiānggǎng 香港	能量、蛋白质、碳水化合物、总脂肪、饱和脂肪、反式脂肪、糖、钠

Source: http://www.topcanchina.org/src/2012-07/10005623.html

*总 zǒng total *膳食 shànshí dietary

Questions:

❶ What is one nutrient that every country requires on its label?

❷ Name two countries that both have energy, protein, and trans fat on the label.

❸ Compare the nutrients required on labels by Taiwan and Australia and state one difference.

❹ Compare the nutrients on the labels required by Hong Kong and Singapore and name two things that are the same.

❺ Name two countries that both require sugar content to be reported.

❻ Which country requires reporting a nutrient that no other country requires and what is it?

2. Read the following sentences and decide whether the meaning of 除了……以外 is "except for" or "in addition to." Then, if it means "except for," state what item is left out; if it means "in addition to," name the two or three items that go together.

❶ 除了马克以外，每个人都喜欢吃甜点。

❷ 除了包子以外，饺子和馒头也都是面食。

❸ 除了吃饭以外，我们还要吃水果。

❹ 除了周末以外，他每天都跑步。

❺ 除了咖啡以外，他什么饮料都喝。

❻ 除了维生素C以外，橙子还有很多膳食纤维。

❼ 豆类制品除了铁和钙以外，还有很多的蛋白质。

❽ 除了看电视以外，我什么都不想做。

❾ 除了星期五晚上以外，我都有时间。

❿ 牛肉除了卡路里以外，脂肪和蛋白质都很高。

⓫ 苹果很有营养，除了以钙外，也有很多维生素A和维生素B。

⓬ 除了奶类和豆类之外，你也要吃鱼肉蛋类的食物。

3. Look at the pictures and write a sentence comparing the pictures and using the word 有的.

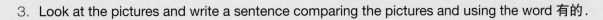

有的苹果是红色的，有的苹果是绿色的。 Or
有的人喜欢吃红苹果，有的人喜欢吃绿苹果。

The joule (焦耳, jiāo'ěr), symbol J, is a unit of energy, work, or amount of heat in the International System of Units. It is equal to the energy expended in applying a force of one newton through a distance of one meter or in passing an electric current of one ampere through a resistance of one ohm for one second. It is named after the English physicist James Prescott Joule (1818–1889).

The kilojoule (千焦耳, qiānjiāo'ěr), symbol kJ, is equal to one thousand (10^3) joules. Nutritional food labels in certain countries express energy in standard kilojoules (kJ). Because joules refer to heat, you may see the designation on some Chinese food labels or labels in other countries. To help you understand the relationship, think of it this way. A small calorie or gram calorie is approximately the energy needed to increase the temperature of 1 gram of water by 1 kelvin at standard atmospheric pressure. This is approximately 4.2 joules.

hǎochù
吃蔬菜对身体好 / 有好处。
Eating vegetables is good for our health.

suīrán
虽然可乐很好喝,

dànshì
但是糖份很高。
Though coke tastes good, it contains a lot of sugar.

生 词

NEW WORDS

健康 adj.		jiànkāng	healthy
虽然…但是… pron.	雖然…但是…	suīrán...dànshì...	although...(but)
对……好 n.	對……好	duì...hǎo	good for...
对……有好处 n.	對……有好處	duì...yǒu hǎochù	is beneficial to...

Words you have learned

suān	kǔ	xián
酸 adj. sour	苦 adj. bitter	咸 adj. salty
tián	là	dàn
甜 adj. sweet	辣 adj. spicy	淡 adj. bland

When mentioning that something is good for you, use the expression 对你好 / 有好处. For example, to say that eating apples is good for your health, you can say, 吃苹果对身体好 / 有好处. Here 对 has the meaning of "toward" so that the action of eating apples is good "towards" or "for" you.

Examples: ❶ 少油，少盐，少糖对身体好 / 有好处。
Having less oil, salt, and sugar are good for our health.

❷ 多说，多听，多写，对学中文好 / 有好处。
Speaking more, listening more, and writing more are good for learning Chinese.

❸ 每天喝八杯水，对健康好 / 有好处。
Drinking eight glasses of water every day is good for your health.

To create a sentence where one part contrasts with another, use the expression 虽然…但是…. In English you do not need to use the word "but" after the first clause to show contrast; however, in Chinese you must use 但是 after the clause with 虽然.

Examples: ❶ 虽然冰淇淋蛋糕很好吃，但是要少吃。
Though ice cream cake is tasty, we should eat less of it.

❷ 虽然牛排的蛋白质很高，但是脂肪也很高。
Though steak is high in protein, its fat content is also very high.

❸ 虽然鸡蛋营养价值很高，但是有很高的胆固醇。
Though eggs are high in nutritional value, they are also high in cholesterol.

Try This!

1. Look at the following pictures and create a sentence about the food using 虽然…但是… and another sentence using the 对…好/有好处 pattern.

> 虽然我喜欢吃薯条，但是卡路里很高。Or
> 虽然我喜欢吃薯条，但是对健康不好。

2. Write down three healthy foods and three unhealthy foods that you ate in the past week. Then survey at least eight members of the class and ask them to name one healthy food they ate and one unhealthy food they ate. Ask them the questions "你吃了什么健康的食品？你吃了什么不健康的食品？" and write down their answers. Afterwards, put their responses in Chinese into the following categories.

食物 (Category of food)	健康	不健康
蔬菜类		
水果类		
肉类		
奶制品		
饮料		
甜点		

GETTING SICK

nǎlǐ   shūfu
你哪里不舒服？
Where do you feel discomfort?

dùzi   tòng
我肚子痛。
I have a stomach ache.

A Seeing the doctor

zěnme   le
你怎么了？
What's the matter with you?

jiǎowàn   niǔshāng
我的脚腕扭伤了。
I sprained my ankle.

生 词

NEW WORDS

怎么了 q.w.	怎麼了	zěnme le	what	扭伤 v.	扭傷	niǔshāng	sprain
舒服 adj.		shūfu	comfortable	擦伤 v.	擦傷	cāshāng	graze, scratch
生病 v.		shēngbìng	fall sick	受伤 v.	受傷	shòushāng	be injured

Common illnesses

头疼 phr.	頭疼	tóu téng	headache	咳嗽 phr.		késòu	cough
牙疼 phr.		yá téng	toothache	打喷嚏 phr.	打噴嚏	dǎpēntì	sneeze
背疼 phr.		bèi téng	backache	流鼻涕 phr.		liú bítì	running nose
肚子疼 phr.		dùzi téng	stomach ache	拉肚子 phr.		lādùzi	diarrhea
喉咙疼 phr.	喉嚨疼	hóulong téng	sore throat	消化不良 phr.		xiāohuà bù liáng	indigestion
胸口疼 phr.		xiōngkǒu téng	chest pain	胃口不好 phr.		wèikǒu bù hǎo	have no appetite
感冒 phr.		gǎnmào	flu	呼吸困难 phr.	呼吸困難	hūxī kùnnan	have difficulty breathing
发烧 phr.	發燒	fāshāo	fever				

227

生词 NEW PHRASES
Parts of the body

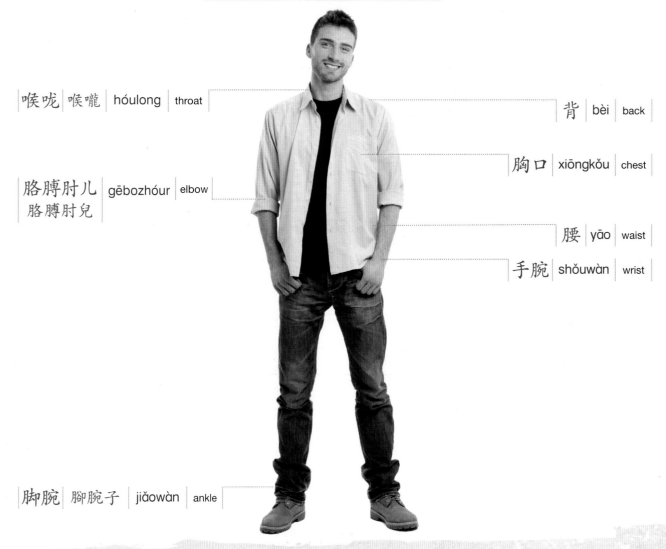

| 喉咙 | 喉嚨 | hóulong | throat |

| 背 | bèi | back |
| 胸口 | xiōngkǒu | chest |

| 胳膊肘儿 | gēbozhóur | elbow |
| 胳膊肘兒 | | |

| 腰 | yāo | waist |
| 手腕 | shǒuwàn | wrist |

| 脚腕 | 腳腕子 | jiǎowàn | ankle |

LANGUAGE FOCUS

你哪里不舒服？ is commonly used to ask someone where his or her bodily discomfort is. Alternatively, the question word 怎么了 can be used to form a general question asking how someone is.

To answer these questions in the context of physical discomfort, place the word or phrase describing the sickness right after the subject.

Examples: ❶ 我头疼。
I have a headache.

❷ 弟弟拉肚子。
My younger brother has diarrhea.

❸ 哥哥的手腕扭伤了。
My older brother sprained his wrist.

1. With a partner, look at the following pictures and act out a role play. One student will pretend to be the doctor and ask what is wrong. The other student will pretend that he/she is the person in the picture and describe the symptom. Then switch roles.

Example:

Student A: 怎么了？你哪儿不舒服？

Student B: 我肚子疼。

2. Read the dialog and decide if the five statements are true or false.

医生：你怎么了？哪儿不舒服？

马克：我咳嗽、打喷嚏、流鼻涕，还发烧。

医生：什么时候发烧的？

马克：昨天晚上。

医生：量体温了吗？
　　　liáng　tǐwēn
measure body temperature

马克：量了。三十九度八。

医生：你感冒了。需要多喝水，多休息。
　　　　　　　　　xūyào　　　　　　　xiūxi
　　　　　　　　　need　　　　　　　　rest

马克：谢谢医生。

① 马克虽然咳嗽、打喷嚏，但是没有流鼻涕。

② 马克是昨天晚上发烧的。

③ 医生说，马克需要少喝水，多休息。

④ 马克没有量体温。

⑤ 马克感冒了。

gěi　　kāiyào
我 给 你 开 药。
I'll prescribe some medicine for you.

生 词

NEW WORDS

给 prep.	給	gěi	to, for
次 m.w.		cì	(referring to the number of times an action occurs) time
片 m.w.		piàn	capsule
开药 v.	開藥	kāiyào	prescribe medicine
打针 v.	打針	dǎzhēn	give an injection

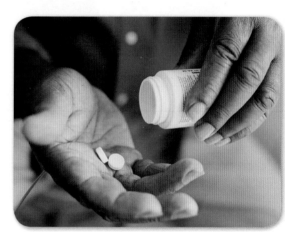

cì
每 天 吃 三 次 药。
Take the medicine three times a day.

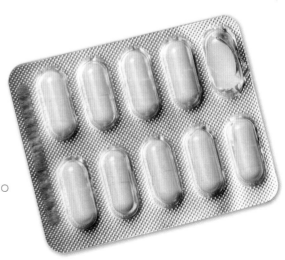

piàn
每 天 三 次，每 次 一 片。
Three times a day; one capsule each time.

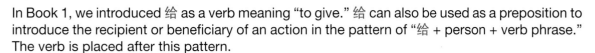
In Book 1, we introduced 给 as a verb meaning "to give." 给 can also be used as a preposition to introduce the recipient or beneficiary of an action in the pattern of "给 + person + verb phrase." The verb is placed after this pattern.

Examples: ❶ 医生给我打针。 The doctor gives me an injection.

❷ 妈妈给妹妹买衣服。 Mom buys clothes for my younger sister.

When you wish to discuss how frequently an activity should take place or has taken place, use the measure word 次. It denotes the number of times an action occurs. A number precedes 次 to form a frequency phrase, such as 一次 (one time), 三次 (three times). The frequency phrase can be placed before the object of a verb:

Examples: ❶ 每天吃两次药。 Take the medicine twice a day.

❷ 每个星期吃一次冰淇淋。 Have ice cream once a week.

Sometimes the object can move to the beginning of the sentence:

Examples: ❶ 感冒药一天吃三次。 Take the flu medicine three times a day.

❷ 冰淇淋每个星期吃一次。 Have ice cream once a week.

On medicine bottles, the dosage will read either 每次三片 or 一次三片 which means to take three pills each time or at one time take three pills. The meaning is the same. What does 每天三次 / 一天三次 mean? How frequently should the medicine be taken?

CULTURAL HIGHLIGHTS

Acupuncture

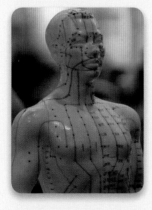

The first known record of acupuncture is found in a book that is over 4,700 years old called 黄帝内经 (Huáng Dì Nèi Jīng) or "Yellow Emperor's Classic of Internal Medicine." It is said to be the oldest medical textbook in the world and was compiled from earlier theories by Shennong (神农, Shénnóng), who is considered the father of Chinese medicine. Shennong documented theories about circulation, pulse, and the heart over 4,700 years ago.

According to Shennong, the body had an energy force, called *qi* (气), running throughout it. *Qi* consisted of all essential life activities which include the spiritual, emotional, mental, and physical aspects of life. A person's health was influenced by the flow of *qi* in the body along with the universal forces of yin and yang. If the flow of *qi* is insufficient, unbalanced, or interrupted, the yin and yang become unbalanced, and illness may occur. *Qi* travels throughout the body along "meridians" or special pathways or channels that are the same on both sides of the body. There are 14 main meridians that run vertically up and down the body and 12 organ meridians in each half of the body. In addition, there are two unpaired midline meridians. In acupuncture, the belief is that there are specific points where the meridians come to the surface of the skin and are easily accessible by "needling" or acupressure. Placing needles or pressure at these points is a way of restoring the even circulation of *qi* and creating a balance between yin and yang. In recent years, acupuncture has been gaining favor with Western doctors and many people are turning to using acupuncture or acupressure to relieve pain.

1. Look at the following pictures, read the instructions below the pictures, and indicate whether the following statements are true (T) or false (F).

zhǐténgyào		tāngshí		zhēnjiǔ
止疼药	感冒药	止咳药水	中药	针灸
Pain medicine		Cough medicine	Chinese medicine	Acupuncture

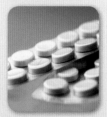    

每四小时一次，
一次两片

一次一片，
一天三次

每次一汤匙，
tāngshí
tablespoon
每天三次

每天两次，
吃早饭以前，
睡觉以前

每天一次，
每次四十分钟

❶ 止疼药每四小时一次，每次一片。

❷ 感冒药每天三次，每次一片。

❸ 止咳药水一天三次，每次一汤匙。

❹ 中药一天两次，早饭以后，睡觉以前。

❺ 针灸每天一次，每次四十五分钟。

2. Read the following dialog and answer the questions.

李医生：你哪里不舒服？

张安：我喉咙疼。

李医生：你疼了几天了？

张安：我疼了三天了，还有点咳嗽和流鼻涕。

李医生：你感冒了，我给你开药。

张安：我需要请假吗？
xūyào
need

李医生：你不能去上学，得在家休息两天，多喝水，少吃油。
bù néng
cannot
xiūxi
rest
这是你的感冒药，每天三次，每次一片。

张安：是吃饭以前吃还是吃饭以后吃？

李医生：吃饭以后吃。

张安：谢谢，李医生！

❶ 李医生和张安在什么地方？
a.在家　　　　b.在诊所　　　　c.在图书馆　　　d.在药房　　　（　　）

❷ 张安不舒服了几天了？
a.一天　　　　b.两天　　　　　c.三天　　　　　d.四天　　　　（　　）

❸ 李医生要张安做什么？
a.回去上课　　b.在家休息　　　c.多运动　　　　d.去买药　　　（　　）

❹ 张安要在什么时候吃药？
a.去上学以前　b.吃饭以后　　　c.睡觉以前　　　d.放学以后　　（　　）

❺ 张安每天吃几次药？
a.一次　　　　b.两次　　　　　c.三次　　　　　d.四次　　　　（　　）

DO YOU KNOW . . . 你知道吗？

Many centuries ago Chinese medicine (中医, zhōngyī) developed a theory of avoiding eating specific foods based on the yin-yang theory. The yin (feminine) and the yang (masculine) represent two opposing principles of nature. Yang foods are believed to increase the body's heat (raise the metabolism), while yin foods are believed to decrease the body's heat (lower the metabolism). The idea is that the two principles need to be in balance. Every category of food  has its own quality; some food is called "hot" food and some is called "cold" food. The "hot" and "cold" properties are believed to be innate, not external (resulting from heating or freezing).

For example, though iced chocolate is cold on the surface, it is considered a "hot" food. So, if your illness is caused by the imbalance of feminine and masculine energies, you have to be careful about the food you eat. If the masculine energy is overcoming the feminine energy, the person needs to avoid "hot food." "Cold food" will help to relieve the symptoms. Examples of "hot foods" are peaches, lamb, garlic, onions, and ginger; examples of "cold foods" are lemons, green beans, pears, cucumbers, melon, and salt.

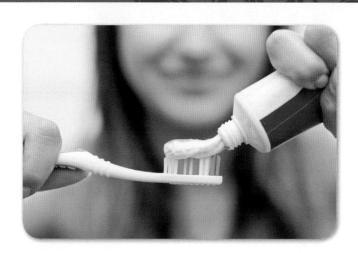

yòng yágāo
我 用 牙膏 刷牙 。
I use toothpaste to brush my teeth.

A Maintaining daily hygiene

生 词

NEW WORDS

用 v.		yòng	to use
卫生 n.	衛生	wèishēng	hygiene
习惯 n.	習慣	xíguàn	habit

yòng xǐfàyè
她 用 洗发液 洗头发 。
She uses hair shampoo to wash her hair.

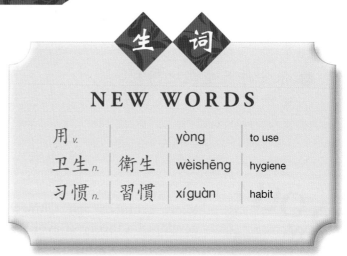

LANGUAGE FOCUS

用 is a verb that means to use or utilize an object to complete an action. For example, you say "用牙刷刷牙," that is, you use a toothbrush to brush your teeth.

COMMON TOILETRIES	HEALTHY HABITS	COMMON TOILETRIES	HEALTHY HABITS

COMMON TOILETRIES

féizào
肥皂 n.
soap

mùyùyè
沐浴液 n.
body wash

xǐfàyè
洗发液 n.
洗 髮 液
hair shampoo

yágāo
牙膏 n.
toothpaste

yáshuā
牙刷 n.
toothbrush

yáxiàn
牙线 n.
牙線
dental floss

HEALTHY HABITS

xǐ shǒu
洗手 phr.
wash your hands

xǐzǎo
洗澡 phr.
take a bath

xǐtóu
洗头 phr.
洗 頭
wash your hair

shuāyá
刷牙 phr.
brush your teeth

qīngjié yáchǐ
清洁牙齿 phr.
清 潔 牙 齒
clean your teeth

COMMON TOILETRIES

shùkǒushuǐ
漱口水 n.
mouth wash

shūzi
梳子 n.
comb

máojīn
毛巾 n.
towel

miànjīnzhǐ
面巾纸 n.
面 巾 紙
kleenex, tissue

zhǐjiadāo
指甲刀 n.
nail cutter

HEALTHY HABITS

shùkǒu
漱口 phr.
rinse your mouth

shūtóu
梳头 phr.
梳 頭
comb your hair

cā shēntǐ
擦身体 phr.
擦 身 體
wipe your body

cā bítì
擦鼻涕 phr.
blow your nose

jiǎn zhǐjia
剪指甲 phr.
cut your nails

Try This!

1. Here is a list of common items that are part of our everyday life. Create a sentence to describe what you do with these objects.

   Example: 牙膏 ___我用牙膏刷牙。___

   ❶ 肥皂　　　❺ 牙刷　　　❾ 面巾纸
   ❷ 梳子　　　❻ 牙线　　　❿ 漱口水
   ❸ 洗发液　　❼ 指甲刀　　⓫ 水
   ❹ 毛巾　　　❽ 沐浴液　　⓬ 笔

2. Create a table of all of the daily hygiene habits that you do and when you do them. Make sure that you do at least 10 habits during the day.

什么时候	卫生习惯
吃饭以前	洗手

3. Imagine that you are going to take a weekend trip and will be away from your house. Write up your list of at least eight toiletries that you will pack in your suitcase. After you have made up your list, explain to a classmate why you are taking those items with you. For example, if you pack toothpaste, tell your partner, "我用牙膏刷牙。"

yīnggāi

吃饭以前应该先洗手。

We should wash our hands before meals.

guòdù

我们不应该过度运动。

We should not over exercise.

生 词

NEW WORDS

应该 aux. v.	應該	yīnggāi	should, ought to
运动 v.	運動	yùndòng	exercise
健身 v.		jiànshēn	train the body
休息 v.		xiūxi	rest
过度 adj.	過度	guòdù	excessively, too much
太 adv.		tài	too
早睡早起 phr.		zǎo shuì zǎo qǐ	go to sleep early, get up early
做体检 phr.	作體檢	zuò tǐjiǎn	have a physical/body check up

237

In order to say that you should, must, or are supposed to do something, use the word 应该:

Examples: ❶ 我们应该多运动。   We should exercise more.

❷ 我们应该多吃水果。   We should eat more fruits.

The negative form is 不应该:

Examples: ❶ 我们不应该吃太多。   We shouldn't eat too much.

❷ 我们不应该喝太多可乐。   We shouldn't drink too much cola.

1. Look at the following activities and state in Chinese when you would most likely do the activity. You may state a meal, a time, a date, or a day.

> *Example:* 吃水果   早饭，午饭，晚饭，零食

❶ 刷牙   ❷ 做运动   ❸ 洗澡   ❹ 洗手   ❺ 理发

❻ 吃蔬菜   ❼ 喝水   ❽ 睡觉   ❾ 起床   ❿ 吃零食

2. In Chinese, write up your daily schedule with the times you do the activities in the middle column and whether they are healthy for you or not. Put in at least 10 activities that you do during the day and make sure that at least four of them are healthy activities. Use the table below to organize your day's activities.

什么时候	活动	健康还是不健康

3. Imagine that you are in health class and are required to give a short talk about what you must to do stay healthy. Write a short speech of five to eight sentences about what you should do to maintain a healthy lifestyle.

xiǎoshí
你每天运动几小时？
How long do you exercise every day?

我每天运动半小时。
I exercise for half an hour every day.

生词

NEW WORDS

| 分钟 n. | 分鐘 | fēnzhōng | minute |
| 小时 n. | 小時 | xiǎoshí | hour |

Word you have learned bàn
半 v. half

她每天刷几次牙？
How often does she brush her teeth every day?

她每天刷两次牙。
She brushes her teeth twice a day.

分钟, 小时, and 天 are common units of time. They can be used after numbers to form phrases that indicate duration:

❧ 五分钟 five minutes ❧ 三小时 three hours ❧ 两天 two days

To ask about how long someone does an activity, place the question word 几小时 after the verb. If the verb takes an object, place the question word between them; 的 may be added after the question word:

Examples: ❶ 你每天上网几小时？ How long do you go online every day?

❷ 他每天看几小时(的)电视？ How long does he watch TV every day?

In reply, replace the question word with the duration phrase:

Examples ❶ 我每天上网两小时。 I go online for two hours every day.

❷ 他每天看一小时(的)电视。 He watches TV for an hour every day.

In the earlier section, you learned how to use 次 to indicate frequency. To ask about how frequently someone does an activity, place the question word 几次 after the verb. If the verb takes an object, place the question word between them. In the reply statement, 几次 is replaced by the frequency phrase.

Questions	Answers
❧ 你每星期运动几次？ How often do you exercise every week?	我每星期运动三次。 I exercise three times a week.
❧ 他每个月看几次电影？ How often does he go to the movies every month?	他每个月看两次电影。 He goes to the movies twice a month.

CULTURAL HIGHLIGHTS

Chinese Therapeutic Massage - Tuina

Tuina (推拿, tuīná) is a Chinese therapeutic approach guided by Traditional Chinese Medicine (TCM) and was first used to treat pediatric diseases through massage manipulations. A very important component of Chinese medicine, it is often used in conjunction with acupuncture and herbal prescriptions.

The practitioner may brush, knead, roll/press, or rub the areas between each of the joints to attempt to open the body's defensive qi (卫气, wèiqì) and get the energy moving in the meridians and the muscles. The practitioner can then use a range of motion, traction, and massage, with the stimulation of acupressure points. These techniques are believed to aid in the treatment of both acute and chronic musculoskeletal conditions, as well as many non-musculoskeletal conditions.

Today Tuina has become very advanced in its treatment for many diseases and is used in many hospitals in China in the front line of healthcare.

1. Survey at least 10 members of your class and ask them the following questions:

   ❶ 你每星期运动多长时间？　　　❺ 你每天打几小时的电话？

   ❷ 你每天睡几小时的觉？　　　　❻ 你每星期上网聊天几小时？

   ❸ 你每天看几小时的电视？　　　❼ 你每星期做几小时的作业？

   ❹ 你每天上网几小时？　　　　　❽ 你每个月买几次东西？

   Create a table like the one below where you write one of your classmate's names and the answer to each question.

Student's Name	❶	❷	❸	❹	❺	❻	❼	❽

   When you have all of the answers, make a separate pie chart or a bar graph for the answers to at least three of the questions.

2. Imagine that you and another classmate are running a fitness center where you train celebrities. You are the personal trainer for a celebrity who will play a new role in an action film and your partner is the nutritional expert. The celebrity needs to look very fit, be agile and flexible, be able to do some of her own stunts, and have a glowing complexion. Between the two of you, devise a diet plan and exercise routine for her so that in six weeks she will be ready to start the film. Write down the specifics of what she has to eat and do and how often. You can present your plan to the class.

Reading *in Context*

STEP 1 EATING WELL

Two students talking about foods they like

马克：张安，你喜欢吃快餐吗？

张安：喜欢，非常喜欢。

马克：你喜欢吃什么快餐？

张安：我喜欢吃肯德基、麦当劳什么的。你呢？你喜欢吃麦当劳和肯德基吗？

马克：喜欢，但是我妈妈说不要多吃。

张安：为什么？

马克：她说，这些快餐虽然好吃，但是多吃对健康不好。也不要常常喝可乐、雪碧什么的，因为这些饮料的糖份很高，常喝对身体也不好。

张安：那我们还是少吃快餐吧。

马克：是的。除了快餐，你还喜欢吃什么？

张安：我喜欢吃中国菜！

马克：我也很喜欢。明天中午我们一起去中餐馆吃午饭吧。

张安：好！

kuàicān	fast food
Kěndéjī	Kentucky Fried Chicken
Màidāngláo	MacDonald's
shuō	say
chángcháng	often
Xuěbì	Sprite
yìqǐ	together

STEP 2 GETTING SICK

Seeing the doctor

医生：请坐，你怎么了？

丁强：医生，我可能感冒了。

医生：发烧吗？

丁强：我觉得有点儿发烧。

医生：量量体温吧。

（量体温）

医生：我看看多少度。38.7度，你发烧了。你咳嗽吗？

丁强：咳嗽，喉咙也疼。

医生：流鼻涕吗？

丁强：流鼻涕，头也很疼。

医生：你得打针。

丁强：医生，我不想打针，给我开(一)些药，行吗？

医生：行。你想吃中药还是西药？

丁强：我想吃中药。

医生：好。我给你开一点儿中药，再开一点儿西药。回家多喝水。

丁强：谢谢医生。

STEP 3 DEVELOPING HEALTHY HABITS

Two students talking about health and exercise

安琪：芳芳，这几天没见到你。你还好吗？

芳芳：我这几天感冒了，还发高烧。今天好多了。

安琪：那就好，你应该多休息，还要多喝水。

芳芳：我觉得是因为我很少运动，所以容易生病。

安琪：你最后一次运动是什么时候？

芳芳：我想大概是两个月前。

安琪：那你真的应该多运动了。我每个星期一、三、五跑步半小时，星期六和朋友打网球一小时。你什么时候有空？我们一起去跑步。

芳芳：跑步太累了，我比较喜欢打网球。

安琪：那也行，我们就这个星期六去打网球吧。

芳芳：好，星期六见！

dàgài	about
zhēnde	really
yǒukòng	free

Step Up!

1. Read the following menu from a Chinese restaurant and decide which dishes you will order for your class's teacher appreciation banquet. Make sure that the meal is balanced with the following food groups: 主食, 开胃菜 (kāiwèicài, appetizer), 肉类, 蔬菜, 海鲜. Circle or check off the dishes that you are ordering. You have a budget of $250 for the entire class's meal and the $250 includes beverages.

美食园 电话：61234567

特色小炒 (tèsè xiǎochǎo) — yuán 元

白切鸡（半只）(báiqiējī bànzhī)	35元
三杯鸡（半只）(sānbēijī bànzhī)	35元
烧鸡（半只）(sháojī bànzhī)	35元
香煎粉肠 (xiāngjiānfěncháng)	30元
椒盐／酸甜排骨 (jiāoyán suāntián páigǔ)	35元
青瓜炒肉片 (qīngguā chǎoròupiàn)	22元
凉瓜炒牛肉 (liánggguā chǎo niúròu)	28元
姜葱炒牛百合 (jiāngcōng chǎo niúbǎihé)	30元
家常豆腐 (jiācháng dòufu)	18元
客家酿豆腐 (kèjiā niàngdòufu)	20元
酿三宝 (niàngsānbǎo)	22元
客家菜甫煎蛋 (kèjiā càifǔ jiāndàn)	18元
番茄炒蛋 (fānqié chǎodàn)	20元

海鲜类 (hǎixiānlèi)

姜葱炒花蟹 (jiāngcōng chǎohuāxiè)	时价
生鱼二食 (shēngyú èrshí)	时价
豉汁蒸带子 (chǐzhī zhēngdàizi)	时价
清蒸鲈鱼 (qīngzhēng lúyú)	时价
豉汁蒸鲇鱼 (chǐzhī zhēng niányú)	时价
清蒸桂花鱼 (qīngzhēng guìhuāyú)	时价

蒸类 (zhēnglèi)

咸鱼蒸五花肉 (xiányú zhēng wǔhuāròu)	32元
豉汁蒸排骨 (chǐzhī zhēng páigǔ)	32元
冬菇蒸滑鸡（半只）(dōnggū zhēng huájī bànzhī)	35元

煲仔 (bāozǎi)

红烧／鱼香茄子煲 (hóngshāo yúxiāng qiézibāo)	18元
金菇日本豆腐煲 (jīngū rìběn dòufubāo)	20元
客家蛋角煲 (kèjiā dànjiǎobāo)	22元
萝卜牛腩煲 (luóbo niúnánbāo)	32元
梅菜扣肉煲 (méicài kòuròubāo)	32元

铁板 (tiěbǎn)

铁板田鸡 (tiěbǎn tiánjī)	28元
铁板牛肉 (tiěbǎn niúròu)	32元
铁板猪肚 (tiěbǎn zhūdù)	32元

青菜类 (qīngcàilèi)

手拍青瓜 (shǒupāi qīngguā)	10元
蒜茸炒时菜 (suànróng chǎoshícài)	15元
椒丝腐乳炒通菜 (jiāosī fúrǔ chǎotōngcài)	15元
上汤时菜 (shàngtāng shícài)	18元

川菜 (chuāncài)

麻婆豆腐 (mápó dòufu)	18元
酸辣土豆丝 (suānlà tǔdòusī)	18元
干煸豆角 (gānbiān dòujiāo)	20元
鱼香肉丝 (yúxiāng ròusī)	20元
尖椒回锅肉 (jiānjiāo huíguōròu)	28元
辣子鸡 (làzijī)	32元
水煮牛肉 (shuǐzhǔ niúròu)	32元

汤类 (tānglèi)

紫菜蛋花汤 (zǐcài dànhuātāng)	18元
鱼头豆腐汤 (yútóu dòufutāng)	25元
枸杞猪杂汤 (gǒuqǐ zhūzátāng)	25元

主食 (zhǔshí)

三丝炒米粉 (sānsī chǎomǐfěn)	15元
豉油皇炒面 (chǐyóu huángchǎomiàn)	15元
干炒（湿炒）牛河 (gānchǎo shīchǎo niúhé)	15元

2. Using the menu that you have created for the teacher appreciation banquet, work with another classmate and come up with one list of foods that you both like. You will need to eliminate some foods to come up with a joint list. You will also need to revise your menu because, in the $250 budget, you did not include 15% for tips. Between the two of you, come up with a new menu for the banquet that includes beverages and tips.

3. The day after the banquet, you are not feeling well and decide to go to see the doctor. With a partner, create a skit of your visit to the doctor. Be sure to include a description of your symptoms and also the type of treatment or medication that the doctor prescribes. Be sure that the doctor also recommends a health regimen for the patient's future health. There must be at least 20 exchanges of information between the patient and the doctor.

4. Write up a plan for the next six months that you will do to become healthier. Use bullets to detail the information in your plan. Be sure to include foods that you will eat and drink, exercise that you will do, and other healthy habits that you will engage in. Your plan should have at least 10 bulleted items of information.

Fun Time!

Read the proverbs and sayings in Chinese and see if you can figure out their meaning. Then read the proverbs and sayings that are from different cultures but written in English, and see if they match any of the Chinese sayings. Give your reasons for why you think they are similar or not.

Then choose one saying in Chinese that is your favorite and tell another classmate why.

1. Fàn hòu bǎi bù zǒu, huódào jiǔshí jiǔ.
   饭 后 百 步 走, 活 到 九 十 九。

2. Xiào kǒu cháng kāi, qīngchūncháng zài.
   笑 口 常 开, 青 春 常 在。

3. Chīhǎo shuìhǎo, chángshēng bù lǎo.
   吃 好 睡 好, 长 生 不 老

4. Fàn qián xǐshǒu, fàn hòu shùkǒu.
   饭 前 洗 手, 饭 后 漱 口。

5. Yào xiǎng rén chángshòu, duō chī dòufu shǎo chī ròu.
   要 想 人 长 寿, 多 吃 豆 腐 少 吃 肉。

6. Zǎo shuì zǎo qǐ shēntǐ hǎo.
   早 睡 早 起 身 体 好。

7. Fàn chī bāfēn bǎo, dào lǎo wèikǒu hǎo.
   饭 吃 八 分 饱, 到 老 胃 口 好。

8. Měi tiān yì píngguǒ, yīshēng yuǎnlí wǒ.
   每 天 一 苹 果, 医 生 远 离 我。

9. Shǎo chī duō cān, yì shòu yán nián.
   少 吃 多 餐, 益 寿 延 年。

10. Dàsuàn shì gè bǎo, cháng chī shēntǐ hǎo.
    大 蒜 是 个 宝, 常 吃 身 体 好。

1. An apple a day keeps the doctor away.
   (Benjamin Franklin, American)

2. Early to bed and early to rise makes a man healthy, wealthy, and wise.
   (Benjamin Franklin, American)

3. Laughter is the best medicine.
   (American proverb)

4. An ounce of prevention is worth a pound of cure.
   (Benjamin Franklin, American)

5. If you don't take care of your body, where are you going to live?
   (Unknown)

6. Our bodies are our gardens – our wills are our gardeners.
   (William Shakespeare, English)

7. The greatest wealth is health.
   (Virgil, Roman poet)

8. A man too busy to take care of his health is like a mechanic too busy to take care of his tools.
   (Spanish proverb)

9. Fresh air impoverishes the doctor.
   (Danish proverb)

10. From the bitterness of disease man learns the sweetness of health.
    (Catalan proverb)

245

I have learned...

Core Vocabulary

Verbs

生病		shēngbìng	fall sick	打针	打針	dǎzhēn	give an injection
扭伤	扭傷	niǔshāng	sprain	用		yòng	to use
擦伤	擦傷	cāshāng	graze, scratch	运动	運動	yùndòng	exercise
受伤	受傷	shòushāng	be injured	健身		jiànshēn	train the body
开药	開藥	kāiyào	prescribe medicine	休息		xiūxi	rest

Nouns

Food-related

面食	麵食	miànshí	flour products (pasta, pancakes, bread, dumplings, etc.)	卡路里		kǎlùlǐ	calories
主食		zhǔshí	staple foods (rice, noodles, dumplings, etc.)	蛋白质	蛋白質	dànbáizhì	protein
副食		fùshí	non-staple foods (meat and vegetable dishes)	碳水化合物		tànshuǐhuàhéwù	carbohydrate
甜点	甜點	tiándiǎn	dessert	脂肪		zhīfáng	fat
饮料	飲料	yǐnliào	beverages	维生素	維生素	wéishēngsù	vitamin
零食		língshí	snacks	纤维	纖維	xiānwéi	fiber
食品		shípǐn	food products (cooked or processed items)	钠	鈉	nà	sodium
种类	種類	zhǒnglèi	category	钙	鈣	gài	calcium
营养	營養	yíngyǎng	nutrition	铁	鐵	tiě	iron
能量		néngliàng	energy	糖份		tángfèn	sugar content
维生素	維生素	wéishēngsù	vitamin	胆固醇	膽固醇	dǎngùchún	cholesterol

Parts of the body

背		bèi	back	手腕		shǒuwàn	wrist
腰		yāo	waist	脚腕	腳腕子	jiǎowàn	ankle
喉咙	喉嚨	hóulong	throat	胳膊肘儿	胳膊肘兒	gēbozhóur	elbow
胸口		xiōngkǒu	chest				

Common toiletries

肥皂		féizào	soap	洗发液	洗髮液	xǐfàyè	hair shampoo
沐浴液		mùyùyè	body wash	牙膏		yágāo	toothpaste

牙刷		yáshuā	toothbrush	毛巾		máojīn	towel
牙线	牙綫	yáxiàn	dental floss	面巾纸	面巾紙	miànjīnzhǐ	kleenex, tissue
漱口水		shùkǒushuǐ	mouth wash	指甲刀		zhǐjiadāo	nail cutter
梳子		shūzi	comb				

Time

				Others			
分钟	分鐘	fēnzhōng	minute	卫生	衛生	wèishēng	hygiene
小时	小時	xiǎoshí	hour	习惯	習慣	xíguàn	habit

Adjectives

				Measure words			
健康		jiànkāng	healthy	次		cì	*(referring to the number of times an action occurs)* time
有的		yǒude	some	片		piàn	capsule
舒服		shūfu	comfortable	**Auxiliary verb**			
过度	過度	guòdù	excessively, too much	应该	應該	yīnggāi	should, ought to

Question word

				Preposition			
怎么了	怎麼了	zěnme le	what	给	給	gěi	to, for

Adverb

				Particle			
太		tài	too	吧		ba	*(giving suggestions)*

Conjunctions

除了……以外		chúle...yǐwài	except for; in addition to
虽然…但是…	雖然…但是…	suīrán...dànshì...	although...*(but)*

Constructions

对……好	對……好	duì...hǎo	good for...
对……有好处	對……有好處	duì...yǒu hǎochù	is beneficial to...

Phrases
Food-related

谷物类	穀物類	gǔwù lèi	grains	蔬菜类	蔬菜類	shūcài lèi	vegetables *(category)*
奶类	奶類	nǎi lèi	milk category	肉类	肉類	ròu lèi	meats *(category)*
奶制品	奶製品	nǎizhìpǐn	dairy products	海鲜类	海鮮類	hǎixiān lèi	seafood *(category)*
豆类	豆類	dòu lèi	beans *(category)*	油脂类	油脂類	yóuzhī lèi	fats and oils *(category)*
豆制品	豆製品	dòuzhìpǐn	bean products	水果类	水果類	shuǐguǒ lèi	fruits *(category)*

I have learned...

坚果类	坚果類	jiānguǒ lèi	nuts (category)	饱和脂肪	飽和脂肪	bǎohé zhīfáng	saturated fat
食物标签	食物標籤	shíwù biāoqiān	food label	反式脂肪		fǎnshì zhīfáng	trans fat
营养成分	營養成分	yíngyǎng chéngfèn	nutritional content				

Common illnesses

头疼	頭疼	tóu téng	headache	咳嗽		késòu	cough
牙疼		yá téng	toothache	打喷嚏	打噴嚏	dǎpēntì	sneeze
背疼		bèi téng	backache	流鼻涕		liú bítì	running nose
肚子疼		dùzi téng	stomach ache	拉肚子		lādùzi	diarrhea
喉咙疼	喉嚨疼	hóulong téng	sore throat	消化不良		xiāohuà bù liáng	indigestion
胸口疼		xiōngkǒu téng	chest pain	胃口不好		wèikǒu bù hǎo	have no appetite
感冒		gǎnmào	flu	呼吸困难	呼吸困難	hūxī kùnnan	have difficulty breathing
发烧	發燒	fāshāo	fever				

Healthy habits

洗手		xǐ shǒu	wash your hands	擦身体	擦身體	cā shēntǐ	wipe your body
洗头	洗頭	xǐtóu	wash your hair	擦鼻涕		cā bítì	blow your nose
刷牙		shuāyá	brush your teeth	剪指甲		jiǎn zhǐjia	cut your nails
清洁牙齿	清潔牙齒	qīngjié yáchǐ	clean your teeth	早睡早起		zǎo shuì zǎo qǐ	go to sleep early, get up early
漱口		shùkǒu	rinse your mouth	做体检	做體檢	zuò tǐjiǎn	have a physical/ body check up
梳头	梳頭	shūtóu	comb your hair				

◆ SENTENCE PATTERNS ◆

我们喝茶<u>吧</u>。

豆类制品<u>除了</u>铁和钙<u>以外</u>，<u>还有</u>蛋白质。

<u>虽然</u>可乐很好喝，<u>但是</u>糖份很高。

你<u>哪里</u>不舒服？我肚子<u>痛</u>。

每天吃三<u>次</u>药。

她<u>用</u>洗发液洗头发。

吃饭<u>以前应该</u>先洗手。

我每天运动半小时。她每天刷两<u>次</u>牙。

I can do!

Interpretive Communication

❑ I can read and understand the label on Chinese foods and medicine.

❑ I can read a Chinese menu and choose which foods go best together.

❑ I can understand when the doctor tells me how to take my medicine.

❑ I can read and understand a written text on medications and healthy habits.

❑ I can classify foods according to their health benefits.

Interpersonal Communication

❑ I can discuss which foods are healthy and which are not.

❑ I can exchange information about illnesses.

❑ I can inquire about healthy habits and describe how I maintain fitness.

❑ I can ask for and get information on staying healthy.

Presentational Communication

❑ I can create a plan for eating healthy meals.

❑ I can describe the symptoms of an illness.

❑ I can talk about my daily routine and healthy habits.

❑ I can express how often to take medicine and to do exercises.

Cultural Knowledge

❑ I can describe Chinese food labels and compare them with Western labels.

❑ I can talk about a typical healthy Chinese meal.

❑ I can describe some aspects of Chinese acupuncture.

❑ I can talk about some techniques used in Chinese therapeutic massage.

❑ I can compare Chinese medicine with Western medicine.

Connecting with others

与人沟通

COMMUNICATIVE GOALS
- Describing computers and gadgets
- Talking about maintenance and repair
- Describing activities done with others
- Stating the source of news

Cultural Knowledge
- Lenovo and China's Silicon Valley
- E-commerce and instant messaging in China
- News in China

Get ready...

Internet use has been such an integral part of contemporary life; it is hard to imagine life without an Internet connection. Conduct a class poll on the most popular online activities your classmates do per week. First fill in the column labeled "我" and rank the activities in descending order according to the approximate amount of time spent on each of them each week. For example, if you spend the most time on blog writing, put "1" under the column for 写博客.

Use the form below to take a quick class poll on the ranking of the most popular online activities. Your teacher will ask you to report the results to the whole class.

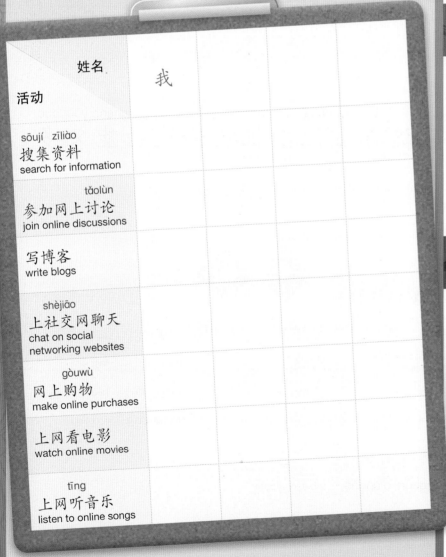

姓名 活动	我					
sōují zīliào 搜集资料 search for information						
tǎolùn 参加网上讨论 join online discussions						
写博客 write blogs						
shèjiāo 上社交网聊天 chat on social networking websites						
gòuwù 网上购物 make online purchases						
上网看电影 watch online movies						
tīng 上网听音乐 listen to online songs						

STEPS *at a glance!*

 STEP 1

USING TECHNOLOGY IN DAILY LIFE

A. Describing computers and gadgets

这台电脑既轻巧又耐用。

B. Talking about maintenance and repair

电脑坏了。电脑修好了。

打印机坏了，所以我买了一台新的。

C. Talking about technical glitches

网断了，现在上不了网。

 STEP 2

COMMUNICATING WITH OTHERS

A. Maintaining contact using technology

我用网络视频电话跟朋友一起聊天。

B. Doing one thing or another

他不是玩网络游戏，就是在网上购物。

 STEP 3

GATHERING INFORMATION

A. Stating the source of news

我看了电视新闻才知道这个消息。他一上网就看到了这条新闻。

B. Using technology to gather information

只要上网查一查，就可以找到资料。

251

píngbǎn   jì qīngqiǎo yòu nàiyòng

这台平板电脑既轻巧又耐用。

This tablet computer is light and durable.

A Describing computers and gadgets

bù zhìnéng shǒujī jì kuàisù gōngnéng yòu duō

这部智能手机既快速功能又多。

This smartphone is fast and multifunctional.

生 词 NEW WORDS

既…又…		jì…yòu…	both…and…	实用 adj.	實用	shíyòng	easy to use
部 m.w.		bù	(used for mobile phones)	快速 adj.		kuàisù	fast
轻巧 adj.	輕巧	qīngqiǎo	light	美观 adj.	美觀	měiguān	beautiful, sleek
耐用 adj.		nàiyòng	durable	功能 n.		gōngnéng	function

IT products

平板电脑 phr.	平板電腦	píngbǎn diànnǎo	tablet computer
智能手机 phr.	智能手機	zhìnéng shǒujī	smartphone
数码相机 phr.	數碼相機	shùmǎ xiàngjī	digital camera
摄像机 phr.	攝像機	shèxiàngjī	video camera

打印机 n.	打印機	dǎyìnjī	printer
键盘 n.	鍵盤	jiànpán	keyboard
鼠标 n.	鼠標	shǔbiāo	mouse
显示屏 n.	顯示屏	xiǎnshìpíng	monitor
耳机 n.	耳機	ěrjī	earphones, headphones

LANGUAGE FOCUS

The construction 既…又… means "both...and" or "as well as." It is placed after the subject to talk about two features of the subject that are of the same importance. The features are each placed after 既 and 又.

For example:

❶ 这个数码相机既轻巧又美观。 This digital camera is light and sleek.

❷ 这台打印机既快速功能又多。 This printer is fast and has many functions.

CULTURAL HIGHLIGHTS

Lenovo and China's Silicon Valley

Lenovo Group Limited (联想集团 Liánxiǎng Jítuán) is a Chinese multinational technology firm with headquarters in Beijing, China, and Morrisville, North Carolina. Lenovo was founded in Beijing in 1984 and incorporated in Hong Kong in 1988 under its previous name, Legend. It sells personal computers, tablet computers, smartphones, workstations, servers, electronic storage devices, IT management software, and smart televisions. In 2005 Lenovo purchased IBM's PC division for $1.75 billion, making it the world's third-largest PC maker. In 2012, Lenovo was the world's second-largest personal computer vendor by unit sales. Lenovo markets the ThinkPad line of notebook computers and the ThinkCentre line of desktops.

Lenovo's headquarters in Beijing is located at Zhongguancun (中关村 Zhōngguāncūn), a technology hub in the Haidian District. Zhongguancun is geographically situated in the northwestern part of Beijing city, in a band between the northwestern Third Ring Road and the northwestern Fourth Ring Road. Zhongguancun is very well known in China, and is often referred to as "China's Silicon Valley."

Many world renowned technology companies, such as Google, Intel, AMD, Oracle Corporation, Motorola, Sony, and Ericsson, built their Chinese headquarters and research centers in Zhongguancun Technology Park. Microsoft has built its Chinese research headquarters in the park at a cost of $280 million. The research facility accommodates 5000 employees and was completed in April, 2011.

Try This!

1. State two possible features of each of the items below using 既…又….

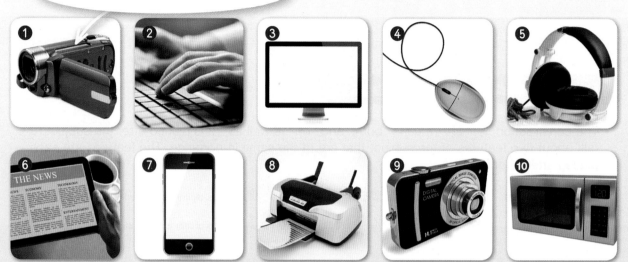

这台摄影机既轻巧又美观。

① ② ③ ④ ⑤

⑥ ⑦ ⑧ ⑨ ⑩

2. Use the words below to make sentences containing 既…又….

Example:

打印机　　便宜　　功能多 ⟶ 这台打印机既便宜功能又多。

❶ 鼠标　　　美观　　耐用　　　_____

❷ 智能手机　方便　　功能多　　_____

❸ 平板电脑　快速　　实用　　　_____

❹ 数码相机　耐用　　轻巧　　　_____

❺ 雨伞　　　好看　　便宜　　　_____

❻ 书桌　　　实用　　美观　　　_____

❼ 牛奶　　　有营养　好喝　　　_____

❽ 我的暑假　轻松　　有趣　　　_____
　　　　　　qīngsōng　yǒuqù
　　　　　　relaxing　interesting

❾ 中国菜　　便宜　　好吃　　　_____

❿ 去夏令营　有用　　好玩　　　_____
　　　　　　　　　　hǎowán
　　　　　　　　　　fun

B Talking about maintenance and repair

huài
电脑坏了。
The computer is broken.

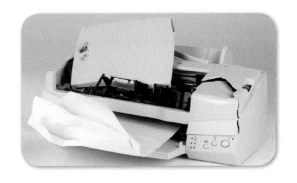

打印机坏了，所以我买了一台新的。
The printer is broken, so I bought a new one.

生 词

NEW WORDS

坏 adj.	壞	huài	broken	修理 v.		xiūlǐ	repair, fix
死机 v.	死機	sǐjī	freeze (computing)	安装 v.	安裝	ānzhuāng	install
中病毒 phr.		zhòng bìngdú	be infected with a computer virus	组装 v.	組裝	zǔzhuāng	assemble

Computers and accessories

主机 n.	主機	zhǔjī	host
硬盘 n.	硬盤	yìngpán	hard disk
U 盘 n.	U 盤	U pán	thumb drive
软件 n.	軟件	ruǎnjiàn	software
防毒软件 phr.	防毒軟件	fángdú ruǎnjiàn	antivirus software
声卡 n.	聲卡	shēngkǎ	sound card
显卡 n.	顯卡	xiǎnkǎ	video card, graphics card
数据线 phr.	數據線	shùjù xiàn	data cable
耳机口 phr.	耳機口	ěrjī kǒu	earphone plug
麦克风口 phr.	麥克風口	màikèfēng kǒu	microphone plug
电源插口 phr.	電源插口	diànyuán chākǒu	power plug

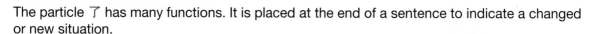
The particle 了 has many functions. It is placed at the end of a sentence to indicate a changed or new situation.

Examples: ❶ 手机坏了。 The mobile phone is broken.

❷ 电脑中病毒了。 The computer is infected with a virus.

❸ 软件安装好了。 The software has been installed.

了 can also be placed after an action verb to indicate the completion of an action.

Examples: ❶ 我买了一台打印机。 I bought a printer.

❷ 他修理好了电脑。 He fixed the computer.

In the examples above, 好 functions as a complement and is placed after a verb to indicate the successful completion of an action.

1. Rearrange the words to form proper sentences.

❶ 好 主机 了 组装

_____

❷ 修理 了 好 打印机

_____

❸ 丁强 的 了 电脑 安装 硬盘 好

_____

❹ 新 安装 的 软件 好 了

_____

❺ U盘 你 要 的 了 买到

_____

❻ 好 显示屏 了 修理

_____

❼ 装好 你 的 声卡 电脑 了

_____

❽ 中病毒 电脑 软件 了 要 防毒 安装

_____

2. Change the action in each sentence into a completed action by adding 了 and an appropriate time word.

Example: 我去图书馆借两本书。 ⟶ 昨天我去图书馆借了两本书。

❶ 哥哥安装防毒软件。

❷ 张安去商店买一个智能手机。

❸ 我组装一台电脑。

❹ 丁强修理一台打印机。

❺ 马克安装一个声卡。

❻ 我们去电影院看一个电影。

❼ 爸爸在银行存一些钱。

❽ 妈妈在超级市场买一些菜。

❾ 安琪在餐馆吃晚餐。

❿ 我去医院做一下体检。

3. Read the following paragraph and answer the questions in Chinese.

上个学期爸爸给我买了一台新电脑。这台电脑是银灰色的，有一个27寸（cùn / inch）的显示屏，机箱上有四个USB插口，还有无线（wúxiàn / wireless）键盘和无线鼠标。我非常喜欢我的新电脑，常常（chángcháng / often）用电脑做作业，上网和朋友聊天。可是（kěshì / but）前天我想和马丁用Skype聊天的时候，电脑显示屏突然（tūrán / suddenly）黑了。我试（shì / try）了好几次，还换（huàn / change）了电源插口，还是打不开显示屏。我很担心（dānxīn / worried），所以给电脑公司（gōngsī / company）打了一个电话。昨天下午，师傅（shīfu / skilled worker）来给我修理电脑了。他检查（jiǎnchá / check）了显示屏，也检查了电源插口。最后（zuìhòu / in the end），他说我的电脑不是显示屏坏了，而是（érshì / but）中病毒了。他告诉（gàosu / tell）我应该安装一个新软件。今天上午我去商店里买了新软件。刚才（gāngcái / just now）新软件已经安装好了。现在我的电脑已经（yǐjīng / already）修好了，我高兴极了！

❶ 我的新电脑是什么颜色的？

❷ 我的新电脑是什么样子（yàngzi / appearance）的？

❸ 我常常用电脑做什么？

❹ 我的电脑有什么问题（wèntí / problem）？

❺ 我自己（zìjǐ / oneself）是怎么修理的？

❻ 电脑公司的师傅是怎么修理的？

❼ 师傅说我的电脑有什么问题？

❽ 他建议（jiànyì / suggest）我怎么做？

❾ 我的电脑现在怎么样？

❿ 你修理过电脑吗？你的电脑出了什么问题？怎么修理的？

liǎo
现在上得了网吗？
Can you access the Internet now?

duàn
网断了，现在上不了网。
The connection is broken and I can't access the Internet now.

kāi
你开得了机吗？
Can you turn on the computer?

chū wèntí
电脑出问题了，我开不了机。
The computer has some problems and I can't turn it on.

NEW WORDS 生 词

断 v.	斷	duàn	disconnect
了 v.		liǎo	*(used after 得 or 不 to indicate the possibility or impossibility of accomplishing something)*
出 v.		chū	occur, arise
问题 n.	問題	wèntí	problem
开机 phr.	開機	kāi jī	turn on *(machine)*
关机 phr.	關機	guān jī	turn off *(machine)*

LANGUAGE FOCUS

In addition to the usages introduced earlier, 了 can function as a potential complement to express the possibility of completing an activity successfully. It can also be used to express the ability to complete an action. As a potential complement, 了 is pronounced as liǎo. The positive form is "verb + 得 + 了," and the negative form is "verb + 不 + 了."

For example: **1** 电脑修得了。   The computer can be fixed.

2 我关不了机。   I can't turn off the computer.

3 我牙疼，吃不了东西。   I have a toothache and can't eat anything.

1. Match the questions with the correct answers. Next, read each pair of question and answer aloud. Pay special attention to the pronunciation of 了 in different cases.

Questions	Answers
1 现在上得了网吗?	a. 电脑有病毒，所以我可能修不了。
2 这台电脑，开得了机吗?	b. 我不吃辣，所以吃不了这个菜。
3 我的电脑，你修得了吗?	c. 网断了，所以现在上不了网。
4 这么多事情，你做得了吗?	d. 现在我放假了，所以我做得了。
5 这个菜很辣，你吃得了吗?	e. 这台电脑的电源插口坏了，所以开不了机了。

2. Rewrite the following sentences using 了.
      ^{liǎo}

    Example: 现在没有电，不能看电视。 ⟶ 现在没有电，看不了电视。
                      can

1 东西太多了，我不能拿。
          take (ná)

2 书房的门坏了，不能开了。

3 我的电脑修好了，能上网了。

4 我没有车，不能去那么远的地方。

5 我很饿，能吃两个三明治。
    hungry (è)

6 我不累，能跑五公里。

7 我的房间很小，不能放这么多东西。
    place (fàng)

8 我的电脑硬盘很大，可以安装这么多软件。

259

3. Read the following paragraph and answer the following questions.

我很喜欢玩电脑游戏，可是我最大的爱好还是上网。上网太有意思了，可以查资料、买东西、看电影、听音乐，还可以和朋友们聊天。我每天上网的时间超过三个小时，我的朋友们都叫我"网迷"。今天早上，我打开电脑，发现上不了网了。我非常着急，马上给电脑公司打了电话。可是电脑公司的师傅来检查了以后说，我的电脑没坏，因为网断了，所以我才上不了网。我又给电话公司打电话，可是他们的师傅说因为工作太多，今天来不了。他还说，明天下午才来得了。这可怎么办呢？我太着急了。

chá zīliào — search for information
péngyou — friend
chāoguò — exceed
wǎngmí — cyber fan
zháojí — anxious
mǎshàng — immediately
shuō — say
how

❶ 我的爱好有什么？

❷ 我为什么最喜欢上网？

❸ 我的朋友们都叫我什么？为什么？

❹ 今天早上我的电脑怎么了？

❺ 我是怎么做的？

❻ 我的电脑为什么上不了网了？

❼ 电话公司的师傅为什么不来给我修理？

❽ 他什么时候才能来？

wǎngluò shìpín diànhuà gēn péngyou yìqǐ
我 用 网 络 视 频 电 话 跟 朋 友 一 起 聊 天 。

I chat with friends using Skype.

A Maintaining contact using technology

liǎnshū   liánxì
姐 姐 用 脸 书 跟 同 学 联 系 。

My older sister connects with her classmates using Facebook.

NEW WORDS

跟 prep.		gēn	with	社交媒体 phr.	社交媒體	shèjiāo méitǐ	social media
一起 prep.		yìqǐ	together with	脸书 n.	臉書	liǎnshū	Facebook
朋友 n.		péngyou	friend	推特 n.		tuītè	Twitter
联系 v.	聯系	liánxì	keep in touch	微博 n.		wēibó	Weibo (microblog)
分享 v.		fēnxiǎng	share	博客 n.		bókè	blog
通话 v.	通話	tōnghuà	talk over the phone	互联网/英特网 n.	互聯網/英特網	hùliánwǎng/yīngtèwǎng	Internet
信息 n.		xìnxī	information	网络视频电话 phr.	網絡視頻電話	wǎngluò shìpín diànhuà	online video call

LANGUAGE FOCUS

The preposition 跟 is used to indicate involvement. It introduces the person with whom the subject does a certain activity, as in the pattern of "跟 + person + (一起) + verb (phrase)." This pattern is placed right after the subject to indicate the person and the activity that the subject and the person do together. 一起 may be omitted without causing ambiguity.

Examples: ❶ 我跟哥哥(一起)玩电脑游戏。
I play computer games with my older brother.

❷ 她跟妹妹(一起)分享信息。
She shares information with her younger sister.

An adverbial phrase or expression can be added before the pattern to provide more details about the activity.

Examples: ❶ 我在网上跟哥哥(一起)玩电脑游戏。
I play computer games with my older brother online.

❷ 她用推特跟妹妹(一起)分享信息。
She shares information with her younger sister using Twitter.

Try This!

1. Look at the pictures and make sentences describing the activity the person is doing and with whom. Use 跟……一起.

芳芳跟姐姐一起聊天。

 ❶ 芳芳 | 姐姐

 ❷ 丁强 | 哥哥

 ❸ 安琪 | 芳芳

 ❹ 张安 | 弟弟

 ❺ 马克 | 丁强

 ❻ 丽丽 | 芳芳

 ❼ 哥哥 | 我

 ❽ 姐姐 | 爸爸

2. Refer to Question 1 and the sentences you have made. Add an adverbial expression to each sentence based on the pictures below.

芳芳用网络视频电话跟姐姐一起聊天。

3. Interview at least five classmates about what they like to do. Ask questions about the hobbies they have, how frequently they do the activity, and with whom. Refer to the sample questions below and record your findings in a table. Then share your findings with the class.

你有什么爱好？　你每个星期……几次？　你跟谁一起……？

姓名 (Category of food)	爱好	次数	跟谁一起做
丁强	打篮球	每星期两次	同学、哥哥

wǎngluò
他不是玩网络游戏，
就是在网上购物。
He is either playing online games or buying things online.

xiàzài　　　gēqǔ
她不是下载网络歌曲，
shàngchuán zhàopiàn
就是上传照片。
She is either downloading songs or
uploading her photos.

生 词

NEW WORDS

Phrases you have learned

fā diànyóu		xiě bókè	
发电邮 *phr.* send emails		写博客 *phr.* write blogs	
shàngwǎng		(shàngwǎng) liáotiān	
上网 *phr.* go online		(上网) 聊天 *phr.* chat online	

Common online activities

听音乐 *phr.*	聽音樂	tīng yīnyuè	listen to music
读博客 *phr.*	讀博客	dú bókè	read blogs
看电邮 *phr.*	看電郵	kàn diànyóu	read emails
网(上)购(物) *phr.*	網(上)購(物)	wǎng(shàng) gòu(wù)	shop online
上传/载照片 *phr.*	上傳/載照片	shàngchuán/zài zhàopiàn	upload photos
下载歌曲 *phr.*	下載歌曲	xiàzài gēqǔ	download songs
搜集资料 *phr.*	搜集資料	sōují zīliào	find information
上社交网 *phr.*	上社交網	shàng shèjiāowǎng	visit social networking sites
玩网络游戏 *phr.*	玩網絡游戲	wán wǎngluò yóuxì	play online games
参加网上讨论 *phr.*	參加網上討論	cānjiā wǎngshàng tǎolùn	join online discussions
打网络视频电话 *phr.*	打網絡視頻電話	dǎ wǎngluò shìpín diànhuà	make online video calls

不是…就是… *conj.* | búshì…jiùshì… | either…or…

The paired conjunctions 不是…就是… express the meaning "it must be this or that." Each conjunction normally precedes a verb phrase that indicates one of the activities.

Examples:

❶ 弟弟不是上社交网，就是读博客。
My younger brother is either surfing social network websites or reading blogs.

❷ 姐姐不是参加网上讨论，就是看电邮。
My older sister is either joining online discussions or reading emails.

Try This!

1. Look at the pictures, and write a sentence describing the activities each of the people does using 不是…就是….

> 丁强不是打网络视频电话，
> 就是上社交网。

❶
丁强

❷
马克

❸
芳芳

❹
安琪

❺
张安

❻
玛丽

❼
哥哥

❽
姐姐

❾
妹妹

2. **Survey** Ask at least five of your classmates two things they like to do on the Internet. Then report your findings to the whole class using 不是…就是….

Examples: ❶ 你在网上喜欢做什么？我在网上喜欢购物，也喜欢聊天。
❷ 安琪不是在网上购物，就是在网上聊天。

姓名	活动一	活动二
安琪	购物	聊天

 CULTURAL HIGHLIGHTS

e-commerce and instant messaging in China

Taobao (淘宝 Táobǎo) and Alibaba (阿里巴巴 Ālǐbābā) are two of the most popular e-commerce sites in China. They were founded by Jack Ma (马云 Mǎ Yún), a Chinese Internet entrepreneur who was the first mainland Chinese entrepreneur to appear on the cover of Forbes Magazine and ranks as one of the world's billionaires.

Taobao Marketplace is a Chinese language website for online shopping, similar to eBay and Amazon, operated in the People's Republic of China by the Alibaba Group. Founded by the Alibaba Group on May 10, 2003, Taobao Marketplace facilitates consumer-to-consumer retail by providing a platform for small businesses and individual entrepreneurs to open online retail stores that generally cater to consumers in mainland China, Hong Kong, Macau, and Taiwan. Taobao features nearly a billion products and is one of the 20 most-visited websites globally.

The Alibaba Group is a privately owned Hangzhou-based family of Internet-based e-commerce businesses that cover business-to-business online marketplaces, retail and payment platforms, shopping search engines, and data-centric cloud computing services. The company began in 1999 with the web domain Alibaba.com, a business-to-business portal to connect Chinese manufacturers with overseas buyers. In 2012, two of Alibaba's portals together handled 1.1 trillion yuan ($170 billion) in sales. The company primarily operates in the People's Republic of China.

Besides e-commerce, instant messaging is extremely popular in China. Tencent QQ (腾讯QQ Téngxùn QQ), popularly known as QQ, is an instant messaging software service developed by Tencent Holdings Limited. QQ also offers a variety of services, including online social games, music, shopping, microblogging, and group and voice chat. As of March 20, 2013, there are 798.2 million active QQ accounts.

xīnwén cái zhīdào xiāoxi

我看了电视新闻才知道这个消息。

I learned about this news only after I watched the TV news.

A Stating the source of news

xīnwén

他一上网就看到了这条新闻。

He saw this news right after he went online.

NEW WORDS 生 词

才 adv.		cái	only then	消息 n.		xiāoxi	news, information
知道 v.		zhīdào	know, learn of	新闻 n.	新聞	xīnwén	news
获得 v.	獲得	huòdé	obtain, get hold of				

News sources

电视新闻 phr.	電視新聞	diànshì xīnwén	TV news
电台广播 phr.	電台廣播	diàntái guǎngbō	radio broadcast
报纸 n.	報紙	bàozhǐ	newspaper
报章报道 phr.	報章報導	bàozhāng bàodǎo	newspaper report
广告 n.	廣告	guǎnggào	advertisement
网上新闻 phr.	網上新聞	wǎngshàng xīnwén	online news

The adverb 才 is used before a verb to indicate that an action or event has just taken place. It conveys a sense of lateness or delay, and indicates that an action or event has occurred too late. It can combine two actions to state that the latter is later than what it is supposed to be.

Examples:
❶ 我早上十点才起床。
I didn't get up until 10 in the morning.

❷ 我听了电台广播才知道这个消息。
I didn't know of this news until I heard the radio broadcast.

You learned the adverb 就 in Lesson 5. In contrast to 才, the primary function of 就 is to stress promptness and indicate that an action or event has occurred early. When used to combine two actions, with the latter taking place shortly after the former, 一 is normally placed before the first verb. 了 is usually placed at the end of sentences with 就.

Examples:
❶ 我早上七点就起床了。
I woke up at 7 in the morning.

❷ 他一看报纸就读到这条新闻了。
He came across this news right after he read the newspaper.

❸ 她一看广告就获得这个信息了。
She obtained this information right after she saw the advertisement.

Try This!

1. Look at the pictures and make sentences stating the source of a news item. For each picture, make a sentence using 才 to indicate delay, and then another sentence using 就 to indicate promptness.

❶

Example:

• 他今天看了电视新闻才知道这个消息。

• 他昨天看电视新闻就知道这个消息了。

•

•

③

· _____

· _____

④

· _____

· _____

⑤

· _____

· _____

2. Fill in the blanks with 才 or 就.

❶ 丁强和张安很早_____认识了。

❷ 我昨晚12点_____睡觉，所以今天有点儿累。

❸ 安琪每天早上七点_____到学校了，马克八点半_____到学校。

❹ 他五岁_____学中文了。

❺ 他吃了晚饭_____去朋友家。

❻ 电脑坏了一个月马克_____拿去修理。

❼ 他一回家_____上网聊天。

❽ 芳芳听了天气预报_____知道下午有雷阵雨。
　　　　　yùbào
　　　　　forecast

❾ 爸爸一看报纸_____知道昨天发生的事了。
　　　　　　　　　　fāshēng　shì
　　　　　　　　　　happen　event

❿ 他看了电视新闻_____获得这个信息。

zhǐyào　　　　chá
只要上网查一查,
　　　　　　　zhǎo
　就可以找到资料。

As long as you do an online search, you will
find the information.

　　tīng　　　shǒu
只要到网上听听这首歌,
　就知道它好听不好听了。

As long as you go online and listen to this song, you will know
whether it sounded good or not.

NEW WORDS 生 词

只要…就… conj.		zhǐyào...jiù...	as long as, provided
查 v.		chá	check
找 v.		zhǎo	find, search
可以 aux.v.		kěyǐ	can, may
能 aux.v.		néng	can, be able to
首 m.w.		shǒu	(used for songs)
好听 adj.	好聽	hǎotīng	nice to listen to
搜索引擎 phr.		sōusuǒyǐnqíng	search engine

The paired conjunctions 只要…就… mean "as long as" or "provided." 只要 is placed at the beginning of a sentence to indicate an essential condition, and 就 leads the second part of the sentence to express the result if the condition is fulfilled. The auxiliary verbs 可以 and 能 can be used interchangeably after 就 to indicate ability or capability.

Examples: ❶ 只要用搜索引擎找一找，就可以找到信息。
As long as you use the search engine, you can find the information.

❷ 只要在报章上看看，就能找到资料。
As long as you read the newspaper, you can find the materials.

In Chinese, to express an action that lasts only for a short duration, the verb can be repeated to form a duplicated verb form "verb + verb." Alternatively, 一 can be inserted between the duplicated verb form to express the same meaning. Read the following examples.

- 看(一)看
- 听(一)听
- 找(一)找
- 查(一)查

CULTURAL HIGHLIGHTS

News in China

Sina Weibo (新浪微博 Xīnlàng Wēibó) is a Chinese microblogging website. It is one of the most popular sites in China, used by over 30% of people on the Internet. Launched in 2009, it has 503 million registered users by the end of 2012. About 100 million messages are posted each day on Sina Weibo, making it an important source of news and information in China.

Users may post with a 140-character limit, mention or talk to other people using the "@UserName" format, and add hashtags with the "#HashName#" format. They can also follow other people to make his/her posts appear in the users' own timeline, re-post with "//@UserName" similar to Twitter's retweet function "RT @UserName," put a post into the favorite list, and verify the account if the user is a celebrity. Users are also allowed to insert graphical emoticons or attach their own image, music, or video files in every post.

Baidu, Inc. (百度 Bǎidù), incorporated on January 18, 2000, is a Chinese web service company headquartered in the Baidu Campus in the Haidian District in Beijing. Baidu offers many services, including a Chinese language-search engine for websites, audio files, and images. It provides an index of over 740 million web pages, 80 million images, and 10 million multimedia files. Baidu offers 57 search and community services including Baidu Baike, an online collaboratively built encyclopedia, and a searchable, keyword-based discussion forum. During the last quarter of 2010, it was estimated that there were 4.02 billion search queries in China, of which Baidu had a market share of 56.6%.

1. Complete the following sentences.

❶ 只要到网上查一查，_____。

❷ 只要看一看电视新闻，_____。

❸ 只要听一听电台广播，_____。

❹ 只要在报纸上看看，_____。

❺ 只要在YouTube上看看，_____。

❻ _____，就可以看到这个广告。

❼ _____，就可以听到最新的交通信息。

❽ _____，就能找到这首歌。

❾ _____，就可以和家人视频聊天。

❿ _____，就可以找到银行的电话号码。

hàomǎ
number

2. Read the dialog and determine whether the following statements are true (T) or false (F).

芳芳：安琪，我暑假会跟家人一起去北京旅行。你知道北京有什么好玩的地方吗？

安琪：我没去过北京，所以不知道有什么好玩的地方。北京是大城市，你只要上网查一查，就可以找到资料。

芳芳：好吧，等下我用百度找一找，应该能找到一些有用的信息。你暑假有什么打算？

Bǎidù
useful

安琪：我想去打工。

芳芳：在哪里打工？

安琪：还没找到工作。你知道有什么好的工作吗？给我介绍一下？

jièshào
recommendation

芳芳：真对不起，我也不知道哪儿有好的工作。但是只要在

zhēn duìbuqǐ
really sorry

报纸上看看，就会找到一些暑期工。你也可以到网上

找一找。

安琪：好，我现在就去买份报纸看看，然后回家上网找

fèn
set

暑期工。

芳芳：祝你暑假愉快！

安琪：也祝你暑假愉快！

❶ 芳芳暑假要跟朋友去北京旅行。   （   ）

❷ 安琪知道北京有什么好玩的地方。   （   ）

❸ 芳芳要用百度查北京的资料。   （   ）

❹ 安琪暑假想去打工。   （   ）

❺ 安琪可以看报纸或听电台广播找暑期工。   （   ）

Reading *in Context*

STEP 1 USING TECHNOLOGY IN DAILY LIFE

Mark is having problems connecting to the Internet.

马克：妈妈，怎么上不了网啊？

妈妈：我也不知道为什么网断了。今天一天都上不了网。

马克：有没有通知？

妈妈：不知道。

马克：我打电话问问。

tōngzhī	notification
wènwèn	enquire
gōngsī	company

（马克给电话公司打电话）

马克：喂，是电话公司吗？

公司：是。

马克：今天怎么上不了网啊？

公司：对不起，今天你们那个小区出了一点儿事故，网络信号不好，我们贴了一个通知，但是现在已经修好了。

wéi	hello
duìbuqǐ	sorry
shìgù	problem
xìnhào tiē	signal post
yǐjīng	already

马克：是吗？可是我家的电脑还是上不了网啊。是不是网又断了？

公司：不可能，我们刚修好。

马克：您能不能现在来我家看看啊？

公司：对不起，现在去不了。师傅们都不在。他们都出去工作了。明天可以。我先给你登记一下，明天一上班就去你家。

马克：好吧。

gāng	just
shīfu	skilled workers
dēngjì	register

STEP 2 COMMUNICATING WITH OTHERS

Ding Qiang and Tony are talking about their cyber friends.

丁强：东尼，你有网友吗？

东尼：有哇。我有好几个网友，有美国网友，也有外国网友。

丁强：你有没有中国网友？

东尼：有一个。

丁强：你们常常联系吗？

东尼：常联系。我每个周末都用网络视频电话跟他聊天。

丁强：我也有一个中国网友，每个周末，我们不是一起玩网络游戏，就是上社交网分享信息。

东尼：我也喜欢玩网络游戏！什么时候把你的中国网友介绍给我，那我们就可以一起玩了。

丁强：好主意！

chángcháng	often
jièshào	introduce
zhǔyì	idea

STEP 3 GATHERING INFORMATION

Here are ways you can use the Internet:

网络让人们的生活发生了变化。离开网络，人们会觉得生活和工作很不方便。那么，人们上网做什么呢？

第一，网民利用因特网浏览新闻。他们关心国内外大事，一上网就可以很快知道世界上发生的大事。

第二，在网上跟朋友聊天，跟同事或网友联系。在网上不但可以聊天，而且还可以用视频跟对方见面。

第三，在网上查找资料。只要你打开电脑，在网上查一下，就能找到你要的资料，比去图书馆方便多了。

ràng 让	shēnghuó 生活	fāshēng 发生	biànhuà 变化	líkāi 离开	lìyòng 利用	liúlǎn 浏览
let	life	occur	change	leave	use	surf
guānxīn 关心	nèi 内	shì 事	shìjiè 世界	tóngshì 同事	jiànmiàn 见面	
show concern	inside	matter	world	colleague	meet face to face	

Step Up!

1. Imagine that your Chinese exchange school e-pal is the editor of his school magazine and the next issue of the magazine plans to focus on the topic of "The Internet and Our Lives." Your Chinese e-pal sent you the following article that a Chinese student wrote. Read it and answer the following questions.

我的网络生活

　　互联网给我们的生活❶带来了方便。只要一上网，就可以知道❷各种不同的新闻，还可以看到很多❸精美的视频画面。我❹需要的各种❺学习资料，在网上都能查到。我最喜欢的就是上QQ、聊聊天、发电邮、玩网络游戏。

　　因为❻平时很忙，所以我到了星期天才能上网。每个星期天，我都会用网络视频电话跟住在北京的姐姐聊天。我们不是聊我的学校生活，就是聊姐姐在北京的工作。打网络视频电话既❼快捷又❽节省电话❾费。我还能❿通过网络摄像机看到远在北京的姐姐呢。除了聊天，我还常在网上看电影、听音乐、玩游戏。

　　通过上网，我还⓫了解到了一些非常有意思的网络⓬用语，例如"伊(ē)妹儿"、"黑客(kè)"、"网虫(chóng)"、"大虾"、"菜鸟"等。每次我和姐姐聊天后⓭总得说"88"、"886"才⓮肯离去，意思就是：⓯拜拜，拜拜了。网络上还有电子银行和网上购物等，它们都很快捷方便。我和爸爸⓰交电话费时，都在电子银行交，只要几⓱秒钟就可以了。走进网络，就⓲像进入了⓳万花筒⓴世界一样㉑精彩。

　　网络给我们带来了㉒便利，㉓改变了我们的生活，我会好好㉔使用网络，让它㉕成为我学习的好㉖帮手。

dàilai ❶ 带来 bring	dàilai ❼ 快捷 fast	zǒng ⓭ 总 always	wànhuātǒng ⓳ 万花筒 kaleidoscope	chéngwéi ㉕ 成为 become
gèzhǒng bùtóng ❷ 各种不同 different types	jiéshěng ❽ 节省 save	kěn ⓮ 肯 willing	shìjiè ⓴ 世界 world	bāngshǒu ㉖ 帮手 helper
jīngměi ❸ 精美 beautiful	fèi ❾ 费 fee	bàibài ⓯ 拜拜 bye	jīngcǎi ㉑ 精彩 exciting	
xūyào ❹ 需要 need	tōngguò ❿ 通过 through	jiāo ⓰ 交 pay	biànlì ㉒ 便利 convenience	
xuéxí ❺ 学习 learning	liǎojiě ⓫ 了解 understand	miǎo ⓱ 秒 seconds	gǎibiàn ㉓ 改变 change	
píngshí ❻ 平时 normal times	yòngyǔ ⓬ 用语 phrase	xiàng ⓲ 像 just like	shǐyòng ㉔ 使用 use	

Adapted from: http://zuowen.sanwen.net/z/314667-wangluoshenghuo-wodi

A. Describe in English the main idea of this article in one sentence. Do not translate from the original Chinese title.

_____

B. Indicate whether the statements below are true (T) or false (F) based on the article.

    zuòzhě
❶ 作者每天都上网。
    author

❷ 作者说网络让生活非常方便，在网上可以看新闻、看视频和找学习资料。

❸ 作者说虽然网络很好，但是很多人买不起电脑，所以上不了网。

❹ 作者最喜欢上网聊天、发邮件和网购。

❺ 作者每个星期六跟姐姐一起在网上聊天。

❻ 北京离作者的家很近。

❼ 作者姐姐在北京工作。

❽ "88" 的意思是 "爸爸"。

❾ 作者的父亲开车去银行交电话费。

2. Your Chinese e-pal encouraged you to submit a short article about the life of a typical American student and the Internet and to do some cross cultural comparisons based on the article you just read. The Chinese article provided you with some understanding of the view of a Chinese student on the Internet and his/her life. You have also thought about your own views on the subject. You now need to find out one classmate's thoughts on this topic.

Talk to one classmate to find out his/her opinions on the use of the Internet. The discussion will provide ideas for the article. During the discussion, share your understanding of what you learned from the article and your own views, and try to learn as much as possible about your classmate's thoughts. The discussion may include your classmate's and your views on how the Internet has changed everyone's life in contemporary society, created popular online activities, and caused both productive and unproductive use of the Internet.

3. Write an article on the topic of "The Internet and the Lives of American Students" similar to the article you just read. In the article, compare and contrast how this Chinese student uses the Internet and how you and your American classmates use the Internet. Be sure to conclude your article by analyzing the similarities and differences between the cultural perspectives and traditions that may have influenced these comparisons.

Fun Time!

Texting (发短信) is very popular in China nowadays. The use of numbers is very common. For example, 0376 means 你生气 (qì) 了, 14 means 意思 and 065 means 原谅 (yuánliàng) 我.

Take a look at some popular text messages in numbers, and then match them with the corresponding characters and meanings. Compare your answers with your classmates to see who got the most number of correct matches.

0	**1**	**2**	**3**	**4**
a) 08376	c) 1414	e) 20999	g) 3321	i) 4242
b) 095	d) 1799	f) 246	h) 3q	

5	**6**	**7**	**8**	**9**
j) 51396	l) 6789	m) 7878	o) 84	r) 918
k) 596		n) 7998	p) 847	s) 9494
			q) 8 错	t) 987

① 乱 (luàn) 七八糟 (zāo) (In a mess)
② 你别生气 (bié shēngqì) 了 (Don't be angry anymore.)
③ 是啊是啊 (Yes.)
④ 三心二意 (Fickle minded)
⑤ 谢谢你 (Thank you.)
⑥ 我要睡觉了 (I'm going to sleep.)
⑦ 不是 (No.)
⑧ 别生气 (Don't be angry.)
⑨ 爱你久久久 (I love you forever.)
⑩ 饿死(èsǐ)了 (I'm famished.)
⑪ 我走了 (I'm leaving.)
⑫ 不错。 (Not bad.)
⑬ 意思意思 (Just a small token.)
⑭ 加油吧 (Come on! All the best.)
⑮ 就是就是 (That's right.)
⑯ 就不去 (Not going.)
⑰ 一起走走 (Let's take a walk.)
⑱ 去吧去吧 (Go.)
⑲ 去走走吧 (Go take a walk.)
⑳ 你找我 (Are you looking for me?)

277

I have learned...

Core Vocabulary
Verbs

死机	死機	sǐjī	freeze (computing)	通话	通話	tōnghuà	talk over the phone
修理		xiūlǐ	repair, fix	知道		zhīdào	know, learn of
安装	安裝	ānzhuāng	install	获得	獲得	huòdé	obtain, get hold of
组装	組裝	zǔzhuāng	assemble	听	聽	tīng	listen, hear
断	斷	duàn	disconnect	上传/载	上傳/載	shàngchuán/zài	upload
了		liǎo	(used after 得 or 不 to indicate the possibility or impossibility of accomplishing something)	下载	下載	xiàzài	download
出		chū	occur, arise	搜集	搜集	sōují	find, search
联系	聯繫	liánxì	keep in touch	查		chá	check
分享		fēnxiǎng	share	找		zhǎo	find, search

Nouns
IT products

摄像机	攝像機	shèxiàngjī	video camera	鼠标	鼠標	shǔbiāo	mouse
打印机	打印機	dǎyìnjī	printer	显示屏	顯示屏	xiǎnshìpíng	monitor
键盘	鍵盤	jiànpán	keyboard	耳机	耳機	ěrjī	earphones, headphones

Computers and accessories

主机	主機	zhǔjī	host	软件	軟件	ruǎnjiàn	software
硬盘	硬盤	yìngpán	hard disk	声卡	聲卡	shēngkǎ	sound card
U盘	U盤	U pán	thumb drive	显卡	顯卡	xiǎnkǎ	video card, graphics card

News sources

报纸	報紙	bàozhǐ	newspaper	广告	廣告	guǎnggào	advertisement

Others

功能		gōngnéng	function	推特		tuītè	Twitter
问题	問題	wèntí	problem	微博		wēibó	Weibo (microblog)
朋友		péngyou	friend	博客		bókè	blog
信息		xìnxī	information	消息		xiāoxi	news, information
脸书	臉書	liǎnshū	Facebook	新闻	新聞	xīnwén	news
照片	照片	zhàopiàn	photos	社交网	社交網	shèjiāowǎng	social networking sites
资料	資料	zīliào	information	讨论	討論	tǎolùn	discussion
互联网/英特网	互聯網/英特網	hùliánwǎng/yīngtèwǎng	Internet				

278

Adjectives

坏	壞	huài	broken	快速		kuàisù	fast
轻巧	輕巧	qīngqiǎo	light	美观	美觀	měiguān	beautiful, sleek
耐用		nàiyòng	durable	好听	好聽	hǎotīng	nice to listen to
实用	實用	shíyòng	easy to use				

Adverb

才	cái	only then

Prepositions

跟	gēn	with
一起	yìqǐ	together with

Conjunctions

不是…就是…	búshì…jiùshì…	either…or…
只要…就…	zhǐyào…jiù…	as long as, provided

Measure words

部	bù	(used for mobile phones)
首	shǒu	(used for songs)

Auxiliary verbs

可以	kěyǐ	can, may	能	néng	can, be able to

Phrases

IT products

平板电脑	平板電腦	píngbǎn diànnǎo	tablet computer	数码相机	數碼相機	shùmǎ xiàngjī	digital camera
智能手机	智能手機	zhìnéng shǒujī	smartphone				

Computers and accessories

防毒软件	防毒軟件	fángdú ruǎnjiàn	antivirus software	麦克风口	麥克風口	màikèfēng kǒu	microphone plug
数据线	數據線	shùjù xiàn	data cable	电源插口	電源插口	diànyuán chākǒu	power plug
耳机口	耳機口	ěrjī kǒu	earphone plug				

News sources

电视新闻	電視新聞	diànshì xīnwén	TV news	报章报道	報章報導	bàozhāng bàodǎo	newspaper report
电台广播	電台廣播	diàntái guǎngbō	radio broadcast	网上新闻	網上新聞	wǎngshàng xīnwén	online news

Internet

社交媒体	社交媒體	shèjiāo méitǐ	social media
网络视频电话	網絡視頻電話	wǎngluò shìpín diànhuà	online video call
搜索引擎		sōusuǒ yǐnqíng	search engine

Others

中病毒	zhòng bìngdú	be infected with a computer virus

I have learned...

开机	開機	kāi jī	turn on (machine)
关机	關機	guān jī	turn off (machine)
听音乐	聽音樂	tīng yīnyuè	listen to music
读博客	讀博客	dú bókè	read blogs
看电邮	看電郵	kàn diànyóu	read emails
网(上)购(物)	網(上)購(物)	wǎng (shàng) gòu (wù)	shop online
上传/载照片	上傳/載照片	shàngchuán/zài zhàopiàn	upload photos
下载歌曲	下載歌曲	xiàzài gēqǔ	download songs
搜集资料	搜集資料	sōují zīliào	find information
上社交网	上社交網	shàng shèjiāowǎng	visit social networking sites
玩网络游戏	玩網絡遊戲	wán wǎngluò yóuxì	play online games
参加网上讨论	參加網上討論	cānjiā wǎngshàng tǎolùn	join online discussions
打网络视频电话	打網絡視頻電話	dǎ wǎngluò shìpín diànhuà	make online video calls
Construction			
既…又…		jì...yòu...	both...and...

❖ SENTENCE PATTERNS ❖

这台平板电脑<u>既</u>轻巧<u>又</u>耐用。

电脑坏<u>了</u>。

打印机坏<u>了</u>，所以我买了一台新的。

网断了，现在<u>上不了</u>网。

我<u>用</u>网络视频电话跟朋友<u>一起</u>聊天。

他<u>不是</u>玩网络游戏，<u>就是</u>在网上购物。

我看了电视新闻<u>才</u>知道这个消息。他<u>一</u>上网<u>就</u>看到了这条新闻。

<u>只要</u>上网查一查，<u>就</u>可以找到资料。

I can do!

Interpretive **Communication**

❑ I can understand when someone talks about computers and gadgets.

❑ I can read and understand short, simple descriptions about common maintenance and repair problems related to computers and gadgets.

❑ I can understand when someone describes and/or writes about activities done with others.

❑ I can understand when people talk about and write about the source of a news item.

Interpersonal **Communication**

❑ I can converse about computers and gadgets.

❑ I can talk to others about simple and common maintenance and repair problems related to computers and gadgets.

❑ I can ask questions and get information about activities done with other people.

Presentational **Communication**

❑ I can give a short presentation on computers and gadgets.

❑ I can describe some experience of activities done with others.

❑ I can talk about my computer, the Internet, social media, and other computer related tasks.

❑ I can write about, introduce, and describe the source of a news item.

Cultural Knowledge

❑ I can talk about Lenovo and China's Silicon Valley.

❑ I can compare popular search engines in China and those in my own country.

❑ I can talk about E-commerce and instant messaging in China.

❑ I can talk about news in China.

Getting along with others

与他人相处

COMMUNICATIVE GOALS

- Identifying household chores
- Stating how to help another person
- Describing simultaneous actions
- Expressing agreement and disagreement
- Stating opinions

Cultural Knowledge

- Ways to set the table
- The value of good neighbors in Chinese culture
- The meaning of "face" in China

Get ready...

What kinds of chores do you do around your home to help out? What kinds of responsibilities do you have? As a class, make a list of 10 chores that you think many students your age would be expected to do (for example, making your bed, washing dishes, mowing the lawn, and helping with the laundry). Then go around the room and survey five classmates to find out which responsibilities they have to do and when (daily, weekly, monthly). If they do the chore (you can ask in English), write their name in the space under 有. Then ask them, "什么时候？" They should answer you in Chinese. As a class, compare your answers to see which chore is done more often than others.

Use the chart below to help you.

Chore	有	什么时候(每天，每周，每个月)
❶ Making your bed		
❷ Setting the table		
❸ Washing the dishes		
❹ Helping with the laundry		
❺ Mowing the lawn		
❻ Cleaning the house		
❼ Babysitting your brother or and sister		
❽ Take out the garbage		

STEPS *at a glance!*

STEP 1

HELPING AT HOME

A. Doing chores around the house
   我帮妈妈洗碗。

B. Offering help at home
   你要是出门的话，我可以帮你喂狗。

STEP 2

BEING A GOOD NEIGHBOR

A. Seeking and offering help
   你可以帮我割草吗?
   当然可以。

B. Helping your neighbors
   我帮邻居把车子洗干净了。

STEP 3

WORKING WITH OTHERS

A. Helping your classmates
   我一边帮他温习功课，一边和他讨论作业。

B. Expressing agreement and disagreement
   你同意我的看法吗?
   我同意。

C. Stating one's opinion
   你说的我不是不同意，只是我觉得有点难。

283

bāng　　　xǐ wǎn
我帮妈妈洗碗。
I'm helping mom wash the dishes.

A Doing chores around the house

dào　　lājī
哥哥帮爸爸倒垃圾。
My older brother is helping dad take out the garbage.

NEW WORDS

帮 v.	幫	bāng	help	帮忙 v./n.	幫忙	bāngmáng	help
帮助 v./n.	幫助	bāngzhù	help	家务 n.	家務	jiāwù	household chores

Household chores

洗碗 phr.		xǐ wǎn	wash dishes
倒垃圾 phr.		dào lājī	take out the garbage
叠衣服 phr.	疊衣服	dié yīfu	fold clothes

烫衣服 *phr.*		tàng yīfu	iron clothes
叠被子 *phr.*		dié bèizi	make *(your)* bed
整理房间 *phr.*	整理房間	zhěnglǐ fángjiān	straighten up *(your)* room
扫地 *v.*	掃地	sǎodì	sweep *(the floor)*
摆碗筷 *phr.*	擺碗筷	bǎi wǎnkuài	set the table *(bowl and chopsticks)*
擦桌子 *phr.*		cā zhuōzi	wipe the table
洗车 *phr.*	洗車	xǐ chē	wash the car
喂狗 *phr.*	餵狗	wèi gǒu	feed the dog
遛狗 *phr.*		liū gǒu	walk the dog
拖地板 *phr.*		tuō dìbǎn	sweep the floor
浇花 *phr.*	澆花	jiāo huā	water flowers or plants
做午饭 *phr.*	做午飯	zuò wǔfàn	make lunch
吸尘 *phr.*	吸塵	xīchén	vacuum
洗厕所 *phr.*	洗廁所	xǐ cèsuǒ	clean the bathroom
割草/打草 *phr.*		gē cǎo/dǎ cǎo	mow the lawn
看孩子 *phr.*		kān háizi	babysit
擦窗 *phr.*		cā chuāng	wash the window

Words you have learned

xǐ yīfu
洗衣服 *phr.* wash clothes, do laundry

LANGUAGE FOCUS

When you wish to say that you want to help your parents with chores around the house, use the expression 帮父母做家务 (bāng fùmǔ zuò jiāwù). You can change the person(s) after 帮 to refer to someone else. The type of chore can also be changed.

Examples: ❶ 我帮妈妈擦桌子。 I'm helping mom wipe the table.
❷ 姐姐帮妈妈叠衣服。 My older sister is helping mom fold clothes.
❸ 哥哥帮爸爸拖地板。 My older brother is helping dad sweep the floor.

Both 帮忙 and 帮助 have the same meaning in English. When someone offers help to another person, he/she may say "我帮助你" or "我帮你," which literally means "I help you." It is also possible to say "我帮你忙," which translates as "I offer assistance to you."

285

Setting the table

only a bowl and chopsticks for each person. This is because most people will take their food from a central tray in the middle of the table and place it in the bowl to eat.

The food is generally put on a round rotating tray that is called a "Lazy Susan" in English. The tray sits in the middle of the table and family members can move the food to the next person without touching the bowls or plates that the food is in.

In fancy restaurants, the table will be set more elaborately with glasses, plates, cups, and possibly bowls. When the guests begin to eat, the napkin is often placed under the plate on the table and drapes onto the person's lap.

In China there are different ways to set the table. When many families eat, they set the table simply by putting out a bowl and chopsticks. There is even a term for that in Chinese, 摆碗筷 (bǎi wǎnkuài) which means to set the table with

Try This!

1. Look at the following pictures of chores that are done around the house. For each chore, make a sentence telling who does the chore and when that person does it (put in the day of the week and the approximate time).

> 弟弟昨天下午五点在洗车。

2. Look at the following pictures and decide what must be done to correct the situation and a person to help. Write a sentence stating that you will help that person to fix the situation in the picture.

帮爷爷浇花。

帮爷爷······

帮妹妹······

帮奶奶······

帮哥哥······

帮妹妹······

帮姐姐······

帮爸爸······

帮阿姨······

DO YOU KNOW ....
你知道吗?

When you set a table in China, there are some rules to follow. Sometimes, the chopsticks are placed horizontally in front of the guest on the plate or can be placed on chopstick holders. The purpose of the chopstick holder is to raise the chopsticks off the table to keep them clean. The holders are often elegant designs which add to the attractiveness of the table.

méi kòng   huà

你要是没空的话，

我可以帮你喂狗。

If you are busy, I can help you feed the dog.

NEW WORDS

生词

要是……的话 *conj.*	要是……的話	yàoshi...dehuà	if
有空 *phr.*		yǒu kòng	free
没空 *phr.*	沒空	méi kòng	not free, busy
出门 *phr.*	出門	chū mén	go out

Words you have learned

shíjiān
时间 *n.* time

LANGUAGE FOCUS

If you wish to talk about a situation that may occur in the future ("if" clause), use the conjunction 要是……的话. In Chinese, part of the conjunction, 要是, comes before the action that occurs in the future (and may even come before the subject) and the second part 的话 comes right after the action. 的话 may be omitted without changing the meaning.

Examples: ❶ 你要是出门(的话)，我可以帮你洗碗。
If you are going out, I can help you do the dishes.

❷ 要是你很累(的话)，我可以帮你拖地板。
If you are tired, I can help you wipe the floor.

1. Complete the following statements with a logical conclusion.

❶ 要是妈妈很忙的话，_____。

❷ 要是我有空的话，_____。

❸ 要是爸爸没空，_____。

❹ 要是姐姐很累的话，_____。

❺ 要是哥哥没有时间，_____。

❻ 要是你有很多家务要做的话，_____。

❼ 要是你没有时间去寄信，_____。

❽ 要是你想去书店买书的话，_____。

2. You would like to find out whether your classmates have been helping their parents with chores at home. Go around the room to interview 10 classmates and ask them their name. Write their name under the number in the boxes on top. Then ask the question "你最常 (cháng, often) 做的三个家务是什么？" After the interview, calculate the percentage of students who do each task and report your findings to the class.

帮父母做家务

家务 / 同学	叠被子	洗碗	倒垃圾	割草	摆碗筷	洗衣服	洗厕所	整理房间	喂宠物	遛狗	bié 别的家务 other chores
❶											
❷											
❸											
❹											
❺											
❻											
❼											
❽											
❾											
❿											
Total %											

你可以帮我割草吗？
Could you help me mow the lawn?

dāngrán
当然可以。
Of course, I can.

A Seeking and offering help

xūyào
你需要帮忙吗？
Do you need help?

是的，谢谢你。
Yes, thank you.

Here are some useful expressions for seeking and offering help. Some common responses are included as well. Study the table to learn more of them.

NEW WORDS

Useful expressions

Seeking help

你可以帮我吗？
Could you help me?

你有时间帮我忙吗？
Do you have time to help me?

请你帮我个忙，好不好？
Could you do me a favor?

Response

dāngrán
当然可以。
Of course, I can.

好，没问题。
No problem.

bàoqiàn
很抱歉，我没有时间。
Sorry, I don't have time.

对不起，我帮不了你。
I'm sorry I can't help you.

Offering help

xūyào
你需要帮忙吗？
Do you need help?

有什么要帮忙的吗？
Is there anything I can help you with?

ràng
让我帮你吧。
Let me help you.

Response

谢谢你帮我。
Thank you for your help.

谢谢你来帮我。
Thank you for coming to help me.

máfan
不好意思，麻烦你了。
I'm sorry to trouble you.

LANGUAGE FOCUS

A common way to ask someone for help is to say "你可以帮我吗？" If you are able to help, say 当然可以 or 没问题. If you are unable to help, you can start with an apology such as 很抱歉 or 对不起, and then further explain why.

需要 (need) is a common word to use for offering help. It is used as a verb and takes an object, which is 帮忙 in this context.

1. Read the following dialog and determine whether the statements afterward are true (T) or false (F).

芳芳：王奶奶，你在做什么？

王奶奶：我在洗衣服。

芳芳：有什么要帮忙的吗？

王奶奶：我自己来，谢谢。要是你有时间的话，帮王奶奶去浇花，可以吗？

芳芳：没问题，我可以帮你！

王爷爷：芳芳，你在做什么？你有时间吗？

芳芳：我在帮王奶奶浇花，你需要帮忙吗？

王爷爷：嗯，我不会发电邮，请你帮我个忙，好不好？

芳芳：好，没问题，我来帮你吧。

王奶奶：芳芳，你现在忙吗？

芳芳：我在帮王爷爷发电邮，你需要帮忙吗？

丁强：王奶奶，我来帮你吧，我可以做什么呢？

王奶奶：要是你有时间的话，你可以帮我倒垃圾吗？

丁强：没问题。我现在就有空，可以帮你去倒。我下午还可以帮王爷爷洗车和割草。

芳芳：王奶奶，吃了午饭以后，我可以帮你洗碗和整理屋子。

❶ 奶奶现在在浇花。　　　　　　（　　）　❹ 王爷爷可以去倒垃圾。　（　　）

❷ 芳芳可以帮王奶奶浇花。　　（　　）　❺ 丁强现在没空帮王爷爷。（　　）

❸ 王爷爷需要芳芳帮她发电邮。（　　）　❻ 丁强说他可以帮忙洗碗。（　　）

NEW WORDS

干净 *adj.*	乾淨	gānjìng	clean
完 *v.*		wán	finish, complete
打扫 *v.*	打掃	dǎsǎo	clean

gānjìng
我帮邻居把车子洗干净了。

I helped my neighbor get his car washed.

LANGUAGE FOCUS

The 把 construction has many different uses. One of the ways to use 把 in a sentence is when you want to show that an object is being acted upon by the subject. In this case, 把 and the object are placed before the verb. It forms a construction: subject + 把 + object + verb phrase.

Examples:
❶ 我把房子打扫干净了。   I cleaned the room.

❷ 他把餐具摆好了。   He set the table.

❸ 哥哥把草割完了。   My older brother mowed the lawn.

Note that in the sentences above, 干净, 好 and 完 function as complements to the preceding verbs to indicate the results of the actions. For example, 打扫干净 means that by the action of cleaning, the result achieved is "clean." 摆好 means that by the action of setting the table, the result is satisfactory. 割完 means that by the action of mowing, the task has been completed.

1. Imagine that your neighbors are going on vacation for two weeks and need your help. Before you agree to help them, you send an email message with questions about what they want you to do, and tell them what you can do. Write five questions about the types of jobs that you will help them do and five statements of the things you can do.

Example: 你需要我帮你割草吗？

我每个星期一可以帮你割草。

2. Look at the following pictures of chores that the person can help his/her neighbor with, and use the 把 construction to form sentences stating that he/she has done these chores.

姐姐帮邻居把衣服洗干净了。

1 姐姐······

2 安琪······

3 我······

4 玛丽······

5 妹妹······

6 马克······

7 弟弟······

8 妹妹······

CULTURAL HIGHLIGHTS

Better a close neighbor than a distant relative

There is a good expression in Chinese, 远亲不如近邻 (yuǎn qīn bùrú jìn lín), which means that although family members are much valued, they are not as beneficial as having a good neighbor. The reason for that is that today relatives often live a distance away, even when in the same city, while a good, close neighbor can help you quickly in an emergency because he/she lives next door.

Years ago, families often lived in the same neighborhood and sometimes in the same complex of houses called a *siheyuan* (四合院, sìhéyuàn), a traditional courtyard residence. Often one *siheyuan* joined another to form the narrow streets or alleys of a *hutong* (胡同, hútòng), one of the most famous types of neighborhoods in Beijing. The word *hutong* actually comes from the Mongolian language and means "town."

Many of the old *hutong* neighborhoods of Beijing have been demolished to make way for new roads and buildings. However, in recent years, some *hutongs* have been designated as protected areas in order to preserve that aspect of Chinese culture. Today it is possible to tour some *hutong* neighborhoods to get a feel for how these close-knit neighborhoods developed in China.

STEP 3
WORKING WITH OTHERS

wēnxí

我一边帮他温习功课，

一边和他讨论作业。

I'm helping him review his school work while discussing the homework assignment with him.

A Helping your classmates

我一边做功课，一边教她数学。

I'm doing my homework while coaching her in math.

NEW WORDS 生 词

一边⋯一边⋯ _conj._	一邊⋯一邊⋯	yìbiān…yìbiān…	at the same time, simultaneously
温习 / 复习 _v._	温習 / 復習	wēnxí / fùxí	review
教 _v._		jiāo	teach, coach

Words you have learned

tǎolùn	gōngkè	zuòyè	liǎotiān
讨论 _v._ discuss	功课 _n._ homework	作业 _n._ homework	聊天 _n._ chat

LANGUAGE FOCUS

The structure 一边⋯一边⋯ can be used to indicate that two things are being done at the same time, either by a person or a group of people. The first 一边 is placed in the first clause before a verb, and the second 一边 in the second clause before another verb.

For example: ❶ 我一边打电话，一边帮丁强买三明治。
I'm making a phone call while helping Ding Qiang buy a sandwich.

❷ 我一边吃午饭，一边教安琪中文。
I'm eating lunch while helping Anqi with her Chinese.

❸ 他们一边做作业，一边听音乐。
They are doing their homework while listening to music.

1. Read the actions below and use the structure 一边⋯一边⋯ to express that they are being done simultaneously.

❶ 帮安琪买可乐　　和大卫聊天 ⟶ 我一边帮安琪买可乐，一边和大卫聊天。

❷ 温习功课　　教丁强英文 ⟶ _____

❸ 讨论作业　　吃午饭 ⟶ _____

❹ 上社交网　　下载歌曲 ⟶ _____

❺ 教芳芳数学　　帮张安温习功课 ⟶ _____

❻ 跑步　　听音乐 ⟶ _____

⑦ 看电邮　　　　发短信　　　　⟶ _____

⑧ 教马克物理　　和安琪讨论作业 ⟶ _____

⑨ 网购　　　　　上社交网　　　 ⟶ _____

⑩ 帮邻居洗车　　和邻居聊天　　 ⟶ _____

2. **Survey** Find out from at least 10 classmates what activities they like to do at the same time. Record your findings in a table and present them to the class using the structure 一边…一边….

Eample: 马克喜欢一边喝咖啡，一边和朋友聊天。

姓名	huódòng 活动 activities
马克	喝咖啡、和朋友聊天。

我们一边喝咖啡，一边聊天。

tóngyì　　　kànfǎ
你同意我的看法吗？
Do you agree with me?

① 我同意。／我不同意。
Yes, I do. / No, I don't.

rènwéi　　shuō　　dàolǐ
② 我认为你说的有道理。
I think what you said makes sense.

xiǎngfǎ
③ 我的想法跟你的不一样。
My view is different from yours.

NEW WORDS

生
词

同意 v.		tóngyì	agree
看法 n.		kànfǎ	point of view
认为 v.	認爲	rènwéi	think, consider
说 v.	説	shuō	say, speak
有道理 adj.		yǒu dàolǐ	makes sense, is reasonable
正确 adj.	正確	zhèngquè	correct, right
想法 n.		xiǎngfǎ	thoughts, ideas

Words you have learned

gēn...... yíyàng
跟……一样 n. the same as

298

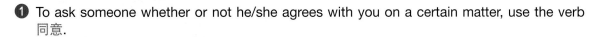

❶ To ask someone whether or not he/she agrees with you on a certain matter, use the verb 同意.

Examples: 我觉得郑和非常聪明，你同意吗？
I think Zheng He is very intelligent. Do you agree?

你同意他的看法吗？
Do you agree with him?

❷ The verb 认为 can be used to express agreement or disagreement.

Examples: 我认为你说的非常正确。
I think what you said is right.

我认为他说的不对。
I think what he said is wrong.

❸ The construction 跟……一样 can be used to compare two points of view.

Examples: 姐姐的想法跟我的一样。
My older sister's view is the same as mine.

他的想法跟我的不一样。
His view is different from mine.

CULTURAL HIGHLIGHTS

The meaning of "face" (面子) in China

In Chinese culture the idea of face is very important. As a result, there are a number of idioms that have developed around the concept of face in Chinese: 人要脸, 树要皮 (rén yào liǎn, shù yào pí) "Humans can't live without face, trees can't live without bark."

The expressions "lose face" and "save face" have come into the English language through Chinese. According to the Online Etymology Dictionary, "lose face" was seen in English around 1876, whereas "save face" appeared around 1898. The expression "save face" does not exist in Chinese and was coined by the British community in China at the end of the 19th century as a direct contrast to the Chinese expression of "lose face" or 丢脸 (diūliǎn). The closest Chinese equivalent to "save face" is the expression 要面子 (yào miànzi) meaning "eager to gain reputation." Another expression related to "saving face" is the expression of "giving face to others" 给面子 (gěi

miànzi). This refers to saving someone's reputation.

It seems that "saving face" is a more important practice in Chinese culture than it is in Western culture. A good part of this has to do with the value that Chinese culture places on social harmony and the decision to avoid criticism. There are some slights that in the West would be viewed as minor and often quickly forgotten but would be considered a faux pas in the East. Where some Americans are viewed as being frank and "straight shooters" in a meeting, they may be viewed as being rude in Chinese culture.

1. Using the following statements, survey at least 10 classmates to see if they agree or disagree with the statements and write down their names in the appropriate columns. Afterwards, make a chart summarizing the results.

yìjiàn 意见 opinion	同意	不同意
❶ 我们的中文功课太多了。		
❷ 学生应该好好学习^{xuéxí}learn。		
❸ 每个中学生都要上大学。		
❹ 我们应该在家帮父母做家务。		
❺ 大家用筷子^{kuàizi}chopsticks吃饭。		
❻ 老师不需要给我们考试。		
❼ 我们不需要吃早饭。		
❽ 我们的校长很有耐心^{yǒu nàixīn,}patient。		
❾ 学校餐厅的食物很好吃。		
❿ 学生应该打扫教室。		

2. **Pair work** Decide if you agree or disagree with the statements above using 认为 or 跟……一样. One student will read a statement and the other will respond to it.

Example:
Student A: 我们的中文功课太多了。
Student B: 我认为你说的很对。/ 我的想法跟你的一样。

你 说 的 我 不 是 不 同 意 ，

① 只 是 我 觉 得 有 点 难 。

I do not disagree with what you said, but I think it may be a bit difficult *(to do)*.

jiànyì
这 个 建 议 好 是 好 ，

búgòu
② 可 是 时 间 可 能 不 够 。

This suggestion is good, but there may not be enough time *(to do it)*.

NEW WORDS

不是不…只是…		bú shì bù...zhǐshì...	it is not that...but...
好是好…可是…		hǎo shì hǎo...kěshì...	*(it)* is good, but...
建议 *n.*	建議	jiànyì	suggestion
不够 *adj.*	不够	búgòu	insufficient, not enough
花时间 *phr.*	花時間	huā shíjiān	time consuming
不实际 *phr.*	不實際	bù shíjì	impractical

301

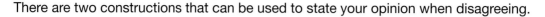
There are two constructions that can be used to state your opinion when disagreeing.

❶ 不是不…只是… is a polite way to express disagreement. 不是不 is used in the first clause to indicate a positive meaning, and 只是 is used in the second clause to signify a change in thought and opinion.

> *Examples:* 🦜 我不是不同意你的看法，只是觉得他说的比较有道理。
> I do not disagree with you, but I feel that what he said makes more sense.
>
> 🦜 我不是不喜欢这里，只是觉得太安静了。
> I do not dislike this place, but I think it's too quiet.

❷ 好是好…可是… is a tactful way of expressing disagreement or pointing out shortcomings. 好是好 is used in the first clause to affirm the subject, and 只是 is used in the second clause to point out the shortcoming. Note that 好 can be replaced by other adjectives depending on the context.

> *Examples:* 🦜 你的建议好是好，可是太花时间了。
> Your suggestion is good, but it is too time consuming.
>
> 🦜 这个社区方便是方便，可是太吵了。
> This community is convenient, but it is too noisy.

Try This!

1. Imagine your classmate gave the following suggestions or views. Use 不是不…只是… to express your disagreement.

❶ 我们应该每天运动一个小时。

❷ 我觉得这个社区很方便。

❸ 这个学校很大，也很新。

❹ 这个中餐馆的食物很好吃。

❺ 我们应该多看书。

❻ 这部智能手机既轻巧，功能又多。

❼ 我们下午去吃快餐吧。

❽ 学校离地铁站只有四百米，我们走路去地铁站吧。

❾ 我觉得上暑期学校很有意思。

❿ 我觉得这个新同学很有才华。

2. Read the dialog and answer the following questions.

马克：芳芳，学校开了一间新餐厅，你到那里吃过了吗？

芳芳：吃过了，我觉得东西有点贵。

马克：东西贵是贵，可是非常好吃，而且份量也很多。
　　　fēnliàng
　　　quantity
　　　tǐng
　　　我觉得挺不错的。
　　　quite

芳芳：但那里离教学楼有点远，吃了午饭再回来上课，
　　　很不方便。

马克：这个我同意。那你比较喜欢去哪里吃饭？
　　　fùjìn
芳芳：我喜欢去图书馆附近的餐厅，那里的食物又便宜
　　　nearby
　　　又好吃。

马克：哦，那里好是好，可是我觉得人太多了。

❶ 马克觉得新餐厅的东西怎么样？
　　a. 便宜　　　　　　　　　　　　　b. 好吃
　　c. 不好吃　　　　　　　　　　　　d. 份量太少　　　　　　（　　）

❷ 芳芳为什么不喜欢新餐厅？
　　a. 东西贵，份量少　　　　　　　　b. 不方便，太吵了
　　c. 东西贵，人太多　　　　　　　　d. 有点远，不方便　　（　　）

❸ 芳芳觉得图书馆附近的餐厅怎么样？
　　a. 食物便宜、好吃　　　　　　　　b. 食物很贵、不好吃
　　c. 食物便宜、份量多　　　　　　　d. 食物很贵、份量少　（　　）

❹ 马克喜欢图书馆附近的餐厅吗？为什么？
　　a. 喜欢，因为那里的东西很好吃。
　　b. 喜欢，因为那里很方便。
　　c. 不喜欢，因为那里的东西份量少。
　　d. 不喜欢，因为那里的人太多了。　　　　　　　　　　　（　　）

STEP 1 HELPING AT HOME

Ding Qiang is describing how he and his sister help their parents with household chores.

我和姐姐平时会帮爸爸妈妈做家务。每天吃完晚饭，姐姐会帮妈妈洗碗，我会帮忙擦桌子。要是妈妈很累的话，我会帮她拖地板。到了周末，要是我有空的话，我会先帮妈妈洗厕所，再帮爸爸洗车。姐姐会帮忙叠衣服、整理房间。做完家务以后，我们一家人喜欢一起去遛狗、散步。我觉得做孩子的应该帮爸爸妈妈分担家务事，这样爸爸妈妈就不会那么辛苦了。

píngshí	sànbù	fēndān	xīnkǔ
平时	散步	分担	辛苦
normally	take a stroll	share	laborious

STEP 2 BEING A GOOD NEIGHBOR

Grandpa Li is going on an overseas trip and seeks Mark's help to take care of things when he's not around.

马克：李爷爷，您后天就要去北京了，行李都收拾好了吗？

行李 xínglǐ luggage
收拾 shōushi pack

李爷爷：都收拾好了，谢谢。马克，你可以帮我个忙吗？

马克：当然可以，您要我做什么？

李爷爷：我不在的这两周，你可以帮我照顾我的狗吗？

马克：好，没问题。有什么需要注意的吗？

注意 zhùyì take note of

李爷爷：Jack 很容易照顾，每天喂一次，遛一次，就行了。

马克：好的。您还有什么需要帮忙的吗？

李爷爷：对了，我还需要你帮我割草。每个周末一次就可以了。

马克：好，没问题。

李爷爷：不好意思，麻烦你了。

马克：别这么说。祝您旅途愉快！

别 bié don't
旅途 lǚtú journey
愉快 yúkuài happy

李爷爷：谢谢！

STEP 3 WORKING WITH OTHERS

Three friends are talking about the Internet.

张安：我觉得互联网真的是这个世纪最伟大的发明。它改变了我们的生活，给我们带来了很大的方便。

世纪 shìjì century
发明 fāmíng invention
改变 gǎibiàn change
生活 shēnghuó life
带来 dàilai bring

安琪：我同意你的看法。现在我们不用出门，就可以一边上网搜集资料，一边和同学在网上讨论作业。

大卫：互联网好是好，但是人们花太多时间在网络上了，我认为这不是很健康。

张安：你说的也有道理，我弟弟就是一个网迷，他每天不是玩网络游戏，就是和网友聊天，一整天对着电脑，跟我们都说不上几句话。

网迷 wǎngmí cyber fan
整 zhěng whole
对 duì face
句 jù sentence
话 huà words

安琪：我哥哥以前也是这样，但爸爸妈妈跟他谈过以后，他慢慢学会控制自己上网的时间。我觉得只要我们能够自律，互联网还是非常有用的。

谈 tán talk
慢慢 mànman slowly
控制 kòngzhì control
能够 nénggòu can
自律 zìlù disciplined

大卫：说的没错！

Step Up!

1. Your school has decided to come up with a campaign to help with the senior citizens in your community and you have been asked to chair the committee that will set the schedule and decide when and where help will be administered. Come up with a schedule for a month of at least 20 tasks that students will undertake, for whom they need to be done (come up with a list of imaginary people for whom they should be done), what time and day of the week they need to be done, and where they need to be done (inside the house, outside the house). For each of the tasks, write on a 3 x 5 file card the name of the senior citizen, the name of the task, the date, and time.

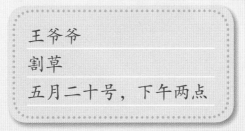

2. Using the schedule of tasks that you came up with in #1, go around the classroom and find someone who is willing and has the time to do the task. In Chinese, ask your classmates, "Can you help Mr. Wang by mowing his lawn at 2 PM on Saturday?" If the person says, "Yes," give him/her the card that represents that task.

3. **Role-play** Your friend has asked you to help with some of the tasks in #1. While you agree that these are meaningful activities, you have your own reservations and constraints. Work with a partner to create a short dialog of at least 10 exchanges, stating your opinions and expressing agreement/disagreement.

4. Below is a short essay of a student for college explaining what he does to help his neighbors. Read the essay and list all the items he does.

我经常帮助我的邻居。每个星期一、三、五，我会
帮邻居王爷爷遛狗和喂狗，要是有空，我还会帮他拖地
板。每个星期二、四，我会帮邻居张阿姨看孩子。因为
作业很多，所以我有时会一边做功课，一边照顾他们。
到了周末，我会帮隔壁的李叔叔洗车，帮李阿姨浇花，
还会帮陈奶奶倒垃圾。我天天都很忙，但是能够帮助
别人，我觉得很开心！

jīngcháng often
zhàogù take care of
gébì next door
nénggòu able to

Fun Time!

zhù rén wéi kuàilè zhī běn
助人为快乐之本 means that helping people is the source of happiness. Look at the following pictures of Chinese people helping others. Write a caption for each picture.

Giving a helping hand

I have learned...

Core Vocabulary

Verbs

帮	幫	bāng	help	让	讓	ràng	let
帮助	幫助	bāngzhù	help	麻烦	麻煩	máfan	trouble, bother
帮忙	幫忙	bāngmáng	help	温习/复习	温習/復習	wēnxí/fùxí	review
扫地	掃地	sǎodì	sweep *(the floor)*	教		jiāo	teach, coach
完		wán	finish, complete	同意		tóngyì	agree
打扫	打掃	dǎsǎo	clean	认为	認爲	rènwéi	think, consider
需要		xūyào	need	说	説	shuō	say, speak

Nouns

帮助	幫助	bāngzhù	help	看法		kànfǎ	point of view
帮忙	幫忙	bāngmáng	help	想法		xiǎngfǎ	thoughts, ideas
家务	家務	jiāwù	household chores	建议	建議	jiànyì	suggestion

Adjectives

抱歉		bàoqiàn	sorry	正确	正確	zhèngquè	correct, right
干净	乾净	gānjìng	clean	不够	不夠	búgòu	insufficient, not enough

Adverb

当然	當然	dāngrán	of course, naturally	

Conjunctions

要是……的话	要是……的話	yàoshi...dehuà	if	
一边…一边…	一邊…一邊…	yìbiān...yìbiān	at the same time, simultaneously	

Phrases

洗碗		xǐ wǎn	wash dishes	洗车	洗車	xǐ chē	wash the car
倒垃圾		dào lājī	take out the garbage	喂狗	餵狗	wèi gǒu	feed the dog
叠衣服	疊衣服	dié yīfu	fold clothes	遛狗		liū gǒu	walk the dog
烫衣服		tàng yīfu	iron clothes	拖地板		tuō dìbǎn	sweep the floor
叠被子	疊被子	dié bèizi	make *(your)* bed	浇花	澆花	jiāo huā	water flowers or plants
整理房间	整理房間	zhěnglǐ fángjiān	straighten up *(your)* room	做午饭	做午飯	zuò wǔfàn	make lunch
摆碗筷	擺碗筷	bǎi wǎnkuài	set the table *(bowl and chopsticks)*	吸尘	吸塵	xīchén	vacuum
擦桌子		cā zhuōzi	wipe the table	洗厕所	洗廁所	xǐ cèsuǒ	clean the bathroom

I have learned...

割草/打草		gē cǎo/dǎ cǎo	mow the lawn	出门	出門	chū mén	go out
看孩子		kān háizi	babysit	有道理		yǒu dàolǐ	makes sense, is reasonable
擦窗		cā chuāng	wash the window	花时间	花時間	huā shíjiān	time consuming
有空		yǒu kòng	free	不实际	不實際	bù shíjì	impractical
没空	沒空	méi kòng	not free, busy				

Conjunctions

不是不…只是…		bú shì bù…zhǐshì…	it is not that…but…
好是好…可是…		hǎo shì hǎo…kěshì…	(it) is good, but…

Useful expressions

你可以帮我吗?	你可以幫我嗎?	Nǐ kěyǐ bāng wǒ ma?	Could you help me?
你有时间帮我忙吗?	你有時間幫我嗎?	Nǐ yǒu shíjiān bāng wǒ máng ma?	Do you have time to help me?
请你帮我个忙，好不好?	請你幫我個忙，好不好?	Qǐng nǐ bāng wǒ gè máng, hǎo bù hǎo?	Could you do me a favor?
你需要帮忙吗?	你需要幫忙嗎?	Nǐ xūyào bāngmáng ma?	Do you need help?
有什么要帮忙的吗?	有什麼要幫忙的嗎?	Yǒu shénme yào bāngmáng de ma?	Is there anything I can help you with?
让我帮你吧。	讓我幫你吧。	Ràng wǒ bāng nǐ ba.	Let me help you.
当然可以。	當然可以。	Dāngrán kěyǐ.	Of course, I can.
好，没问题。	好，沒問題。	Hǎo, méi wèntí.	No problem.
很抱歉，我没有时间。	很抱歉，我沒有時間。	Hěn bàoqiàn, wǒ méiyǒu shíjiān.	Sorry, I don't have time.
对不起，我帮不了你。	對不起，我幫不了你。	Duìbuqǐ, wǒ bāng bù liǎo nǐ.	I'm sorry I can't help you.
谢谢你帮我。	謝謝你幫我。	Xièxie nǐ bāng wǒ.	Thank you for your help.
谢谢你来帮我。	謝謝你來幫我。	Xièxie nǐ lái bāng wǒ.	Thank you for coming to help me.
不好意思，麻烦你了。	不要意思，麻煩你了。	Bù hǎoyìsi, máfan nǐ le.	I'm sorry to trouble you.

❖ SENTENCE PATTERNS ❖

我帮妈妈洗碗。

你要是出门的话，我可以帮你喂狗。

你可以帮我割草吗? 当然可以。

我帮邻居把车子洗干净了。

我一边帮他温习功课，一边和他讨论作业。

你同意我的看法吗? 我同意。

你说的我不是不同意，只是我觉得有点难。

这个建议好是好，可是时间可能不够。

I can do!

Interpretive Communication

❑ I can read and understand information about doing chores in my home.

❑ I can read and understand information about helping someone.

❑ I can understand when someone talks about doing activities at the same time.

Interpersonal Communication

❑ I can converse about helping others and come to a consensus as to when certain activities will occur.

❑ I can discuss opinions with another person.

❑ I can share information about doing two activities at the same time.

Presentational Communication

❑ I can talk about the chores that I do at home and when.

❑ I can write out a list of chores and when they should be done.

❑ I can state whether I agree or disagree with someone.

Cultural Knowledge

❑ I can state various ways to set the table in China.

❑ I can talk about the importance of good neighbors in Chinese culture.

❑ I can discuss the meaning of "face" in China.

Being a global citizen

做一个好公民

COMMUNICATIVE GOALS

- Talking about community workers
- Describing people and getting along with them
- Stating ways to contribute to the community
- Talking about the environment
- Describing how to protect the community

Cultural Knowledge

- The story of Meng Zi
- Project Hope
- The Environmental Hotline in China
- Recycled art

Get ready...

Here is a list of some famous people or organizations who have contributed to making this world a better place. Look at the list and decide which person or organization you believe has made a significant contribution to the world and explain why. If possible, write the reasons in Chinese. If none of these well-known people or organizations is one that you wish to recognize, you may choose another famous person or organization that has made a significant contribution. Then compare your answer with someone else's in the class.

What similarities and differences do you find in your answers?

1. Yuan Longping (袁隆平), a Chinese agricultural scientist
2. Mother Theresa
3. Nelson Mandela
4. Bill Gates
5. Doctors Without Borders
6. The One Foundation (壹基金), by Jet Li
7. Al Gore
8. United Nations Peace Keeping Forces
9. Dr. Albert Schweitzer
10. Steve Jobs
11. Greenpeace
12. Red Cross
13. MADD (Mothers Against Drunk Driving)
14. The Salvation Army

BEING PART OF A COMMUNITY

A. Discovering community workers
   志愿者对我的影响很大。

B. Getting along in the community
   芳芳很有耐心，所以很容易跟她相处。

HELPING THE COMMUNITY

A. Contributing to the community
   张安请我跟他一起去捐血。

B. Protecting the place we live
   空气被污染了。

CREATING A BETTER LIFE

A. Maintaining good daily habits
   我们应该节约用水。

B. Building a greener world
   当你离开房间的时候，应该把灯关掉。

311

zhìyuànzhě   yǐngxiǎng

志愿者对我的影响很大。

The volunteers have a great influence on me.

A Discovering community workers

shòu shìzhǎng

我受市长的影响非常大。

I'm greatly influenced by the mayor.

生 词

NEW WORDS

影响 n.	影響	yǐngxiǎng	influence
受 v.		shòu	receive, be subject to
社会 n.	社會	shèhuì	society
公民 n.		gōngmín	citizen
社区服务 phr.	社區服務	shèqū fúwù	community service
红十字会 phr.	紅十字會	hóngshízìhuì	Red Cross
家长会 phr.	家長會	jiāzhǎnghuì	Parent Association

Professions

图书馆员 n.	圖書館員	túshūguǎnyuán	librarian
志愿者 n.	志願者	zhìyuànzhě	volunteer
公车司机 n.	公車司機	gōngchē sījī	bus driver
急救专家 n.	急救專家	jíjiù zhuānjiā	EMT
救生员 n.	救生員	jiùshēngyuán	life guard
市长 n.	市長	shìzhǎng	mayor

Words you have learned

yīshēng
医生 n. doctor

jǐngchá
警察 n. policeman/policewoman

yīnyuèjiā
音乐家 n. musician

yóudìyuán
邮递员 n. mail carrier

hùshi
护士 n. nurse

xiāofángyuán
消防员 n. fire fighter

yǎnyuán
演员 n. actor

LANGUAGE FOCUS

❶ You learned 对 as a preposition (direct towards) in Lesson 2. It is also used to express that a person has influence on someone else or something:

Person A + 对 + Recipient + 的 + 影响 + degree adverb + adjective

> 我父母对我的影响非常大。
> My parents have a lot of influence on me.
> *(literally, My parents toward me have influence a lot.)*

Look at the following sentence and determine its meaning.

> 这个人对音乐界的影响很大。

To state that someone does not have influence on someone else, use 没有 in the sentence:

> 我父母对我没有影响。
> My parents do not have any influence on me.

To state that someone does not have much influence on someone else, use 不 before the adjective. You can also add the degree adverb 太 after 不 to moderate the tone:

For example:
> 我父母对我的影响不大。
> My parents do not have much influence on me.

> 我父母对我的影响不太大。
> My parent do not have too much influence on me.

❷ To state the same idea using the passive voice, use the verb 受 to create a sentence like the following:

> 我受我父母的影响非常大。
> I am influenced a lot by my parents. *(literally, I receive [from] my parents influence a lot.)*

Since 受 functions as a verb in this instance, place 不 before 受 to create a negative meaning.

> 我不受我父母的影响。

This construction using 受 can be combined with 因为…所以… to form the following sentence.

> 因为我受到李老师的影响，所以我成为中文老师。

1. Look at the list of the following people. State whether or not that person has any influence on you using 对 and 受. In some cases, you may wish to give a specific name to that person.

> *Example:* 中文老师 ⟶ 我的中文老师，王老师，对我的影响很大。
> or
> ⟶ 我受我的中文老师王老师的影响很大。

| ❶ 志愿者 | ❷ 市长 | ❸ 爸爸 | ❹ 妈妈 | ❺ 爷爷 |
| ❻ 奶奶 | ❼ 朋友 | ❽ 医生 | ❾ 图书馆员 | ❿ 校长 |

2. You are the organizer of a major community fair that will be held this summer on July 4th. You are responsible for sending out invitations to people in your community to request that they attend. You will need to do some research (on the Internet, in a phone directory, or elsewhere) to find out the names of the following people in your community. Next to their role, write down the name of at least one person in your community who has that job and whom you would like to invite.

❶ 市长 _____   ❻ 校车司机 _____

❷ 消防员 _____   ❼ 急救专家 _____

❸ 图书馆员 _____   ❽ 救生员 _____

❹ 护士 _____   ❾ 邮递员 _____

❺ 警察 _____   ❿ 医生 _____

314

nàixīn   róngyì   xiāngchǔ

她很有耐心，所以很容易跟她相处。

She is very patient, so it is easy to get along with her.

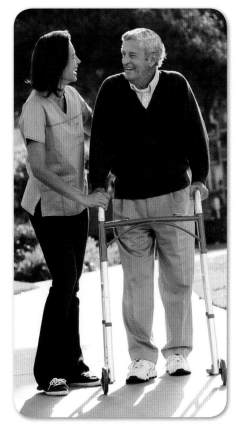

生 词

NEW WORDS

相处 v.	相處	xiāngchǔ	get along (with someone)
性格 n.		xìnggé	personality, disposition
脾气 n.	脾氣	píqì	temper
别人 n.		biéren	other people

Personality traits

有耐心 phr.		yǒu nàixīn	be patient
有爱心 phr.	有愛心	yǒu àixīn	kind-hearted
有礼貌 phr.	有禮貌	yǒu lǐmào	be courteous, polite
开朗 adj.	開朗	kāilǎng	cheerful, outgoing
诚实 adj.	誠實	chéngshí	be honest
热心 adj.	熱心	rèxīn	enthusiastic; eagerness
大方 adj.		dàfang	generous
多心 adj.		duōxīn	suspicious
刻薄 adj.		kèbó	mean
挑剔 adj.		tiāotī	picky, fastidious
爱管闲事 phr.	愛管閑事	ài guǎn xiánshì	nosy

Words you have learned

róngyì
容易 adj. easy

nán
难 adj. difficult

xiǎoqì
小气 adj. petty

lǎnduò
懒惰 adj. lazy

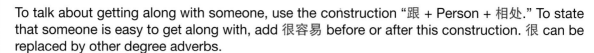

To talk about getting along with someone, use the construction "跟 + Person + 相处." To state that someone is easy to get along with, add 很容易 before or after this construction. 很 can be replaced by other degree adverbs.

Examples: ❶ 安琪很开朗，所以很容易跟她相处。

Anqi is very cheerful, so it is easy to get along with her.

❷ 张安很友善，所以跟他相处非常容易。

Zhang An is very friendly, so it is easy to get along with him.

To state that someone is hard to get along with, add 很难 or 很不容易 before or after this construction. Other degree adverbs can also be used.

Examples: ❶ 马克脾气很坏，所以很难跟他相处。

Mark has a bad temper, so it is hard to get along with him.

❷ 芳芳很挑剔，所以跟她相处非常不容易。

Fangfang is very picky, so it is hard to get along with her.

CULTURAL HIGHLIGHTS

The story of Meng Zi

Meng Zi (孟子, 372 – 289 BC, also called Mencius) was born in the city of Zou, Shan Dong Province. His father died when he was three years old so his mother, Zhang, had to raise him by herself. At first they lived near a cemetery where the children saw many funerals and religious processions. Meng Zi and the other children would imitate the ceremonies and sometimes even join in. Zhang felt that this was not a good place to raise her son so she moved.

Next they moved to a marketplace. Here, Meng Zi began imitating the business people around him. In ancient times, businessmen were not considered people with high social standing in Chinese society, and Meng Zi's behavior upset his mother very much. So, she decided to move again.

This time they moved to an area close to a school. Here Meng Zi saw people treating each other well and also reading a lot. On the first day of every month, officials, scholars, and other students would go to the Confucius temple to learn about and discuss Confucius' theories. Meng Zi started to imitate the behavior he saw around him and also the study habits of the students. Noting the good effect that this environment was having on Meng Zi, his mother decided that this was the place where her son should live. Meng Zi later grew up to be a great Confucian scholar.

This story is an example of the Chinese belief that where and how one grows up has a huge effect on a child. In many cases, Chinese parents have been known to sacrifice a great deal in order to raise their children.

1. Read the following traits of the various individuals and decide if you think they make that person easy or hard to get along with (相处). Then write a sentence stating that because of that trait you get along well with or do not get along well with that person.

   Example: 大卫　脾气很坏

   ⟶ 大卫的脾气很坏，所以不容易跟他相处。

   ❶ 芳芳　　　　　友善　　　　　❾ 张老师　　　　诚实
   ❷ 他哥哥　　　　挑剔　　　　　❿ 小东的姑姑　　小气
   ❸ 我表弟　　　　爱管闲事　　　⓫ 小南　　　　　热心
   ❹ 马克　　　　　爱帮助人　　　⓬ 玛丽　　　　　没礼貌
   ❺ 安妮的妹妹　　没耐心　　　　⓭ 安琪的姐姐　　多心
   ❻ 小红的弟弟　　懒惰　　　　　⓮ 这个新同学　　刻薄
   ❼ 丁强　　　　　性格开朗　　　⓯ 张安　　　　　大方
   ❽ 李明　　　　　脾气坏

2. You are on the selection committee to fill some positions in your community. Next to the position that needs to be filled, write at least three traits or characteristics that are important for this person to have.

   For example: 图书馆员 ⟶ 喜欢看书、有耐心、友善、

   容易跟别人相处、性格开朗、热心

   ❶ 消防员 ⟶ _____

   ❷ 警察 ⟶ _____

   ❸ 校长 ⟶ _____

   ❹ 市长 ⟶ _____

   ❺ 校车司机 ⟶ _____

   ❻ 训狗师 ⟶ _____
   　　xùngǒushī
   　　dog trainer

   ❼ 救生员 ⟶ _____

   ❽ 邮递员 ⟶ _____

   ❾ 家教 ⟶ _____
   　　jiājiào
   　　private tutor

   ❿ 护士 ⟶ _____

HELPING THE COMMUNITY

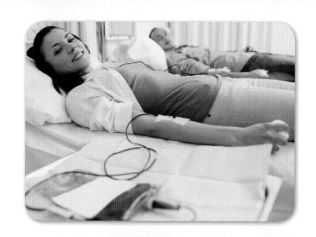

juān xiě
张安请我跟他一起去捐血。
Zhang An asked me to go donate blood with him.

A Contributing to the community

jiào
老师叫我们去
老人中心做义工。
Our teacher asked us to go to the senior center to do volunteer work.

生 词

NEW WORDS

请 v.	请	qǐng	invite, ask, treat
叫 v.		jiào	order, ask
让 v.	讓	ràng	let, allow

Words you have learned

bāngmáng
帮忙 help

zuò yìgōng
做义工 do volunteer work

Volunteer work

做志愿者 phr.	做志願者	zuò zhìyuànzhě	volunteering
做家教 phr.		zuò jiājiào	tutoring
捐款 phr.		juān kuǎn	donate money, make a donation
筹款 phr.	籌款	chóu kuǎn	raise funds
捐血 phr.		juān xiě	donate blood
建学校 phr.	建學校	jiàn xuéxiào	build schools
盖房子 phr.	蓋房子	gài fángzi	build houses

Charitable organizations

慈善机构 *phr.*	慈善機構	císhàn jìgòu	charitable organization
收留所 *phr.*		shōuliú suǒ	shelter
救助站 *phr.*		jiùzhù zhàn	rescue center
慈善厨房 *phr.*	慈善廚房	císhàn chúfáng	soup kitchen
敬老院 *phr.*	敬老院	jìnglǎo yuàn	nursing home
社区中心 *phr.*	社區中心	shèqū zhōngxīn	community center
老人中心 *phr.*		lǎorén zhōngxīn	senior center
儿童福利院 *phr.*	兒童福利院	értóng fúlì yuàn	children's welfare organization
流浪狗救助站 *phr.*		liúlàng gǒu jiùzhù zhàn	homeless dog shelter
防止虐待动物协会 *phr.*	防止虐待動物協會	fángzhǐ nüèdài dòngwù xiéhuì	ASPCA

LANGUAGE FOCUS

In Chinese, sentences may contain more than one verb. When the object of the first verb also functions as the subject of the second verb, it is called a pivotal sentence. The two verbs pivot, or revolve, around the object/subject.

For example: Mark asked <u>me</u> to help him buy a sandwich. "Me" functions as the object of the verb "asked" and also as the subject for the verb "buy." In Chinese, the sentence would be:

 马克请我帮他买三明治。

There are three verbs most often associated with pivotal sentences. They are 请, 让, and 叫. They all carry the meaning of asking someone to do something, and commonly occur as the first verb in pivotal sentences. Of the three, 请 is the most polite and most formal. 让 has more of a meaning of letting someone do something, whereas 叫 implies an order or making someone do something.

Look at the following sentences and try to determine the meaning.

> 妈妈让我做家务。

> 我请你喝饮料。

> 老师叫我去敬老院做义工。

1. In each picture, you will see a type of volunteer work that you can do to demonstrate that you are a good world citizen. Using the information given, state who asked you to do the activity and when you will do it. You may also state the place where you volunteer your service. Use the construction 因为…所以… in your answer.

因为老师让我去医院做义工，所以我每个星期五晚上去。

① 老师……

② 母亲……

③ 父亲……

④ 李叔叔……

⑤ 英语老师……

⑥ 市长……

⑦ 校长……

⑧ 中文老师……

2. Imagine that your community has just suffered a severe disaster (tornado, hurricane, earthquake, snow storm, major accident, etc.). You are the president of the student council and have been asked by the principal to organize student volunteers to help rebuild the community. You need to write a press release/advertisement/poster for the school newspaper which requests that students sign up to help in various areas. Make sure your release has at least five areas where students can volunteer, where they need to go to sign up, and when the service will be needed.

DO **YOU** KNOW …
你知道吗？

In 1989, a Chinese public service project called Project Hope, 希望工程 (Xīwàng gōngchéng), was organized by the China Youth Development Foundation (CYDF) and the Communist Youth League (CYL) with the goal of creating schools in poor rural areas of China. In some areas, the parents are too poor to send their children to school. Through Project Hope, more than 16,000 primary schools have been built and more than three million children have received scholarships to attend school. Many people in China and abroad have contributed to this project.

bèi   wūrǎn
空气被污染了。
The air is polluted.

nòngzāng
公园被他们弄脏了。
The park was made dirty by them.

NEW WORDS

生
词

被 prep.		bèi	(passive marker) by
环境 n.	環境	huánjìng	environment
空气 n.	空氣	kōngqì	air
二氧化碳 phr.		èryǎnghuàtàn	carbon dioxide
饮用水 phr.	飲用水	yǐnyòng shuǐ	drinking water
工业 n.	工業	gōngyè	industry
废气 n.	廢氣	fèiqì	exhaust
废物 n.	廢物	fèiwù	waste
资源 n.	資源	zīyuán	resources
能源 n.		néngyuán	energy
污染 v/n.		wūrǎn	be polluted; pollution
排放 v/n.		páifàng	emit; emissions
弄脏 phr.	弄髒	nòngzāng	make dirty
用光 phr.		yòngguāng	used up
严重 adj.	嚴重	yánzhòng	serious

Environmental issues

全球变暖 _phr._	全球變暖	quánqiú biàn nuǎn	global warming
空气污染 _phr._	空氣污染	kōngqì wūrǎn	air pollution
饮用水污染 _phr._	飲用水污染	yǐnyòng shuǐ wūrǎn	water pollution
工业废物污染 _phr._	工業廢物污染	gōngyè fèiwù wūrǎn	industrial waste pollution
二氧化碳排放 _phr._		èryǎnghuàtàn páifàng	carbon dioxide emissions
工业废气排放 _phr._	工業廢氣排放	gōngyè fèiqì páifàng	industrial emissions
汽车废气排放 _phr._	汽車廢氣排放	qìchē fèiqì páifàng	car emissions
电子废物 _phr._	電子廢物	diànzǐ fèiwù	computer waste
冰川融化 _phr._		bīngchuān rónghuà	melting glaciers

LANGUAGE FOCUS

In Chinese, to form a passive sentence, first say the item being acted upon (subject), then use the word for "by" (被, called passive markers) with the doer (agent/person/thing) who did the action, followed by the verb or verb phrase:

subject + 被 + doer + verb (phrase)

Examples: ❶ 饮用水被工业废物污染了。
The water is polluted by industrial waste.

❷ 环境被人们污染了。
The environment is polluted by people.

Sometimes the doer may be omitted if the context is clear.

Examples: ❶ 饮用水被污染了。
The water is polluted.

❷ 环境被污染了。
The environment is polluted.

Try This!

1. Look at the following pictures of problems in the environment. What do you think the pictures represent in terms of problems? Write a problem label for each picture. Then on a scale of 1 – 5 (1 being not at all and 5 being a major problem), rate each picture according to how serious you think the problem is either in your community or in the world.

Example:

→ 饮用水污染

1 —— 2 —— 3 —— ④ —— 5

没有问题　　　　　　有问题

❶

_____

1 —— 2 —— 3 —— 4 —— 5

没有问题　　　　　有问题

❹

_____

1 —— 2 —— 3 —— 4 —— 5

没有问题　　　　　　有问题

❷

_____

1 —— 2 —— 3 —— 4 —— 5

没有问题　　　　　有问题

❺

_____

1 —— 2 —— 3 —— 4 —— 5

没有问题　　　　　　有问题

❸

_____

1 —— 2 —— 3 —— 4 —— 5

没有问题　　　　　有问题

❻

_____

1 —— 2 —— 3 —— 4 —— 5

没有问题　　　　　　有问题

2. Read the following sentences and change them to the passive voice.

❶ 工业废物污染了饮用水。　❺ 东尼骑走了自行车。

❷ 张安花光了钱。　　　　　❻ 弟弟吃光了苹果。

❸ 工业废气污染了空气。　　❼ 人们污染了环境。

❹ 妹妹弄脏了桌子。　　　　❽ 汽车废气污染了环境。

jiéyuē

我们应该节约用水。
We should save water.

A Maintaining good daily habits

làngfèi diànchí

你们不要浪费电池。
Don't waste batteries.

NEW WORDS 生 词

分类 v.	分類	fēnlèi	classify	楼梯 n.	樓梯	lóutī	staircase
节约 v.	節約	jiéyuē	save, economize	筷子 n.		kuàizi	chopsticks
减少 v.	減少	jiǎnshǎo	reduce	餐具 n.		cānjù	eating utensils
步行 v.		bùxíng	walk	塑料 n.		sùliào	plastic
浪费 v.	浪費	làngfèi	to waste	随手 adv.	隨手	suíshǒu	conveniently
付账 v.	付賬	fùzhàng	pay bills	多余 adj.	多餘	duōyú	surplus, superfluous
拼车 v.	拼車	pīnchē	car pool	随身 adj.	隨身	suíshēng	carry with you
打包 v.		dǎbāo	get take out	低碳生活 phr.		dītàn shēnghuó	low carbon life
携带 v.	攜帶	xiédài	bring along	碳足迹 phr.	碳足迹	tàn zújì	carbon footprint
使用 v.		shǐyòng	use	一次性 adj.		yícìxìng	one-time
电池 n.	電池	diànchí	battery	瓶装 phr.	瓶裝	píngzhuāng	packed in bottles
环保 n.	環保	huánbǎo	environmental protection				
电梯 n.	電梯	diàntī	elevator				

Words you have learned
yīnggāi
应该 should, ought to

wǎngshàng fù zhàng

网 上 付 账

網 上 付 賬

pay bills online

duō zuò gōngjiāochē

多 坐 公 交 车

多 坐 公 交 車

ride on a *(public)* bus more frequently

duō zuò dìtiě

多 坐 地 铁

多 坐 地 鐵

ride the subway more frequently

bùxíng shàng xiàbān

步 行 上 下 班

walk to and from work

bú zuò diàntī

不 坐 电 梯

不 坐 電 梯

not take the elevator

duōyú fàncài dǎbāo

多 余 饭 菜 打 包

多 餘 飯 菜 打 包

pack up left-over food
(get a doggie bag in a restaurant)

lājī fēnlèi

垃 圾 分 类

垃 圾 分 類

separate garbage into categories

zhǐzhāng liǎngmiàn yòng

纸 张 两 面 用

紙 張 兩 面 用

use the front and back side of paper

shǎo mǎi yīfu

少 买 衣 服

少 買 衣 服

buy less clothes

duō chī shūcài shǎo chī ròu

多吃蔬菜少吃肉

eat more vegetables and less meat

qí zìxíngchē

骑自行车

騎自行車

ride a bicycle

suíshǒu guān dēng

随手关灯

隨手關燈

turn off the lights as you leave

suíshǒu guān shuǐlóngtóu

随手关水龙头

隨手關水龍頭

turn off the faucet

yòng tàiyángnéng rèshuǐqì

用太阳能热水器

用太陽能熱水器

use a solar water heater

búyòng yīcìxìng kuàizi

不用一次性筷子

not use one-time chopsticks

gēn péngyou pīnchē

跟朋友拼车

跟朋友拼車

car pool with friends

LANGUAGE FOCUS

If you believe that there are activities that people should do, use the modal verb 应该 plus the verb. To tell someone to save electricity, say 应该省电。 (Remember that 应该 has the meaning of "should.")

> 我们应该多坐地铁。 We should ride the subway more frequently.
> 你们应该跟朋友拼车。 You should car pool with friends.

When you order people not to do something in Chinese (the command form in English), use the structure 不要 followed by a verb. You learned that 要 means "want," but when it is used negatively before another verb, it creates a negative command. For example, a parent might say, "不要跑" or "不要浪费水." The translation in English is "Don't + action verb."

Look at the following sentences and guess their meaning:

> 不要去。
> 不要开车去。
> 不要吃猪肉。
> 不要污染空气。

1. There are a number of things that you should do in order to maintain an eco-friendly lifestyle (低碳 生活). Complete the following chart with at least 10 suggestions to reduce your carbon footprint (碳足迹). Five suggestions include what you <u>should</u> do (应该) to reduce your carbon footprint and another five suggestions should be what you <u>should not</u> (不要) do so that you reduce your carbon footprint.

应该	不要

2. Read the following text and discuss with one of your classmates which actions you both can take in your daily lives to reduce your carbon footprints.

xíngdòng
低碳行动
action

qì hòu biànhuà yǐjīng chéngwéi
现在气候变化已经成为全球的热点问题，我们可以
climate change already became

sùshí
从身边的小事做起："每周绿色出行一天，每周素食一
vegetarian

天，每周手洗一次衣服，每周少看一小时电视，每周少

搭一次电梯、每周少喝一瓶瓶装水。"如果能做得到，

每一个人就可以为地球减少排放二氧化碳。
Earth

3. Study the chart below, and match the actions in the first column with the corresponding actions in the first row by writing what you believe you can do. Write 做得到 for the actions you can do, and 做不到 for the actions that you cannot do.

低碳行动	每周绿色出行一天	每周素食一天	每周手洗一次衣服	每周少看一小时电视	每周少搭一次电梯	每周少喝一瓶瓶装水
不吃肉		做得到				
步行回家						
上下楼走楼梯						
不用洗衣机洗衣服						
坐公交车和地铁						
多吃蔬菜						
骑自行车						
随身携带水瓶						
少看电视						
不坐电梯						
节约用水						
节约用电						
减少使用塑料瓶						
拼车上学						

DO YOU KNOW . . .
你知道吗?

Hotline for Environmental Protection in China

In China there is a pollution hotline number to call if you want to report a problem about noise, waste, gas, dust, or sewage. The number is 010-12369 and was launched back in 2009. The hotline allows people to lodge a complaint from 8 AM to 8 PM, Monday through Friday.

dāng

当你离开房间的时候，

diào

应该把灯关掉。

When you leave the room, you should turn off the lights.

yǐhòu

用完电脑以后，应该关机。

After using the computer, *(you)* should shut it down.

生　词

NEW WORDS

当 *prep.*	當	dāng	when
离开 *v.*	離開	líkāi	leave *(a place)*
关掉 *v.*	關掉	guāndiào	turn off
计划 *v.*	計劃	jìhuà	plan
自备 *v.*	自備	zìbèi	bring along
断电 *v.*	斷電	duàndiàn	turn off the power
节能 *v.*	節能	jiénéng	saves energy
回收 *v.*		huíshōu	recycle
灯泡 *n.*	燈泡	dēngpào	light bulb
电风扇 *n.*	電風扇	diànfēngshàn	electric fan
空调 *n.*	空調	kōngtiáo	air-conditioner
行程 *n.*		xíngchéng	route, itinerary
购物袋 *n.*	購物袋	gòuwùdài	shopping bag

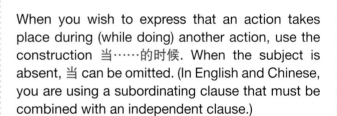

LANGUAGE FOCUS

When you wish to express that an action takes place during (while doing) another action, use the construction 当……的时候. When the subject is absent, 当 can be omitted. (In English and Chinese, you are using a subordinating clause that must be combined with an independent clause.)

❧ 当你刷牙的时候，你应该把水龙头
关掉。
When you brush your teeth, you should turn off the water.

❧ 刷牙的时候，你应该把水龙头关掉。
Turn off the water when brushing your teeth.

When you wish to express that an action takes place before or after another action, use the words 以前 and 以后.

❧ 倒垃圾以前，你应该把垃圾分类。
Before you throw out the garbage, you should sort it.

❧ 看完电视以后，你应该把电视机关掉。
After you watch television, you should turn it off.

1. Find your carbon footprint 碳足迹. Here is a list of behaviors that are part of our everyday life. Read the list and decide which of the behaviors you do on a regular basis (有) and those that you do not (没有). For each 有 response, give yourself five points, and for each 没有 response, give yourself one point. Add up all of your points to find your carbon footprint.

热门调查 diàochá popular survey ： 你的生活低碳吗？	有	没有		有	没有
❶ 随手关灯			⓫ 把垃圾分类回收		
❷ 双面使用纸张			⓬ 种植绿色植物		
❸ 出门前3分钟关空调			⓭ 去超市自己带购物袋		
❹ 少吃肉多吃蔬菜			⓮ 用一次性餐具和纸杯		
❺ 多坐公共交通工具 gōngjù tool			⓯ 跟朋友拼车		
❻ 把普通灯泡换成节能灯 pǔtōng ordinary huànchéng change			⓰ 电脑不用时关机		
❼ 网上付账购物			⓱ 每周少开一天车		
❽ 减少使用塑料袋			⓲ 使用节能电器		
❾ 刷牙时你习惯把水关掉			⓳ 随身携带水瓶		
❿ 在公园跑步代替用 跑步机 dàitì replace treadmill			⓴ 上下楼走楼梯		

2. After you have completed Exercise #1 above, use that information to compare your carbon footprint with the carbon footprint of at least eight other people in the class. Ask your classmates what his/her name is and what their carbon footprint is.

Use the question: 你的碳足迹是多少？

名字	碳足迹
❶	
❷	
❸	
❹	
❺	
❻	
❼	
❽	

3. Complete each sentence with a logical answer on how to be eco-friendly. You may use the hints provided or come up with your own answers.

❶ 睡觉以前，_____。(关灯)

❷ 当你吃饭的时候，_____。(一次性筷子)

❸ 当你不用电脑的时候，_____。(关机)

❹ 当你离开教室的时候，_____。(关灯)

❺ 洗完脸以后，_____。(关水龙头)

❻ 当你上学的时候，_____。(拼车)

❼ 天气热的时候，_____。(电风扇)

❽ 开车出门以前，_____。(计划行程)

❾ 购物的时候，_____。(购物袋)

❿ 用完电器以后，_____。(断电)

DO **YOU** KNOW . . . 你知道吗？

In mainland China and in Taiwan the characters for 垃圾 are the same but the pronunciation is different. In China it is pronounced lājī, whereas in Taiwan it is pronounced lèsè.

Reading *in* Context

STEP 1 BEING PART OF A COMMUNITY

Description of a neighbor

我有一个邻居王奶奶，她一个人住，她的孩子都在国外工作。

王奶奶的脾气非常好，很容易跟别人相处。受她的影响，很多老人的脾气都有了改变。大家都喜欢去她家玩。大家都说她是一个快乐的老太太。她说她是一个快乐的老小孩。当别人请她帮忙的时候，只要她能做的，她都去做。王奶奶常说："我们的社会是一个大家庭，家里人和睦，才会幸福。"她还说："人做事不能只想自己，还要考虑别人的感受，要考虑对别人有什么样的影响。"我觉得王奶奶说得特别好。所以我也很喜欢这个快乐的老奶奶。

改变	快乐	家庭	和睦
gǎibiàn	kuàilè	jiātíng	hémù
change	happy	family	harmonious

幸福	考虑	感受	特别
xìngfú	kǎolǜ	gǎnshòu	tèbié
happy	consider	feelings	exceptionally

STEP 2 HELPING THE COMMUNITY

Xiaohai and Xiaohong talking about environmental issues

小海：小红，你看，你们这里的风景多好啊！蓝天、白云、绿树、绿草。

小红：是啊！这里是郊区，一到周末，来这里休闲活动的人很多。

小海：因为这里的空气比城市里干净多了。周末人们都喜欢去干净的环境放松一下。

小红：是啊！所以大家都应该爱护环境，保护环境，让这样的环境多一些。我很担心，这里的人一多，汽车就多了。空气会被污染，环境就被破坏了。

小海：你说得没错。我也有时候看见一些人走后，草地上有一些果皮、碎纸、垃圾什么的。

小红：我打算给社区一个建议，建议每周末搞一次宣传活动，让大家注意保护这里的环境。每个人都不要乱扔垃圾，要爱护花草树木，让空气、环境干净一些，让我们的家园变得更美丽，更干净。

小海：你的想法不错啊！除了宣传这些，还可以组织中小学生做义工，捡垃圾，打扫环境什么的。

fēngjǐng	scenery
jiāoqū	suburbs

xiūxián	huódòng
leisure	activity

gānjìng	clean

fàngsōng	relax

àihù	bǎohù
care for	protect

dānxīn	worried

pòhuài	damaged

guǒpí	suìzhǐ
fruit peel	bits of paper

gǎo	xuānchuán
organize	publicity

zhùyì	mind

zǔzhī	jiǎn
organize	pick

STEP 3 CREATING A BETTER LIFE

A student essay on how to protect the environment

环境污染问题越来越严重。保护环境是我们每一个人的责任。其实，只要我们在生活中做出一些改变，环保并不是一件难事。

出门的时候，我们可以选择多坐公交车、地铁，最好是步行上班、上学。要开车的话，可以跟朋友拼车。买东西的时候，自备购物袋，不要买瓶装水，也不要使用一次性餐具。在家里，看完电视或用完电脑以后，应该随手关机。睡觉以前，要先关灯。

只要我们注意一下生活中的小细节，就能为环保出一份力。

责任	其实	生活	难事	选择	细节
zérèn	qíshí	shēnghuó	nánshì	xuǎnzé	xìjié
responsibility	actually	life	difficult task	choose	details

$\mathcal{S}\!tep\ Up!$

1. Read the following dialog and decide if the statements afterwards are true (T) or false (F).

马克： 丁强你好，你最近怎么样？

丁强： 马克你好，我最近很累，每天晚上都睡不好。

马克： 你怎么了？为什么每天晚上都睡不好？

丁强： 唉，我和张安住一个宿舍，可是，张安每天很晚才回
ài sigh　　　　　　　　　　　　sùshè dormitory
宿舍，回来以后他又很吵，大家都睡不好。

马克： 是吗？那你们没有和他聊过吗？

丁强： 张安的脾气不好，所以很不容易跟他相处。除了每天
回来晚，他还不爱打扫卫生。他从来不清理桌子，也
　　　　　　　wèishēng hygiene　　　　qīnglǐ clean
不倒垃圾。拖地板、扫地、擦桌子、倒垃圾都是我们
做的。

马克： 他从来不做吗？太不应该了。
always

丁强： 是啊！他看起来每天都很忙，都没有空打扫宿舍。

马克： 可是在我看来，大家住在一起，应该互相帮助、互相
　　　　　　　　　　　　　　　　　hùxiāng each other　　shì
尊重。要是我是你的话，我会跟他好好聊聊这件事。
zūnzhòng respect　　　zhírìbiǎo　　　　　　　　　　　matter
你们有没有值日表？
　　　　rotating schedule

丁强： 有啊！可是他还是从来不干活。你有别的建议吗？
　　　　　　　　　　　gànhuó work

马克： 你们可以跟他的父母说说。

丁强： 我们请过他的父母帮忙，可是，他不听他父母的话。

马克： 我有一个更好的办法，你们可以跟老师说说，请老师
　　　　gèng even more　bànfǎ solution
帮你们。

丁强： 看起来，我们只好去找老师帮忙了。

❶ 马克每天晚上都睡不好。　（　　）

❼ 丁强每天都很忙。　（　　）

❷ 丁强最近很累。　（　　）

❽ 马克建议丁强好好跟张安聊聊打扫宿舍的事。　（　　）

❸ 丁强每天晚上很吵，所以张安晚上都睡不好。　（　　）

❾ 丁强从来没有跟张安聊过打扫宿舍的事。　（　　）

❹ 丁强和张安聊过每天很晚回宿舍的事。　（　　）

❿ 丁强的宿舍没有值日表。　（　　）

❺ 张安不容易相处。　（　　）

⓫ 丁强找张安的父母帮忙，可是张安不受父母的影响。　（　　）

❻ 除了每天回来晚，张安还不清理桌子、不倒垃圾、不拖地板也不扫地。　（　　）

⓬ 丁强要去找老师帮忙。　（　　）

2. Choose a partner with whom you would like to work. You are both members of the Environmental Club and have been asked to come up with a list of the most important things that you can do for your school to make it a Greener School. The two of you will devise a list of 10 activities that everyone can do to create a more eco-friendly environment in the school. Once you have a list of at least 10 activities, discuss which ones are the most important and then come to a consensus on the importance of the activities on your list. Rate them from 1 being the most important to 10 being the least important. (If you have more than 10 items, put all of them in order so that they all have a ranking.)

3. You are the chairperson of the Committee for Creating a Greener School, an important committee of the Environmental Club. You have just received the reports from different members of your committee concerning their ranking of activities to create a greener school. From these rankings, create a brochure or pamphlet to distribute to students in your school to help launch a school-wide campaign to create a greener school and, thus, a better world. On the brochure, be sure to inform the members of the student body of things that they can do in school to reduce their carbon footprint. Make sure that you state at least five different suggestions for ways to improve your school and provide pictures of the activities that students can engage in.

Fun Time!

Recycled art

Thanks to the research and theories of the physicist Albert Einstein, we often say that "nothing disappears, everything transforms." Because of the huge amount of garbage that is created in the world every day, many artists have taken to creating new types of art using recycled trash. There are a number of Chinese artists who used recycled products to do amazing things.

One well known Chinese artist concerned about the environment is Zhu Kefeng. In the early 2000s, Mr. Zhu noticed the effects that many different metals were having on the environment. As a result, he started a project to build a theme park entirely from scrap metals. Mr. Zhu capitalized on the film *Transformers* to create this park that he called the Mr. Iron Robot Theme Park. He completed building the park in Jiaxing City (located in Zhejiang Province) in 2010 with money he had saved from selling his art work and also from selling his apartment in Shanghai. In March of 2012, the Mr. Iron Robot theme park was granted status as a tourist attraction and became the first theme park in China built of recycled iron and steel works.

Young people looking at one of the sculptures in the park.

There are other Chinese artists who have also capitalized on recycling and created very imaginative works of art. Long-Bin Chen from Taiwan has created many sculptures that look like wood or marble but are often made out of paper products. On the left is a sculpture of hurricane made out of magazines and newspapers.

A sculpture of hurricane made from recycled paper.

A suit made out of porcelain shards.

Another Chinese artist, Li Xiaofeng, uses recycled porcelain shards to reassemble them and create dazzling costumes that people can actually wear. (Because they are made of porcelain, the costumes are as heavy as they are beautiful.)

Qiu Zhijie has taken the scrap metal from old oil drums and turned them into aesthetically pleasing sculptures. One of his most well known pieces of art is the "Oil Can Dragon" that you see on the right.

The Oil Can Dragon sculpture.

As the saying goes in English, "One man's trash is another man's treasure." Can you find a way to say that in Chinese? What other productive ways to recycle can you think of?

I have learned...

Core Vocabulary

Verb

受		shòu	receive, be subject to	付账	付賬	fùzhàng	pay bills
相处	相處	xiāngchǔ	get along (with someone)	拼车	拼車	pīnchē	car pool
请	請	qǐng	invite, ask, treat	打包		dǎbāo	get take out
叫		jiào	order, ask	携带	攜帶	xiédài	bring along
让	讓	ràng	let, allow	使用		shǐyòng	use
污染		wūrǎn	be polluted	离开	離開	líkāi	leave (a place)
排放		páifàng	emit; emissions	关掉	關掉	guāndiào	turn off
分类	分類	fēnlèi	classify	计划	計劃	jìhuà	plan
节约	節約	jiéyuē	save, economize	自备	自備	zìbèi	bring along
减少	减少	jiǎnshǎo	reduce	断电	斷電	duàndiàn	turn off the power
步行		bùxíng	walk	节能	節能	jiénéng	saves energy
浪费	浪費	làngfèi	to waste	回收		huíshōu	recycle

Nouns

影响	影響	yǐngxiǎng	influence	工业	工業	gōngyè	industry
社会	社會	shèhuì	society	废气	廢氣	fèiqì	exhaust
公民		gōngmín	citizen	废物	廢物	fèiwù	waste
图书馆员	圖書館員	túshūguǎnyuán	librarian	资源	資源	zīyuán	resources
志愿者	志願者	zhìyuànzhě	volunteer	能源		néngyuán	energy
公车司机	公車司機	gōngchē sījī	bus driver	污染		wūrǎn	pollution
急救专家	急救專家	jíjiù zhuānjiā	EMT	排放		páifàng	emit; emissions
救生员	救生員	jiùshēngyuán	life guard	电池	電池	diànchí	battery
市长	市長	shìzhǎng	mayor	环保	環保	huánbǎo	environmental protection
性格		xìnggé	personality, disposition	电梯	電梯	diàntī	elevator
脾气	脾氣	píqì	temper	楼梯	樓梯	lóutī	staircase
别人		biéren	other people	筷子		kuàizi	chopsticks
环境	壞境	huánjìng	environment	餐具		cānjù	eating utensils
空气	空氣	kōngqì	air	塑料		sùliào	plastic

灯泡	燈泡	dēngpào	light bulb	行程		xíngchéng	route, itinerary
电风扇	電風扇	diànfēngshàn	electric fan	购物袋	購物袋	gòuwùdài	shopping bag
空调	空调	kōngtiáo	air-conditioner				

Adjectives

开朗	開朗	kāilǎng	cheerful, outgoing	挑剔		tiāotī	picky, fastidious
诚实	誠實	chéngshí	be honest	严重	嚴重	yánzhòng	serious
热心	熱心	rèxīn	enthusiastic; eagerness	多余	多餘	duōyú	surplus, superfluous
大方		dàfang	generous	随身	隨身	suíshǒu	carry with you
多心		duōxīn	suspicious	一次性		yícìxìng	one-time
刻薄		kèbó	mean				

Adverbs

Prepositions

随手	隨手	suíshǒu	conveniently	被		bèi	(passive marker) by
				当	當	dāng	when

Phrases

Volunteer work

做志愿者	做志願者	zuò zhìyuànzhě	volunteering	捐血		juān xuě	donate blood
做家教		zuò jiājiào	tutoring	建学校	建學校	jiàn xuéxiào	build schools
捐款	捐款	juān kuǎn	donate money, make a donation	盖房子	蓋房子	gài fángzi	build houses
筹款	籌款	chóu kuǎn	raise funds				

Charitable organizations

慈善机构	慈善機構	císhàn jìgòu	charitable organization
收留所		shōuliú suǒ	shelter
救助站		jiùzhù zhàn	rescue center
慈善厨房	慈善廚房	císhàn chúfáng	soup kitchen
敬老院		jìnglǎo yuàn	nursing home
社区中心	社區中心	shèqū zhōngxīn	community center
老人中心		lǎorén zhōngxīn	senior center
儿童福利院	兒童福利院	értóng fúlì yuàn	children's welfare organization
流浪狗救助站		liúlàng gǒu jiùzhù zhàn	homeless dog shelter
防止虐待动物协会	防止虐待動物協會	fángzhǐ nüèdài dòngwù xiéhuì	ASPCA

337

I have learned...

Environmental issues

全球变暖	全球變暖	quánqiú biàn nuǎn	global warming
空气污染	空氣污染	kōngqì wūrǎn	air pollution
饮用水污染	飲用水污染	yǐnyòng shuǐ wūrǎn	water pollution
工业废物污染	工業廢物污染	gōngyè fèiwù wūrǎn	industrial waste pollution
二氧化碳排放		èryǎnghuàtàn páifàng	carbon dioxide emissions
工业废气排放	工業廢氣排放	gōngyè fèiqì páifàng	industrial emissions
汽车废气排放	汽車廢氣排放	qìchē fèiqì páifàng	car emissions
电子废物	電子廢物	diànzǐ fèiwù	computer waste
冰川融化		bīngchuān rónghuà	melting glaciers

Eco-friendly habits

网上付账	網上付賬	wǎngshàng fù zhàng	pay bills online
多坐公交车	多坐公交車	duō zuò gōngjiāochē	ride on a (public) bus more frequently
多坐地铁	多坐地鐵	duō zuò dìtiě	ride the subway more frequently
步行上下班		bùxíng shàng xiàbān	walk to and from work
不坐电梯	不坐電梯	bú zuò diàntī	not take the elevator
多余饭菜打包	多餘飯菜打包	duōyú fàncài dǎbāo	pack up left-over food (get a doggie bag in a restaurant)
垃圾分类	垃圾分類	lājī fēnlèi	separate garbage into categories
纸张两面用	紙張兩面用	zhǐzhāng liǎngmiàn yòng	use the front and back side of paper
少买衣服	少買衣服	shǎo mǎi yīfu	buy less clothes
多吃蔬菜少吃肉		duō chī shūcài shǎo chī ròu	eat more vegetables and less meat
骑自行车	騎自行車	qí zìxíngchē	ride a bicycle
随手关灯	隨手關燈	suíshǒu guān dēng	turn off the lights as you leave
随手关水龙头	隨手關水龍頭	suíshǒu guān shuǐlóngtóu	turn off the faucet
用太阳能热水器	用太陽能熱水器	yòng tàiyángnéng rèshuǐqì	use a solar water heater
不用一次性筷子	不用一次性筷子	búyòng yīcìxìng kuàizi	not use one-time chopsticks
跟朋友拼车	跟朋友拼車	gēn péngyou pīnchē	car pool with friends

Others

社区服务	社區服務	shèqū fúwù	community service
红十字会	红十字會	hóngshízìhuì	Red Cross
家长会	家長會	jiāzhǎnghuì	Parent Association
有耐心		yǒu nàixīn	be patient
有爱心	有愛心	yǒu àixīn	kind-hearted
有礼貌	有禮貌	yǒu lǐmào	be courteous, polite
爱管闲事	愛管閑事	ài guǎn xiánshì	nosy
二氧化碳	二氧化碳	èryǎnghuàtàn	carbon dioxide
饮用水	飲用水	yǐnyòng shuǐ	drinking water
弄脏	弄髒	nòngzāng	make dirty
用光		yòngguāng	used up
低碳生活		dītàn shēnghuó	low carbon life
碳足迹	碳足迹	tàn zújì	carbon footprint
瓶装	瓶裝	píngzhuāng	packed in bottles

SENTENCE PATTERNS

志愿者<u>对</u>我的影响很大。

芳芳很有耐心，所以很容易<u>跟</u>她<u>相处</u>。

张安<u>请</u>我<u>跟</u>他一起去捐血。

空气<u>被</u>污染了。

我们<u>应该</u>节约用水。

<u>当</u>你离开房间的<u>时候</u>，应该把灯关掉。

I can do!

Interpretive Communication

❑ I can read and understand information about helping others.

❑ I can read and understand information about community workers.

❑ I can understand when someone talks about community service.

❑ I can understand when someone talks about the environment and ways to protect it.

Interpersonal Communication

❑ I can converse about the influence that different people have on me.

❑ I can converse about how to get along with people in my community.

❑ I can converse about contributing to the community.

❑ I can converse about how to make the environment greener.

Presentational Communication

❑ I can state the required traits or qualities of different community workers.

❑ I can write a press release to request help in disaster relief.

❑ I can write and tell about ways to reduce my carbon footprint.

Cultural Knowledge

❑ I can retell the story of Meng Zi.

❑ I can talk about Project Hope.

❑ I can state the number for the Environmental Hotline in China.

❑ I can talk about how recycled material can be used to create works of art.

APPENDICES

Vocabulary Index 生词索引

345

Simplified	Traditional	Pinyin	English	Page
看医生 *phr.*	看醫生	kàn yīshēng	see a doctor	170
看法 *n.*		kànfǎ	point of view	298
考试 *n.*	考試	kǎoshì	exam, test	17
棵 *m.w.*		kē	(used for trees)	98
科目 *n.*		kēmù	subject	70
咳嗽 *phr.*		késòu	cough	227
可爱 *adj.*	可愛	kě'ài	cute	66
可能 *aux. v.*		kěnéng	may, might, probably	192
可以 *aux.v.*		kěyǐ	can, may	270
刻薄 *adj.*		kèbó	mean	315
课程表 *n.*	課程表	kèchéngbiǎo	course schedule	62
课间操 *n.*	課間操	kèjiāncāo	exercises between classes	62
课外活动 *phr.*	課外活動	kèwài huódòng	extra-curricular activities	62
空气 *n.*	空氣	kōngqì	air	321
空气污染 *phr.*	空氣污染	kōngqì wūrǎn	air pollution	322
空调 *n.*	空調	kōngtiáo	air-conditioner	329
裤子 *n.*	褲子	kùzi	trousers, pants	131
块 *m.w.*	塊	kuài	(used for things that come in solid pieces)	95
块 *m.w.*	塊	kuài	(used for things that are shaped like sheets)	133
会计师 *n.*	會計師	kuàijìshī	accountant	184
快速 *adj.*		kuàisù	fast	252
筷子 *n.*		kuàizi	chopsticks	324

L

Simplified	Traditional	Pinyin	English	Page
拉肚子 *phr.*		lādùzi	diarrhea	227
来 *v.*	來	lái	come	40
兰花 *n.*	蘭花	lánhuā	orchid	105
篮球场 *n.*	籃球場	lánqiúchǎng	basketball court	153
懒惰 *adj.*	懶惰	lǎnduò	lazy	200
浪费 *v.*	浪費	làngfèi	to waste	324
老人中心 *phr.*		lǎorén zhōngxīn	senior center	319
雷阵雨 *n.*	雷陣雨	léizhènyǔ	thunderstorm	123
冷 *adj.*		lěng	cold	123
离开 *v.*	離開	líkāi	leave (a place)	329
礼拜 *n.*	禮拜	lǐbài	week	14
理发店 *n.*	理髮店	lǐfàdiàn	hairdresser's salon	153
例如…等		lìrú…děng	for example…etc.	104
联系 *v.*	聯系	liánxì	keep in touch	261

Simplified	Traditional	Pinyin	English	Page
连衣裙 *n.*	連衣裙	liányīqún	dress	131
脸书 *n.*	臉書	liǎnshū	Facebook	261
凉快 *adj.*	涼快	liángkuai	(pleasantly) cool	123
凉鞋 / 拖鞋 *n.*	涼鞋	liángxié / tuōxié	sandals, slippers	132
辆 *m.w.*	輛	liàng	(used for bicycles, cars, etc.)	98
了 *v.*		liǎo	(used after 得 or 不 to indicate the possibility or impossibility of accomplishing something)	258
了不起 *adj.*		liǎobùqǐ	amazing	200
邻居 *n.*	鄰居	línjū	neighbor	98
零食 *n.*		língshí	snacks	214
菱形 *n.*		língxíng	diamond (shape)	107
领带 *n.*	領帶	lǐngdài	tie	133
遛狗 *phr.*		liù gǒu	walk the dog	285
流鼻涕 *phr.*		liú bítì	running nose	227
流浪狗救助站 *phr.*		liúlàng gǒu jiùzhù zhàn	homeless dog shelter	319
楼 *n.*	樓	lóu	floor, story	83
楼上 *n.*	樓上	lóushang	upstairs	83
楼梯 *n.*	樓梯	lóutī	staircase	324
楼下 *n.*	樓下	lóuxia	downstairs	83
炉子 *n.*	爐子	lúzi	stove	96
落地灯 *n.*	落地燈	luòdìdēng	standing lamp	91
旅游 *n.*	旅游	lǚyóu	travel, tour	23
旅游业 *n.*	旅游業	lǚyóuyè	tourism industry	192

M

Simplified	Traditional	Pinyin	English	Page
麻烦 *v.*	麻煩	máfan	trouble, bother	291
码 *m.w.*	碼	mǎ	yard	166
马桶 *n.*	馬桶	mǎtǒng	toilet	96
买 *v.*	買	mǎi	buy	23
买菜 *phr.*	買菜	mǎi cài	buy groceries	170
买药 *phr.*	買藥	mǎi yào	buy medicine	169
麦克风口 *phr.*	麥克風口	màikèfēng kǒu	microphone plug	255
毛巾 *n.*		máojīn	towel	235
毛衣 *n.*		máoyī	sweater	130
帽子 *n.*		màozi	hat, cap	133
玫瑰花 *n.*		méiguīhuā	rose	105
没空 *phr.*	沒空	méi kòng	not free, busy	288
没意思 *adj.*	沒意思	méi yìsi	not interesting	27
美观 *adj.*	美觀	měiguān	beautiful, sleek	252

热心 adj.	熱心	rèxīn	enthusiastic; eagerness	315
认识 v.	認識	rènshi	know someone, be acquainted with	4
认为 v.	認爲	rènwéi	think, consider	298
认真 adj.	認真	rènzhēn	serious	200
容易 adj.		róngyì	easy	62
肉类 phr.	肉類	ròu lèi	meats (category)	215
如果 就 conj.		rúguǒ…jiù…	if…then…	195
软件 n.	軟件	ruǎnjiàn	software	255

S

三角形 n.		sānjiǎoxíng	triangle	107
散步 phr.		sànbù	take a stroll	170
扫地 v.	掃地	sǎodì	sweep (the floor)	285
沙发 n.	沙發	shāfā	sofa	91, 95
商场 n.	商場	shāngchǎng	mall	153
商店 n.		shāngdiàn	retail outlet, shop	188
商人 n.		shāngrén	businessman	185
伤心 adj.	傷心	shāngxīn	sad, heart-broken	29
上 v.		shàng	go or come up	88
上班 v.		shàngbān	go to work	40
上传/载 v.	上傳/載	shàngchuán/zài	upload	264
上社交网 phr.	上社交網	shàng shè jiāowǎng	visit social networking sites	264
少 adj.		shǎo	few, less	62
社会 n.	社會	shèhuì	society	312
设计 v.	設計	shèjì	design	196
社交媒体 phr.	社交媒體	shèjiāo méitǐ	social media	261
社交网 n.	社交網	shèjiāowǎng	social networking sites	264
社区 n.	社區	shèqū	community	153
社区服务 phr.	社區服務	shèqū fúwù	community service	312
社区中心 phr.	社區中心	shèqū zhōngxīn	community center	319
摄氏度 n.	攝氏度	shèshìdù	Celsius degree	125
摄像机 n.	攝像機	shèxiàngjī	video camera	252
深粉色 n.		shēnfěnsè	dark pink	108
深红色 n.	深紅色	shēnhóngsè	dark red	108
深黄色 n.	深黃色	shēnhuángsè	dark yellow	108
深蓝色 n.	深藍色	shēnlánsè	dark blue	108
深绿色 n.	深綠色	shēnlǜsè	dark green	108
深色 n.		shēnsè	dark color	108

伸张 v.	伸張	shēnzhāng	uphold	196
深紫色 n.		shēnzǐsè	dark purple	108
什么时候 q.w.	什麼時候	shénme shíhou	when; what time	17
生病 v.		shēngbìng	fall sick	227
声卡 n.	聲卡	shēngkǎ	sound card	255
生气 adj.	生氣	shēngqì	angry	29
时候 n.	時候	shíhou	time	17
时间 n.	時間	shíjiān	time, period	17
时间表 n.	時間表	shíjiānbiǎo	time table/schedule	62
食品 n.		shípǐn	food products (cooked or processed items)	214
食品业 n.	食品業	shípǐnyè	food industry	192
时尚界 n.	時尚界	shíshàngjiè	fashion industry	192
食物 n.		shíwù	food	104
食物标签 phr.	食物標簽	shíwù biāoqiān	food label	220
实用 adj.	實用	shíyòng	easy to use	252
使用 v.		shǐyòng	use	324
是……的		shì…de	(used to emphasize time, location, and means)	46
市长 n.	市長	shìzhǎng	mayor	312
收留所 phr.		shōuliú suǒ	shelter	319
收银员 n.	收銀元	shōuyínyuán	cashier	185
首 m.w.		shǒu	(used for songs)	270
手表 n.	手錶	shǒubiǎo	watch	133
手套 n.		shǒutào	gloves	133
手腕 n.		shǒuwàn	wrist	228
受 v.		shòu	receive, be subject to	312
售货员 n.	售貨員	shòuhuòyuán	salesperson	185
受伤 v.	受傷	shòushāng	be injured	227
蔬菜类 phr.	蔬菜類	shūcài lèi	vegetables (category)	215
书店 n.	書店	shūdiàn	book store	153
舒服 adj.		shūfu	comfortable	227
书架 n.	書架	shūjià	bookshelf	91
梳头 phr.	梳頭	shūtóu	comb your hair	235
书桌 n.	書桌	shūzhuō	desk	91
梳子 n.		shūzi	comb	235
鼠标 n.	鼠標	shǔbiāo	mouse	253
暑假 n.		shǔjià	summer vacation	4
暑假作业 phr.	暑假作業	shǔjià zuòyè	summer assignments	23
暑期学校 phr.	暑期學校	shǔqī xuéxiào	summer school	23

演戏 *phr.*	演戲	yǎnxì	act	196
严重 *adj.*	嚴重	yánzhòng	serious	321
阳台 *n.*	陽臺	yángtái	balcony	83
腰 *n.*		yāo	waist	228
药房 *n.*	藥房	yàofáng	pharmacy	153
要是……的话 *conj.*	要是……的話	yàoshi... dehuà	if	288
衣柜 *n.*	衣櫃	yīguì	wardrobe	91
医药业 *n.*	醫藥業	yīyàoyè	health industry	192
医院 *n.*	醫院	yīyuàn	hospital	153
医治 *v.*	醫治	yīzhì	cure, treat, heal	196
一次性 *adj.*		yícìxìng	one-time	324
一会儿 *n.*	一會兒	yíhuìr	a little while	4
一边……一边… *conj.*	一邊……一邊…	yìbiān...yìbiān	at the same time, simultaneously	296
一点 *num.*	一點	yìdiǎn	slightly, a little	62
义工 *n.*	義工	yìgōng	volunteer work	23
一起 *prep.*		yìqǐ	together with	261
艺术家 *n.*	藝術家	yìshùjiā	artist	185
艺术界 *n.*	藝術界	yìshùjiè	arts profession	192
一些 *num.*		yìxiē	some	98
一直 *adv.*		yìzhí	straight, straight ahead	163
阴天 *n.*	陰天	yīntiān	overcast	123
因为…所以… *conj.*	因爲…所以…	yīnwèi...suǒyǐ	because...therefore...	55
音乐会 *n.*	音樂會	yīnyuèhuì	musical concerts	196
音乐家 *n.*	音樂家	yīnyuèjiā	musician	185
音乐界 *n.*	音樂界	yīnyuèjiè	music profession	192
银白色 *n.*	銀白色	yínbáisè	silver white	107
银行 *n.*	銀行	yínháng	bank	153
银行出纳员 *n.*	銀行出納員	yínháng chūnàyuán	bank teller	185
银行家 *n.*	銀行家	yínhángjiā	banker	185
银灰色 *n.*	銀灰色	yínhuīsè	silver gray	107
饮料 *n.*	飲料	yǐnliào	beverages	214
饮用水 *phr.*	飲用水	yǐnyòng shuǐ	drinking water	321
饮用水污染 *phr.*	飲用水污染	yǐnyòng shuǐ wūrǎn	water pollution	322
英尺 *m.w.*		yīngchǐ	foot	166
应该 *aux. v.*	因該	yīnggāi	should, ought to	237
英里 *m.w.*		yīnglǐ	mile	166
营养 *n.*	營養	yíngyǎng	nutrition	220
营养成分 *phr.*	營養成分	yíngyǎng chéngfèn	nutritional content	220

影响 *n.*	影響	yǐngxiǎng	influence	312
硬盘 *n.*	硬盤	yìngpán	hard disk	255
勇敢 *adj.*		yǒnggǎn	brave, courageous	200
用 *v.*		yòng	to use	234
用光 *phr.*		yòngguāng	used up	321
邮递员 *n.*	郵遞員	yóudìyuán	mail carrier	185
邮局 *n.*	郵局	yóujú	post office	153
游泳衣 *n.*		yóuyǒngyī	swimsuit	130
油脂类 *phr.*	油脂類	yóuzhī lèi	fats and oils (category)	215
有爱心 *phr.*	有愛心	yǒu àixīn	kind-hearted	315
有才华 *phr.*	有才華	yǒu cáihuá	talented	200
有创意 *phr.*	有創意	yǒu chuàngyì	creative	200
有道理 *phr.*		yǒu dàolǐ	makes sense, is reasonable	298
有的 *adj.*		yǒude	some	220
有点儿 *adv.*	有點兒	yǒudiǎnr	a little, a bit	123
有恒心 *phr.*	有恒心	yǒu héngxīn	persistent	200
有空 *phr.*		yǒu kòng	free	288
有礼貌 *phr.*	有禮貌	yǒu lǐmào	be courteous, polite	315
有耐心 *phr.*		yǒu nàixīn	be patient	315
有学问 *phr.*	有學問	yǒu xuéwèn	learned, scholarly, academic	200
有意思 *adj.*		yǒu yìsi	interesting	27
友善 *adj.*		yǒushàn	friendly	200
有用 *adj.*		yǒuyòng	useful	66
娱乐界 *n.*	娛樂界	yúlèjiè	entertainment profession	192
羽绒服 *n.*	羽絨服	yǔróngfú	down jacket	130
雨天 *n.*		yǔtiān	rainy day	123
雨衣 *n.*		yǔyī	raincoat	130
浴缸 *n.*		yùgāng	bathtub	96
圆形 *n.*	圓形	yuánxíng	circle	107
院子 *n.*		yuànzi	yard	98
运动 *n.*	運動	yùndòng	sports	196
运动 *v.*	運動	yùndòng	exercise	237

Z

再 *conj.*		zài	then, after	161
早操 *n.*		zǎocāo	morning exercises	62
早睡早起 *phr.*		zǎo shuì zǎo qǐ	go to sleep early, get up early	237
早自习 *n.*	早自習	zǎozìxí	morning study	62

怎么 q.w.	怎麼	zěnme	how	40
怎么了 q.w.	怎麼了	zěnme le	what	227
盏 m.w.	盞	zhǎn	(used for lamps)	94
张 m.w.	張	zhāng	(used for beds, tables, sofas, etc.)	95
找 v.		zhǎo	find, search	270
照顾 v.	照顧	zhàogù	take care of	196
照片 n.		zhàopiàn	photos	264
着 part.	著	zhe	(placed after verbs to indicate a continuing action or state)	98
这么 adv.	這么	zhème	so, like this	127
诊所 n.	診所	zhěnsuǒ	clinic	153
正方形 n.		zhèngfāngxíng	square	107
整理房间 phr.	整理房間	zhěnglǐ fángjiān	straighten up (your) room	285
正确 adj.	正確	zhèngquè	correct, right	298
正义 n.	正義	zhèngyì	justice	196
正直 adj.		zhèngzhí	just, righteous	200
知道 v.		zhīdào	know, learn of	267
脂肪 n.		zhīfáng	fat	220
植物 n.		zhíwù	plants	105
指甲刀 n.		zhǐjiǎdāo	nail cutter	235
只要…就… conj.		zhǐyào…jiù…	as long as, provided	270
治安 n.		zhì'ān	peace and order	196
智能手机 phr.	智能手機	zhìnéng shǒujī	smartphone	252
志愿者 n.	志願者	zhìyuànzhě	volunteer	312
中筒袜 n.	中筒襪	zhōngtǒngwà	crew socks	132
种类 n.	種類	zhǒnglèi	category	214
种 v.	種	zhòng	to plant, grow	98
中病毒 phr.		zhòng bìngdú	be infected with a computer virus	255
周末 n.		zhōumò	weekend	14

主机 n.	主機	zhǔjī	host	255
主食 n.		zhǔshí	staple foods (rice, noodles, dumplings, etc.)	214
主卧室 n.	主臥室	zhǔwòshì	master bedroom	83
资料 n.	資料	zīliào	information	264
资源 n.	資源	zīyuán	resources	321
自备 v.	自備	zìbèi	bring along	329
自私 adj.		zìsī	selfish	200
棕色 n.		zōngsè	brown	107
走 v.		zǒu	walk	40
走廊 n.		zǒuláng	corridor; aisle	83
走路 v.		zǒulù	walk	42
最近 n.		zuìjìn	recently	4
坐 v.		zuò	go by, travel by	40
做菜 phr.		zuòcài	cook	196
坐出租车 phr.	坐出租車	zuò chūzūchē	take a cab, taxi	41
坐船 phr.		zuò chuán	go by ship	41
坐地铁 phr.	坐地鐵	zuò dìtiě	take the subway	41
坐飞机 phr.	坐飛機	zuò fēijī	go by airplane	41
坐公交车 phr.	坐公交車	zuò gōngjiāochē	take a public bus	41
坐火车 phr.	坐火車	zuò huǒchē	take a train	41
做家教 phr.		zuò jiājiào	tutoring	318
作曲 phr.		zuò qǔ	compose music	196
做体检 phr.	做體驗	zuò tǐjiǎn	have a physical/ body check up	237
做午饭 phr.	做午飯	zuò wǔfàn	make lunch	285
坐校车 phr.	坐校車	zuò xiàochē	take a school bus	41
做志愿者 phr.	做志願者	zuò zhìyuànzhě	volunteering	318
足球场 n.	足球場	zúqiúchǎng	soccer field	153
组装 v.	組裝	zǔzhuāng	assemble	255

Abbreviations for Parts of Speech

n.	noun		m.w.	measure word		conj.	conjunction
v.	verb		q.w.	question word		num.	numeral
adj.	adjective		pron.	pronoun		part.	particle
adv.	adverb		prep.	preposition		aux.v.	auxiliary verb

Key Sentence Patterns 主要句型

354

她用洗发液洗头发。

吃饭以前应该先洗手。

我每天运动半小时。她每天刷两次牙。

这台平板电脑既轻巧又耐用。 280

电脑坏了。

打印机坏了，所以我买了一台新的。

网断了，现在上不了网。

我用网络视频电话跟朋友一起聊天。

他不是玩网络游戏，就是在网上购物。

我看了电视新闻才知道这个消息。

他一上网就看到了这条新闻。

只要上网查一查，就可以找到资料。

我帮妈妈洗碗。 308

你要是出门的话，我可以帮你喂狗。

你可以帮我割草吗？当然可以。

我帮邻居把车子洗干净了。

我一边帮他温习功课，一边和他讨论作业。

你同意我的看法吗？我同意。

你说的我不是不同意，只是我觉得有点难。

这个建议好是好，可是时间可能不够。

志愿者对我的影响很大。 339

芳芳很有耐心，所以很容易跟她相处。

张安请我跟他一起去捐血。

空气被污染了。

我们应该节约用水。

当你离开房间的时候，应该把灯关掉。

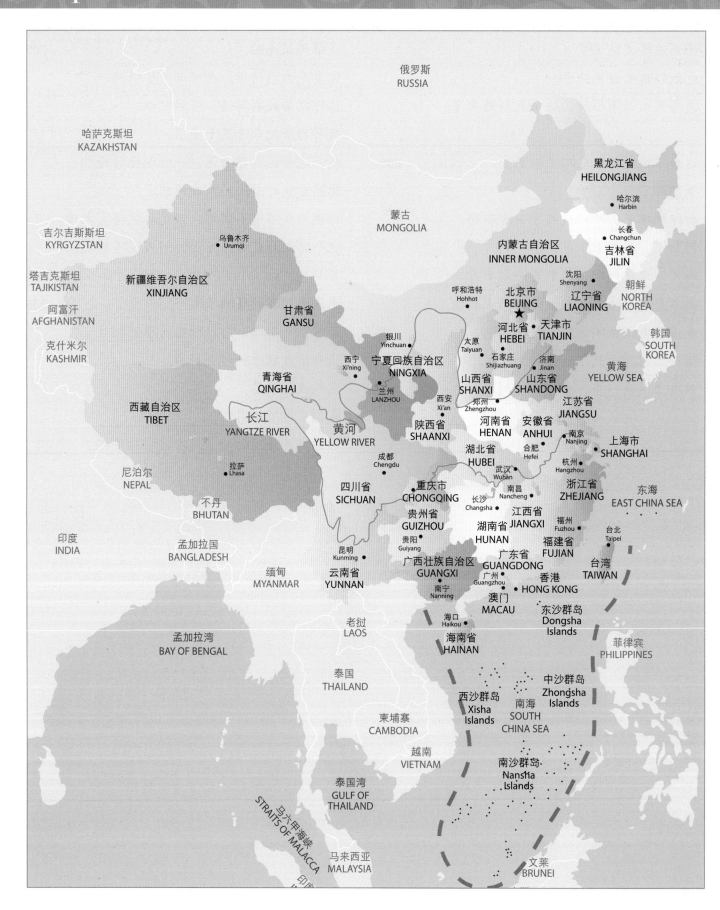

Photo Credits

Every reasonable effort has been made to acquire permission for copyright material in this text, and to acknowledge such indebtedness accurately. Any errors or omissions called to the publisher's attention will be corrected in future printing.

Cover: Yukmin/Asia Images/Getty Images

Pages: vi (t to b) BananaStock/Thinkstock, Paul Bradbury/OJO Images/Getty Images, Wang Leng/Asia Images/Getty Images, Lane Oatey/Blue Jean Images/Getty Images, Jean Heguy/First Light/Getty Images; **vii** (t to b) Digital Vision/Thinkstock, Asia Images Group/Getty Images, XiXinXing/Thinkstock, Thinkstock Images/Comstock/Thinkstock, Paul Burns/Photodisc/Getty Images; **1** BananaStock/Thinkstock; **4** Simone Becchetti/ the Agency Collection/Getty Images; **5** David Hogsholt/Getty Images News/Getty Images; **6** (l to r, t to b) Ryan McVay/Photodisc/Thinkstock, Stockbyte/Thinkstock, Jetta Productions/Lifesize/Thinkstock, Barry Austin/Digital Vision/Thinkstock, Dick Luria/ Photodisc/Thinkstock, Hemera/Thinkstock; **8** (t to b) TongRo Images/Thinkstock, iStockphoto/Thinkstock, Wavebreak Media/Thinkstock; **11** (t to b) Zhang Bo/E+/Getty Images, iStockphoto/Thinkstock, iStockphoto/Thinkstock, TongRo Images/Thinkstock; **13** iStockphoto/Thinkstock; **14** Comstock/Thinkstock; **16** (t to b) iStockphoto/ Thinkstock, Zhang Bo/E+/Getty Images; **20** (t to b) Goodshoot/Thinkstock, Hemera/ Thinkstock; **22** (t to b) Top Photo Group/Thinkstock, iStockphoto/Thinkstock; **23** (l to r, t to b) iStockphoto/Thinkstock, Jupiterimages/Brand X Pictures/Thinkstock, Wavebreak Media/Thinkstock, Wavebreak Media/Thinkstock, Hemera/Thinkstock, Jupiterimages/ Creatas/Thinkstock, Michael Blann/Digital Vision/Thinkstock, iStockphoto/Thinkstock, Pixland/Thinkstock, iStockphoto/Thinkstock, Jupiterimages/Creatas/Thinkstock; **24** TAO Images Limited/Getty Images; **25** (l to r, t to b) Digital Vision/Thinkstock, Stockphoto/ Thinkstock, Jupiterimages/Creatas/Thinkstock, Jupiterimages/Comstock/Thinkstock, Thinkstock Images/Comstock/Thinkstock, iStockphoto/Thinkstock, iStockphoto/ Thinkstock, iStockphoto/Thinkstock, Photodisc/Thinkstock, iStockphoto/Thinkstock; **27** Goodshoot/Thinkstock; **28** (l to r, t to b) Hemera/Thinkstock, iStockphoto/Thinkstock, Brand X Pictures/Thinkstock, Stockphoto/Thinkstock, Stockbyte/Thinkstock, Jetta Productions/Lifesize/Thinkstock, iStockphoto/Thinkstock, iStockphoto/Thinkstock; **29** iStockphoto/Thinkstock; **30** (t to b, l to r) iStockphoto/Thinkstock, Stockbyte/Thinkstock, iStockphoto/Thinkstock, iStockphoto/Thinkstock, iStockphoto/Thinkstock, Digital Vision/ Thinkstock, iStockphoto/Thinkstock, iStockphoto/Thinkstock, iStockphoto/Thinkstock; **31** BananaStock/BananaStock/Thinkstock; **34** (t to b) http://bbs.gaofen.com/ topic-xiaoxun.html, http://www.rredu.com.cn/blog/u/kevin52141/archives/2009/679. html, http://en.wikipedia.org/wiki/File:Harvard_Wreath_Logo_1.svg, https://www. facebook.com/pages/Livingston-Public-Schools/125981870771736; **38** Paul Bradbury/ OJO Images/Getty Images; **40** (l to r) iStockphoto/Thinkstock, Top Photo Group/ Thinkstock; **41** (l to r, t to b) Zoonar/Thinkstock, iStockphoto/Thinkstock, iStockphoto/ Thinkstock, Jupiterimages/Comstock/Thinkstock, iStockphoto/Thinkstock, iStockphoto/ Thinkstock, Top Photo Group/Thinkstock, iStockphoto/Thinkstock, Big Cheese Photo/ Thinkstock; **42** (l to r) Jupiterimages/Photos.com/Thinkstock, Jupiterimages/Creatas/ Thinkstock, iStockphoto/Thinkstock; **43** (t to b) Jupiterimages/Photos.com/Thinkstock, iStockphoto/Thinkstock, Thinkstock/Comstock/Thinkstock, iStockphoto/Thinkstock, iStockphoto/Thinkstock; **44** (l to r, t to b) George Doyle/Stockbyte/Thinkstock, iStockphoto/Thinkstock, Darrin Klimek/Digital Vision/Thinkstock, Jupiterimages/ Comstock/Thinkstock, John A. Rizzo/Photodisc/Thinkstock, iStockphoto/Thinkstock, Top Photo Group/Thinkstock, iStockphoto/Thinkstock, Stockbyte/Thinkstock, Hemera/ Thinkstock, iStockphoto/Thinkstock, iStockphoto/Thinkstock, Hemera/Thinkstock, iStockphoto/Thinkstock, Brand X Pictures/Thinkstock, Ryan McVay/Photodisc/ Thinkstock, Ryan McVay/Photodisc/Thinkstock, iStockphoto/Thinkstock; **46** (t to b) Thinkstock/Comstock/Thinkstock, Darrin Klimek/Digital Vision/Thinkstock, iStockphoto/ Thinkstock, Jupiterimages/Photos.com/Thinkstock; **47** Comstock Images/Comstock/ Thinkstock; **48** (l to r, t to b) iStockphoto/Thinkstock, Top Photo Group/Thinkstock, Comstock/Thinkstock, iStockphoto/Thinkstock, Eyecandy Images/Thinkstock, Jupiterimages/Comstock/Thinkstock, **49** (t to b) Purestock/Thinkstock, Stockbyte/ Thinkstock, iStockphoto/Thinkstock, iStockphoto/Thinkstock; **52** (t to b) Jupiterimages/ Creatas/Thinkstock, Thomas Northcut/Stockbyte/Thinkstock, Hemera/Thinkstock, iStockphoto/Thinkstock; **53** (l to r) iStockphoto/Thinkstock, iStockphoto/Thinkstock; **54** (l to r, t to b) iStockphoto/Thinkstock, iStockphoto/Thinkstock, iStockphoto/Thinkstock, iStockphoto/Thinkstock, iStockphoto/Thinkstock, Digital Vision/Thinkstock, iStockphoto/ Thinkstock, Jupiterimages/Comstock/Thinkstock, Goodshoot/Thinkstock, iStockphoto/ Thinkstock, Jupiterimages/Photos.com/Thinkstock; **55** XiXinXing/Thinkstock; **56** (t to b, l to r) Jupiterimages/Brand X Pictures/Thinkstock, Jupiterimages/Polka Dot/Thinkstock, Polka Dot Images/Polka Dot/Thinkstock, iStockphoto/Thinkstock, iStockphoto/ Thinkstock, Jupiterimages/Pixland/Thinkstock, Blue Jean Images/Photodisc/Thinkstock; **57** iStockphoto/Thinkstock; **58** (t to b) iStockphoto/Thinkstock, iStockphoto/Thinkstock, Thomas Northcut/Photodisc/Thinkstock, iStockphoto/Thinkstock; **60** (l to r, t to b) iStockphoto/Thinkstock, Keith Brofsky/Photodisc/Thinkstock, Photodisc/Photodisc/ Thinkstock, Ingram Publishing/Thinkstock, iStockphoto/Thinkstock, Medioimages/ Photodisc/Photodisc/Thinkstock, Photos.com/Thinkstock, Digital Vision/Thinkstock, iStockphoto/Thinkstock, iStockphoto/Thinkstock, Stockbyte/Thinkstock, TongRo Images/Thinkstock, iStockphoto/Thinkstock, Thinkstock Images/Comstock/Thinkstock, iStockphoto/Thinkstock, Comstock/Thinkstock; **61** (l to r, t to b) Jupiterimages/ Comstock/Thinkstock, Stockbyte/Thinkstock, iStockphotoThinkstock, iStockphoto/ Thinkstock, iStockphoto/Thinkstock, iStockphoto/Thinkstock, iStockphoto/Thinkstock, Stockbyte/Thinkstock, iStockphoto/Thinkstock, iStockphoto/Thinkstock, iStockphoto/ Thinkstock, Hemera/Thinkstock, iStockphoto/Thinkstock, George Doyle/Stockbyte/ Thinkstock, Stockbyte/Stockbyte/Thinkstock, iStockphoto/Thinkstock, iStockphoto/ Thinkstock, Ryan McVay/Photodisc/Thinkstock, iStockphoto/Thinkstock, Hemera/ Thinkstock, Fuse/Thinkstock, iStockphoto/Thinkstock; **62** iStockphoto/Thinkstock; **65** (l to r, t to b) iStockphoto/Thinkstock, Jupiterimages/Creatas/Thinkstock, Thomas Northcut/Digital Vision/Thinkstock, Comstock/Thinkstock, iStockphoto/Thinkstock, Creatas/Thinkstock, Stockbyte/Thinkstock, Creatas Images/Creatas/Thinkstock, Jupiterimages/Pixland/Thinkstock, Ryan McVay/Photodisc/Thinkstock, BananaStock/ Thinkstock, TongRo Images/Thinkstock, Comstock Images/Comstock/Thinkstock, Medioimages/Photodisc/Photodisc/Thinkstock, iStockphoto/Thinkstock, Wavebreak Media/Thinkstock; **66** (t to b) iStockphoto/Thinkstock, iStockphoto/Thinkstock; **67** (l to r, t to b) Comstock/Thinkstock, TongRo Images/Thinkstock, Hemera/Thinkstock, Chris Amaral/Digital Vision/Thinkstock; **68** (l to r, t to b) iStockphoto/Thinkstock, iStockphoto/ Thinkstock, Jupiterimages/Comstock/Thinkstock, VStock/Thinkstock, Jupiterimages/ Creatas/Thinkstock, iStockphoto/Thinkstock, Steffen Kugler/Getty Images News/Getty Images, Science Photo Library/SPL Creative/Getty Images, Jupiterimages/Goodshoot/ Thinkstock, Thinkstock/Comstock/Thinkstock, Digital Vision/Digital Vision/Thinkstock, iStockphoto/Thinkstock; **70** (t to b) Iain Masterton/Photographer's Choice/Getty Images, Comstock Images/Comstock/Thinkstock; **71** (l to r, t to b) Wavebreak Media/Thinkstock, Jupiterimages/Brand X Pictures/Thinkstock, Jupiterimages/Polka Dot/Thinkstock, iStockphoto/Thinkstock, btrenkel/E+/Getty Images, iStockphoto/Thinkstock, iStockphoto/Thinkstock, iStockphoto/Thinkstock, iStockphoto/Thinkstock, BananaStock/Thinkstock, iStockphoto/Thinkstock, iStockphoto/Thinkstock, Heinz Kluetmeier/Contributor/Sports Illustrated/Getty Images; **72** (l to r, t to b) Jupiterimages/ Photos.com/Thinkstock, Sean Gallup/Getty Images News/Getty Images, Chip Somodevilla/Getty Images News/Getty Images, Andrew D. Bernstein/National Basketball/Getty Images, Harry How/Getty Images Sport/Getty Images, Mike Hewitt/ Getty Images Sport/Getty Images, FogStock/Thinkstock, iStockphoto/Thinkstock, Fuse/ Thinkstock, iStockphoto/Thinkstock; **73** Paul Bradbury/OJO Images/Getty Images; **74** George Doyle/Stockbyte/Thinkstock; **76** (l to r) iStockphoto/Thinkstock, Jupiterimages/ Brand X Pictures/Thinkstock; 80 Wang Leng/Asia Images/Getty Images; **81** (t to b) View Stock/Getty Images, iStockphoto/Thinkstock; **82** (t to b) iStockphoto/Thinkstock, iStockphoto/Thinkstock, Top Photo Group/Thinkstock; **84** (t to b) Top Photo Group/ Thinkstock, iStockphoto/Thinkstock; **85** (t to b) iStockphoto/Thinkstock, iStockphoto/ Thinkstock; 87 iStockphoto/Thinkstock; **88** (t to b) Chuck Schmidt/E+/Getty Images,Todd Warnock/Lifesize/Thinkstock; **89** Jack Barnes/Britain On View/Getty Images; **90** (t to b) Goodshoot/Thinkstock, Jupiterimages/Brand X Pictures/Thinkstock, iStockphoto/Thinkstock, Siri Stafford/Lifesize/Thinkstock, Ryan McVay/Photodisc/ Thinkstock, David De Lossy/Photodisc/Thinkstock; **91** (t to b) iStockphoto/Thinkstock, iStockphoto/Thinkstock; **92** (t to b, l to r) Hemera/Thinkstock, iStockphoto/Thinkstock, iStockphoto/Thinkstock, iStockphoto/Thinkstock, Blend Images/Thinkstock; **93** (t to b, l to r) Jupiterimages/Comstock/Thinkstock, iStockphoto/Thinkstock, iStockphoto/ Thinkstock, Top Photo Group/Thinkstock, iStockphoto/Thinkstock, iStockphoto/ Thinkstock, iStockphoto/Thinkstock, iStockphoto/Thinkstock, iStockphoto/Thinkstock, Hemera/Thinkstock, iStockphoto/Thinkstock, Noel Hendrickson/Lifesize/Thinkstock; **94** (l to r, t to b) Hemera/Thinkstock, Hemera/Thinkstock, George Doyle/Stockbyte/ Thinkstock, iStockphoto/Thinkstock, iStockphoto/Thinkstock, iStockphoto/Thinkstock, Stockbyte/Thinkstock; **95** (l to r, t to b) iStockphoto/Thinkstock, Thomas Northcut/ Photodisc/Thinkstock, iStockphoto/Thinkstock, iStockphoto/Thinkstock, iStockphoto/ Thinkstock, Hemera Technologies/PhotoObjects.net/Thinkstock; **96** (t to b, l to r) Hemera/Thinkstock, iStockphoto/Thinkstock, iStockphoto/Thinkstock, Hemera/ Thinkstock, George Doyle/Stockbyte/Thinkstock, Stockbyte/Thinkstock; **97** (t to b, l to r) iStockphoto/Thinkstock, iStockphoto/Thinkstock, iStockphoto/Thinkstock, iStockphoto/ Thinkstock, iStockphoto/Thinkstock; **98** (l to r) iStockphoto/Thinkstock, iStockphoto/ Thinkstock; **99** (l to r, t to b) Jupiterimages/Polka Dot/Thinkstock, Jupiterimages/Photos. com/Thinkstock, iStockphoto/Thinkstock, iStockphoto/Thinkstock, iStockphoto/ Thinkstock, Jupiterimages/Photos.com/Thinkstock, iStockphoto/Thinkstock, iStockphoto/Thinkstock; **101** (t to b) iStockphoto/Thinkstock, Stockbyte/Thinkstock; **102** (l to r) iStockphoto/Thinkstock, Zoonar/Thinkstock, iStockphoto/Thinkstock, iStockphoto/Thinkstock; **103** (l to r, t to b) Hemera/Thinkstock, Hemera Technologies/ PhotoObjects.net/Thinkstock, iStockphoto/Thinkstock, iStockphoto/Thinkstock, iStockphoto/Thinkstock, Hemera/Thinkstock, Hemera Technologies/PhotoObjects.net/ Thinkstock, iStockphoto/Thinkstock, iStockphoto/Thinkstock, **104** (l to r) Martin Poole/ Digital Vision/Thinkstock, iStockphoto/Thinkstock; **105** (l to r) iStockphoto/Thinkstock, iStockphoto/Thinkstock, iStockphoto/Thinkstock, iStockphoto/Thinkstock, Hemera/ Thinkstock; **109** (l to r) iStockphoto/Thinkstock, iStockphoto/Thinkstock; **110** (t to b) iStockphoto/Thinkstock, Stockbyte/Thinkstock, iStockphoto/Thinkstock, iStockphoto/ Thinkstock, iStockphoto/Thinkstock, Hemera/Thinkstock, Hemera Technologies/Photos. com/Thinkstock; **111** (t to b, l to r) iStockphoto/Thinkstock, Dorling Kindersley RF/ Thinkstock, iStockphoto/Thinkstock, Hemera/Thinkstock, iStockphoto/Thinkstock, iStockphoto/Thinkstock, iStockphoto/Thinkstock, iStockphoto/Thinkstock, Hemera/ Thinkstock, iStockphoto/Thinkstock, Polka Dot Images/Polka Dot/Thinkstock; **115** iStockphoto/Thinkstock; **120** Lane Oatey/Blue Jean Images/Getty Images; **122** (t to b) Thomas Northcut/Lifesize/Thinkstock, Photos.com/Photos.com/Thinkstock, BJI/Blue Jean Images/Getty Images; **124** TAO Images Limited/TAO Images/Getty Images; **125** (t to b) iStockphoto/Thinkstock, iStockphoto/Thinkstock; **127** (l to r) iStockphoto/ Thinkstock, Digital Vision/Photodisc/Thinkstock; **128** iStockphoto/Thinkstock; **129** XiXinXing/Thinkstock; **130** (l to r, t to b) Thomas Northcut/Photodisc/Thinkstock, Hemera/Thinkstock, Zoonar/Thinkstock, Jupiterimages/Goodshoot/Thinkstock, Stockbyte/Thinkstock, Hemera/Thinkstock, iStockphoto/Thinkstock, iStockphoto/ Thinkstock, iStockphoto/Thinkstock; **131** (l to r, t to b) Thomas Northcut/Photodisc/ Thinkstock, iStockphoto/Thinkstock, Hemera/Thinkstock, Hemera Technologies/ PhotoObjects.net/Thinkstock, iStockphoto/Thinkstock, iStockphoto/Thinkstock; **132** (l to r, t to b) Hemera Technologies/PhotoObjects.net/Thinkstock, Hemera/